Résumé Empower!

SHATTERING THE PAPER CEILING

Tom Washington and Gary Kanter

Mount Vernon Press
Bellevue, Washington

Cover design: Andrew Newman, Andrew Newman Design
Page layout design and typesetting: DesignForBooks.com
Editing: Sigrid Asmus
Technical assistance: Bob Hayes, hayesonline.com

ISBN 978-0-931213-18-2

Library of Congress Cataloging in Publication Data:
Washington, Tom, 1949-
Kanter, Gary, 1949-
Resume empower!.
Bibliography: p.
1. Resumes (Employment) I. Title.
HF5383.W316   2009   650.14   84-20779

Dedication

To Lois—my friend and love.

— TW

This book is dedicated to all the people who have shared their life stories and, in a very real sense, entrusted their futures to me over the years. I am grateful to all the friends and colleagues who helped me learn my trade in Charlottetown, Nashville, and Washington State. Of course, my debt to my 20-year friend and mentor, Tom Washington is incalculable. Together we learned that opposites can indeed combine without canceling each other out.

To my long-suffering wife, Mary, who long ago stopped wondering what I was doing locked in the back bedroom with the computer running. I hope that's a good thing.

And our two beautiful daughters, Sarah and Carrie, who long ago stopped smirking at me for being locked in the back bedroom with the computer running.

Finally, to our world class dogs and cats who taught us the meaning of the term "value added" when applied to our lives.

— GK

Contents

Part One

CREATING AN EMPOWERING RESUME

Part Two

SAMPLE RESUMES TO USE AS GUIDES

Part Three

USING YOUR RESUME, COVER LETTER, AND MARKETING LETTER

Part Four

APPENDICES

Acknowledgments

Gary and I are especially grateful to numerous friends who volunteered to proofread our manuscript. It is amazing to authors how so many errors can go undiscovered until they are identified and reported by talented eyes.

Our hearty thanks and appreciation go out to Kim Bledsoe, Nick Fascitelli, Beau Hamilton, Susann Joo, Fran Mason, Mike Morris, Laura Paskin, and Bob Thornton for catching those pesky gremlins.

(For those who are good at finding typos, we always "leave" in a few, so if you spot any, please notify me by email: tomw@careerempowering.com. They will be corrected in the next printing.)

Introduction

By Gary Kanter

This book is a 20-year work in progress.

It began with my desire to test the waters of private practice career consulting following a series of public and nonprofit sector positions, providing diverse employment services to special populations in Canada, Tennessee, and Washington State.

Having just left what I assumed was my last social services job, I identified various private employment firms and began contacting the ubiquitous "person with the power to hire" I had sent so many of my previous clients off to find.

Much to my satisfaction, these efforts actually landed meetings with the target market. One of these was with Tom Washington, in the office of his firm, Career Management Resources, Bellevue, WA.

Tom was a young-looking almost 40-something in a smart gray suit with an earnestness about him I had not seen since first meeting my young Tennessee congressman, Al Gore, a decade earlier.

We chatted for over two hours. I left the meeting with the realization that while I knew a lot about employment, I knew relatively little about career counseling and even less about resumes.

Tom eventually contacted me and asked if I would be interested in joining him at CMR, initially as a resume consultant and later, as I learned the program, a full-fledged career counselor.

At the time, I was working part-time as an editor at a small publishing company in downtown Seattle by the famous Pike Place Market.

Not knowing if career counseling was something I was ready to commit to on a full-time basis, we agreed I would ease in, starting three days per week.

Using Tom's book *Resume Power: Selling Yourself on Paper* as a guide, with occasional tutoring by the author, I learned my craft.

I learned that a resume is more than a series of cobbled-together job descriptions punctuated with a bunch of self-aggrandizing statements crammed mercilessly into a single overworked page. I learned that the resume was, first and foremost a statement of *value*, designed to impress the writer as well as the reader. Most workers, Tom maintained, had little understanding of their accomplishments and, as a result, were unable to describe their value to employers.

As if to provide an exclamation point, Tom invited me to my very first meeting of our professional group, *The Puget Sound Career Development Association*. The guest speaker was Bernhard Haldane, whom many consider the godfather of career counseling.

This slight, soft-spoken British-born septuagenarian gazed into the faces of the 40 or so career counselors, consultants, and wannabes (such as me) that comprised his audience and posed the following:

"How many questions does an employer ask at the typical job interview?"

Having a room full of experts naturally resulted in a chorus of conflicting responses.

"Ten."

"Fifteen."

"Twenty."

In response, Haldane, brandished his index finger in the air and said, "One."

"And . . . what is that question?" he asked.

At that point, several of my colleagues got it. "What can you do for me?" they cried in unison.

Haldane nodded in agreement. "How are you going to be valuable to me?" he said, and for emphasis, repeated. "How are you going to be valuable to me?"

Then I, too, got it!

That was my epiphany.

The entire process of client self-discovery and marketing in the job search process came down to a single concept, one word . . . *value!*

From that moment on, my mission as career counselor was to assure my clients understood and appreciated the value they had provided in each of their positions and were able to clearly articulate it both in print and in person.

Value was my new mantra.

Tom and I were on the same page, as it were.

That was nearly two decades ago. In that time, I have worked with hundreds of career and outplacement clients in defining new occupations. I have also worked with thousands of resume clients. Resume consulting became my specialty.

The resume, I decided, is a process not a product. As such, each of my clients is required to actively participate in the preparation and writing. Utilizing this team effort, we consistently prove that the whole is indeed greater than the sum of the parts. By use of trial and error, we find the exact wording and phrasing to define the client's true *value* in each employment setting. The result is not only a strong resume, but the foundation of a strong interview. Everything on the resume has been tested and proven. The client can present it unafraid that some part of it is going to unravel at the interview. On the contrary, everything in the resume is there to be expanded with additional description, context, and value.

As stated, Tom and I are pretty much in agreement as to what makes a strong resume. We have a format that, with certain variations, has served our clients well through the years. Yes, we even consider ourselves "experts" in the field. Tom is the author of three earlier books in the field and both of us have written numerous articles for national and regional publications. We have facilitated countless classes, workshops, and seminars. We have no corner, however, on all the world's knowledge and wisdom pertaining to resumes.

What we have is experience and lots of opinions based upon what we have seen through the decades. We also have the humility to understand and appreciate the work and opinions of others. Resume creation is art . . . not science; the simple measure of what constitutes an effective resume is whether it works or not! Does it result in interviews?

Tom and I do not agree on all aspects of the resume . . . content, structure, and various other issues. Throughout *Resume Empower!* we will present examples of our divergent opinions and allow the readers to make up their own minds as to which one, if either, of us to follow . . . or find their own truth.

That is the true purpose of this book . . . to offer information and strategies that will *empower* you to create the resume and the presentation you deserve.

GARY KANTER
SAMMAMISH, WA
11/25/08

Tips on How to Read and Use Résumé Empower!

Introduce yourself to *Resume Empower* by skimming pages 3-91. Familiarize yourself with the sections of a typical resume, particularly those covered from pages 3–75. Some sections, such as special projects, awards, and licenses, are not used often, but can be very beneficial for some. Then flip through the resume section just to observe some of the samples and what they look like. If a section does not seem useful to your situation, skip it and go on to those that will.

Certain portions do not need to be read intensively. In education, for example, we show different models to select from. If you have a bachelors degree and some graduate credits, but no graduate degree, we have a model for you. The models work and will save you time.

The resume is a *u-build-it* process. We strongly suggest using a Qualifications section because it can greatly strengthen your resume. Pages 33–75 are crucial because they demonstrate how to write a job narrative that will cause people to want to meet you. This section also shows you how to bring your job successes and results into the resume. This is the single most important thing that will cause your resume to stand out above the rest.

Some portions should be skipped entirely. For example, in the portion on creating an electronic resume, we take you through it step-by-step to be sure your text/ASCII resume is created perfectly. If you already know how to do it, skip that portion.

Resume Empower is your tool. Reading it and then using the advice will take time. For all of us, our time is valuable, but when it comes to producing an effective resume, time is an investment. Getting the job you want, with the income you desire, may hinge on one particular hiring manager, liking what he or she sees, and inviting you for an interview. The extra time you spend reading *Resume Empower* and writing your resume, can pay huge dividends.

Good fortune to you as you go through what we have presented to you.

PART ONE

Creating an
Empowering Résumé

The Résumé Is a Process

Forget everything you have ever learned about resumes. Most of it is mythology.

The process of creating an empowering resume goes far beyond the simple act of cobbling together your job narratives and mailing them in response to want ads. In fact, there are at least six benefits to writing a top-quality resume:

1. You will feel more marketable and better armed to attack the job market.
2. Knowing you look good on paper builds self-esteem and self-confidence.
3. You will obtain more interviews and become more confident in your presentations.
4. The resume can be used as the interview script or roadmap by both you and the employer.
5. Your resume will serve as a *calling card*, enabling people to remember you, contact you, and refer you to others.
6. It will help your prospective boss justify the decision to hire you.

In the pages ahead, we are going to provide hints and strategies you can use to create a resume that has real impact. You'll be making dozens of decisions as you construct your resume; the information and examples provided will enable you to make the right decisions and make them quickly. There is no single right way to do anything, but there are ways to build a resume that looks good, reads well—and, most importantly, has impact that will capture the imagination of the reader.

An empowering resume is not just a resume. It represents you. Take the time to create a resume that presents the best you have to offer. A resume won't get you a job, but it can help get interviews. Or, to put it another way, a good resume won't guarantee an interview, but a mediocre one will cost you some. Set your mind on spending whatever time it takes to produce a resume that truly sells you.

What Makes an Empowering Résumé?

*You never get a second chance to make a
good first impression* — UNKNOWN

Eye Appeal

The empowering resume is visually appealing. Lasting impressions can be formed during the first few seconds your resume is read. That's how long it takes someone to view the layout, observe the quality of the printing and type, and note the color and quality of the paper. Of course most of this takes place on an subconscious level. These days, a resume will often be scanned electronically the first time through, but eventually a human being is going to read it, bringing in all the internal prejudices that entails. If the reader detects misspellings, clumsy or verbose writing, or a confusing layout, the resume will be gone quicker than you can say "oooops!"

Accentuate the Positive

I do not place modesty among the virtues — SHERLOCK HOLMES

The empowering resume presents you at your best, yet does not exaggerate your qualifications. Each item is carefully selected to promote you in the eyes of the reader. The resume exudes value, providing positive information about you. Make positive statements about yourself; throw false humility overboard.

Impact and Drama

You are telling a story. Write with impact. Impact is achieved when you accurately describe and *project* your desired image. Your full potential will come across only when you write with confidence. The empowering resume provides valuable information quickly and is easy to read. Each sentence expresses a fact, impression, or idea designed to sell you. Don't fret if it doesn't come out perfectly the first time. Even the most famous and prolific authors find themselves writing and rewriting the same line or paragraph numerous times. When you are reasonably certain that it is close to what you want, read it as if for the first time. Is it interesting? Exciting? Boring? Make your decision and edit accordingly.

Results

An empowering resume showcases results and accomplishments. It is your statement of value, your "features and benefits," as it were.

EMPOWERING RESUME PRINCIPLES IN FACT & FICTION

The Non-Laws of Resume Writing

There is no greater subject for debate (other than politics and religion perhaps) than the resume. But while most so-called *laws of resume writing* are a matter of opinion, there are certain principles you can use to guide your efforts.

Ethics

As previously noted, overselling yourself can be a serious mistake and is to be avoided. Your strongest presentation does not describe you as being *better* than you are but as *good* as you are! An honest presentation will invariably lead to a stronger interview, and will eliminate the fear of being "busted."

One Page or Two?

Perhaps the single most common question we hear regarding resumes is "Should it be one page or two?" This non-argument is the result of the exasperation suffered by generations of employers. Besieged by endless numbers of poorly written efforts, one day they threw up their hands and declared, "If I'm going to read a lousy resume, I'd rather read a poorly written one-pager than a poorly written two-pager." Or something like that.

The empowering resume is interesting, well-written, attractively laid out, and contains useful information; and it will be read.

In principle, a resume should be as long as necessary to tell your story. We have seen resumes where the writers attempted to squeeze 25 years of experience onto a single unhappy page. These people had several key positions but were only able to devote a few uninformative lines to each. And, as more and more information was shoehorned in, certain physical reactions naturally occurred, resulting in the *incredible shrinking fonts* and narrowing margins. By the time they were posted, they were so illegible nobody without a strong magnifying glass could read them.

And if someone actually read them, so much valuable information had been jettisoned that any impact it had, was already neutered.

The Secret to Creating a Multipage Resume Is in the Layout.

Most of your key information should appear on page one. That means a quick scan of your first page will reveal your objective, a Qualifications statement, level of education, a sense of your experience and accomplishments, and, usually, your current or most recent positions. Page two normally contains the earlier positions and additional supporting material.

> By the way, most career professionals and HR managers merely suggest that most resumes be kept to one or two pages.

Sometimes, a three-page resume is appropriate. This happens most frequently when the candidate's work history contains several projects. The *curriculum vitae* or CV, historically the resume format of choice among academics and medical professionals, is often three pages or longer due to the plethora of presentations, publications, committees, and degrees it includes.

For the standard job seeker, two pages are usually sufficient to tell the story. The critical concerns, then, become: What do we include? What do we exclude? This can be a painful predicament. But as we will see, not an unmanageable one.

(If you're interested, take a look at How to Create a Two-Page Resume with Three Pages on page 110.)

By the way, most of the resumes you'll see in Resume Empower! were originally two pages, shortened to provide sufficient variety and examples without creating a tome the size of *War and Peace*.

How to Begin

Before your resume is complete, you will have made dozens of important decisions. This book is designed to help you make those decisions quickly and easily. Each section of a resume is explained in detail with complete instructions in the writing and presentation strategies. Examples and options are provided so you can determine what works best for you. Examples throughout the book explain and demonstrate particular points. Skim pages 3 to 91 quickly. Then return to study each section as you begin to write that portion. Highlight examples that are especially applicable to you.

How Interview Decisions Are Made: It all starts with rejection.

Have you ever wondered how employers decide who will get interviews from the numerous responses they receive to posted job announcements?

Through rejection!

Before seriously considering the merits of the received resumes, there is an initial culling process. Despite all the multitudinous reports describing how many seconds and nanoseconds reviewers devote to each resume, it is a fairly personal and idiosyncratic process.

Visual integrity is perhaps the most obvious manner. A resume with obvious typos, spelling mistakes, grammatical errors, and a blatant lack of certain skills or experience, is pretty much assured a one-way trip to the *round file*. Some reviewers, however, are so obsessive in certain areas that they will reject candidates for violating some rules they've formed that no one else cares about and should make no difference.

The plain vanilla truth of the matter is that we don't know how any given reviewer will respond to any given resume on any given day.

We do know that out of a batch of 80 resumes, perhaps only 20 will be placed in the "I'm interested" pile and read in greater detail. Half of these will be disqualified through a more objective system such as a review of actual qualifications. After further consideration, perhaps six will be selected for interviewing purposes.

MARK TWAIN, ORSON WELLES, AND YOU: YOU CAN'T PLEASE EVERYONE — SO DON'T TRY!

What do *Huckleberry Finn, A Tale of Two Cities, War and Peace, Citizen Kane, Gone With the Wind*, and *Jaws* have in common?
They are all classics of world literature and film.

Does that mean everyone enjoyed viewing or reading them? Hardly. *Huckleberry Finn* has sometimes been decried as racist; *A Tale of Two Cities* as boring, and *War and Peace* intolerably long. *Citizen Kane* was too cerebral; *Gone With the Wind* too pretentious; and *Jaws* too scary for younger viewers.

In other words, these popular and immortal icons of art did not please everybody.

Did the authors and filmmakers set out to appeal to everyone? Hardly. They set out to tell the best story they could in the best way that they could. Did they expect universal acclaim? Of course not!

So, if *Huckleberry Finn, A Tale of Two Cities, War and Peace, Citizen Kane, Gone with the Wind*, and *Jaws* were not designed or expected to satisfy everyone's taste, why must your resume?

When you create your resume, you are creating your own work of art. You are the author, artist, *auteur*. Create it for yourself, not for every junior human resources flack who might review it. If it pleases you and makes you feel marketable, you have created your masterpiece. Cut yourself the same slack as you would Mark Twain, Charles Dickens, and Orson Welles: Don't try to please everybody.

The Objective:
To Have or Have Not

Setting an objective can demonstrate that you are focused.

Objectives do little good, however, if they are not specific enough. If you use an objective that states: "Position utilizing my people skills" it's simply too general. It clarifies nothing, and won't give the employer a clue about what you are looking for.

The following objective is somewhat better, in that it describes a job utilizing certain skills, and for some people it might provide just the right information. "Objective: Seek a position utilizing my administrative, customer service, and project management skills."

While an objective can be very helpful, avoid the common mistake of trying to cram too much into it such as, "Seeking responsible accounting management position with a large progressive firm offering opportunity for growth and promotion, where skills in human relations and effective written communications will prove beneficial." Sounds trite and overblown, no?

In most cases, your objective is the job you are applying for and your resume will be read accordingly, with or without this addition. That means its real purpose is in the focus it demonstrates, especially if you are transitioning into a different career or discipline. In these cases the objective shows you are truly serious about the job and not just *shotgunning* resumes all over Dodge City.

An objective can serve to keep you focused while you write the resume. Before starting, write out your objective; you can alter or delete it later.

Simple objectives are probably the most effective. Software Engineer, Administrative Assistant, Bookkeeper, Chemist, or Construction Superintendent get the point across with the least amount of hyperbole.

Stating an objective on your resume is a way to demonstrate your focus. A resume that says, "I'll do anything, just give me a job" will get you nowhere. If your objective reads "Sales Representative" but you have limited or no experience, everything that follows must demonstrate your *potential* for that position.

PARALLEL OBJECTIVES

If you are considering positions that are closely related, you might try something like this:

OBJECTIVE: Office Manager/Administrative Assistant/Executive Secretary

As these three positions are similar, it is likely the candidate is qualified for each. In fact, job titles are often used interchangeably and one firm's Administrative Assistant is another's Executive Secretary. Using all three titles as parallel objectives covers all the bases.

Never pair unrelated job titles such as Secretary/Sales Representative, Teacher/Real Estate Agent, Flight Attendant/Bookkeeper. It's fine to simultaneously be seeking diverse positions, but not in the same resume.

If you have a professional credential by your name and are looking for a traditional position in that field, consider using it as your objective. For example:

Catherine Toopsly, CPA
Dehlia Bohannon, RN
Jihan Refelda, PE

Some candidates prefer to use their professional designations as part of the heading. In the examples below, the type of position being sought is pretty clear.

Tom Wells

International Marketing Professional

2398 Saxon Drive
Birmingham, Alabama 35209
206.876.9867
tomwells@ditto.com

Tom Wells

2398 Saxon Drive
Birmingham, Alabama 35209
206-876-9867
tomwells@ditto.com

International Marketing Professional

Jack Gleason CPA

34 Elm Street
Charles Town, West Virginia 25414
(304) 555-6362
jgleason@shenandoah.com

Highly experienced CFO / VP of Finance

Laticia Collins

4236 Penny Lane
Ottawa, Ontario, Canada M3K 4C9
613.555-5674
Laticia424@maple.com

Registered Nurse with ten years' OR experience

Entry-level Positions

Phrases such as "Seeking entry-level chemistry position" are usually appropriate when the candidate's education or experience warrant it, or for those making a career change and willing to start at the beginning.

When Not to Use a Job Title

Sometimes stating an exact job title is *not* advised. This is particularly true in management. If you are currently a human resources manager considering any one of the following positions: Training and Development Specialist, Director of Training and Development, or Vice President of Human Resources, you might want to create an objective that incorporates all of these titles, such as "OBJECTIVE: Human Resources Management." Using the term *management* does not limit you to a specific job title, while Human Resources demonstrates your professional focus.

When to Use an Objective

To sum up, use an objective if your goal can be simply stated with a job title, professional credential, or a descriptive phrase. Occasionally you will find it better to omit an objective and let your cover letter and the tone of your Qualifications section indicate your goal. Though most resumes will benefit from an objective, it is certainly not a requirement.

The Qualifications Section: Capturing Your Essence

The Qualifications section can do more than any other section to create a favorable first impression and will set the tone for the rest of the resume. It is a summary of your skills and experience and includes blatantly positive affirmations about you that will be demonstrated in context later in the resume. A well-written Qualifications section should compel the reader to learn more about you by reading the entire resume!

This section should capture the *essence* of who you are and what you have to sell. Any point that is not crucial should either be eliminated or considered for inclusion in your cover letter.

Studying the following examples will help you understand the function of the Qualifications section. A sample job has been included with each example to demonstrate how they fit together.

Example 1

OBJECTIVE: Marine Sales

QUALIFICATIONS

Outstanding sales record. Highly knowledgeable in all facets of sailboats, powerboats, commercial fishing vessels, and marine hardware. Strong ability to introduce new product lines to distributors, dealers, and boat builders. Top-selling rep in the country for four major marine manufacturers.

EMPLOYMENT

Bellkirk Marine, San Diego, California 6/03 to Present

MANUFACTURERS' REPRESENTATIVE – Represent 27 lines throughout California, Nevada, and Arizona. Increased the number of accounts with distributors, dealers, and boat builders from 35 to 96 and have increased sales 85%. Since 2004 have been the top-selling rep for four major manufacturers.

Qualifications example #1 includes a summary and an accomplishment. It starts off with a simple but strong statement: "Outstanding sales record." It then goes on to describe the areas of expertise.

The top accomplishment (as the top-selling representative in the country for four manufacturers) has been included twice—in Qualifications and the job narrative. It is a valuable statement worth repeating.

Example 2

OBJECTIVE: Supermarket Management
QUALIFICATIONS

Strong management background. With a 21-store district, increased profits 32% and oversaw the construction of four new stores. During 17 years in management, coordinated the grand openings of 13 stores and produced some of the most profitable new stores with three different chains.

EMPLOYMENT

Fine Food Centers, Tulsa, Oklahoma 5/88 to Present

DISTRICT MANAGER 9/95 to Present. Responsible for profit and loss analysis, wage and salary administration, merchandising, store layout, advertising, and buying for 21 stores in the district. Supervised the remodeling of five stores and the construction of four stores. Developed in-house cleaning and repair services, saving $150,000 annually. Through improved merchandising and customer service, increased sales per store 28% and profits 32%.

Qualifications example #2 begins with a bold statement, "Strong management background," and then proceeds to back it up with evidence. Immediately you realize this person has been very successful and you want to know more about her. One fact comes right out of her current position (the 32% increase in profits). The second statement (concerning the success of 13 store openings) is a summary that comes from her entire management background. If this summary had not been stated so clearly in a Qualifications section, it might have been easily overlooked, even during a careful reading of the entire resume. Because the coordination of a grand opening is an extremely valuable skill, it deserves prominence in Qualifications.

Example 3

Qualifications statements work great for those with little work experience. Sometimes volunteer experience works perfectly, as in the case of this recent college grad.

OBJECTIVE: Marketing and Event Planning

QUALIFICATIONS

- Strong background in event planning, promotion, and facilitation along with award-winning customer service experience.
- Consistently exceed expectations. For a major fund-raising event, significantly exceeded attendance and revenue goals.
- Proven ability to manage multiple tasks, projects, and assignments simultaneously.
- Effective public speaker and writer with the ability to clearly present complex information.
- Solid leader with the ability to train and mentor teams of employees and volunteers.
- Demonstrated ability to quickly learn and utilize new methods, systems, and procedures.
- Respected by customers, employers, and associates for initiative, follow up, and creating great experiences.

Northwest Wine Country, **Eugene, Oregon 2006**

<u>EVENT COORDINATOR / PUBLICATION EDITOR</u> — As a volunteer, managed all logistics for a statewide wine-tasting festival to benefit the University of Oregon's scholarship program. Coordinated participation of 95 wineries from throughout the state. Prepared venue layout and setup areas. Assigned and supervised a team of 150 volunteers. Served as the foundation's representative to all wineries, vendors, and guests. Managed setup and operation of an onsite wine store inventory from all participating wineries. Oversaw security and accounting of all receipts and remaining inventory. Event drew over 1,500 guests, surpassing expectations in attendance by 40% and revenue for the scholarship program by 48%.

Wrote, edited, and published a 60-page glossy color program guide. Worked closely with corporate and individual sponsors to format ads and recognition pieces. Guide received exceptional feedback for quality and appearance.

Writing Your Qualifications Section

Write your Qualifications section last.

It can be the most difficult section to write and requires the most care. Once you have the Employment section completed you will know better what needs to be included in your Qualifications section.

As you prepare for writing about your qualifications, review the resume and determine which points should be selected. Use these qualifications to introduce yourself to the reader and to provide an overview of why you are qualified for the position. To do this, ask yourself, "What makes me qualified for this position?" Or "What has made me successful in this field?" In Qualifications it is permissible to repeat or paraphrase points made elsewhere in the resume.

While relatively short, the Qualifications section is typically the most difficult to write. Because it can strengthen the overall effectiveness of the resume, it deserves a great deal of attention and effort. An hour or two spent writing and editing this section is not too much.

Presenting Qualifications Statements

> **TOM:** I like short, hard-hitting Qualifications sections. I try to capture the essence of what will impact employers. As a result, most Qualifications sections I write are one or two paragraphs with three to six lines each. If there are three distinct areas that need to be sold, then I may have three paragraphs with three to four lines each. People making career changes, or those seeking positions without having the traditional background, may need three or four paragraphs to bring out all of their related experience. Even so, the emphasis should still be on conciseness and impact. See pages 177, 189, and 202 for examples of single-paragraph Qualifications statements, and pages 182, 187, and 216 for examples of three or more paragraphs.

> **GARY:** I prefer a bulleted list of qualifications because each entry stands out, allowing the reader to do a quick visual scan and hone in on any specific attention grabbers. As the job narratives are typically in paragraph mode, the bulleted entries bring some variety to the format.

Write a Qualifications Sketch

To write a compelling Qualifications section, begin by writing a *qualifications sketch*. List the key strengths and assets that you want to convey. After writing the sketch, select the most critical entries. Delete the others and what remains will be the first draft of your Qualifications section. A well thought out qualifications sketch will enable you to write a more impactful Qualifications statement.

The qualifications sketch of a Quality Control Manager might look like this:

1. Ten years in quality control.
2. Familiar with all techniques that have been developed for the electronics industry.
3. Saved money and reduced rejects for three different companies.
4. I work well with other department heads, particularly production, and coordinate and cooperate well with them rather than work against them.
5. I've developed creative programs that really work.
6. I like my work and enjoy a challenge.
7. I'm always looking for a better method, technique, or system; I'm open to new ideas from others.

8. I'm an excellent supervisor. I train my staff well, I listen to them, I maintain high morale, and productivity is always high.
9. I'm hard-working, loyal, reliable, creative, and efficient.

The final version of the quality control manager's Qualifications section might read like this:

QUALIFICATIONS

Strong experience in quality control gained during ten years in supervision and management. For three electronics manufacturers implemented new quality control programs which decreased rejects at each plant by at least 23%.

Develop excellent relations with all department heads and work well with production personnel.

Excellent supervisor. Consistently increase productivity of quality assurance personnel, and, through effective staff training, increase their technical capabilities.

If you review the original points, you will notice that everything is included here either directly or by implication. By reading the Qualifications section in the context of the entire resume, you would certainly pick up that he enjoys a challenge and that he is hard-working, loyal, reliable, creative, and efficient.

Tips for Writing Your Qualifications Sketch

To help you identify the points you want to make in your Qualifications statement, ask yourself these questions.

1. What is the essence of what I want an employer to know about me?
2. If I could convince an employer of just one strength, which would it be?
3. What would a second strength be?
4. What are the two or three strengths that my bosses have most valued?
5. After reviewing several classified ads in my field, which two or three of my key strengths do they consistently address?

Once you answer these questions you will have a good idea of what you want your Qualifications statement to accomplish. You're now ready to create your qualifications sketch.

In writing Qualifications sections there is a tendency to use the words *strong* and *excellent*, such as "Strong experience in quality control" and "Excellent supervisor." Both are *excellent* words, but try not to overuse them. Unfortunately, even exhaustive thesaurus scans have not provided a great many alternatives.

Strong, Excellent, Broad

Other phrases can also be used to make a point. If you use "Excellent experience" in one paragraph, you could use "Broad experience," "Broad background," or "Solid background" in the next. Don't be overly bothered if you use the word *excellent* three times, but more than that would be excessive. Excellent is often the best word because it is not as humble as *good*, or too superlative, as *outstanding* or *exceptional* can be.

A good way to begin a Qualifications paragraph is with a short statement, such as "Excellent management experience." Then, back it up with further details. In this case the follow-up might be "Consistently obtain high productivity from employees," or "Consistently implement new techniques and procedures that increase productivity and lower costs." Another effective backup statement would be: "Proven ability to turn around projects that are behind schedule and over budget." Whatever general statement you make should be explained or reinforced with details. Look at the resumes on pages 176, 180, 187 and 202 and notice how percentages or other statistics have been included in Qualifications. This can be very effective but is not always necessary or possible, particularly if you are making a broad statement about your entire career.

Notice how effective these various backup statements can be when they are paired with the beginning short statement.

> Excellent management experience. Consistently obtain high productivity from employees.
>
> Broad management experience. Consistently implement new techniques and procedures that increase productivity and lower costs.
>
> Solid management experience. Proven ability to turn around projects that are behind schedule and over budget.
>
> Strong background in trucking gained during 20 years of management experience. Recognized for ability to significantly increase market share and quickly increase profitability. At each terminal achieved one of the best on-time records in the industry.

Opening with a short statement provides impact. It hits the reader directly and makes the person want some evidence, which you will provide in your very next sentence. Of course, you need to be able to verify anything you say, such as "Consistently obtain high productivity from employees," either in other sections of your resume or in a personal interview.

Short, To-the-Point Qualifications Statements

OBJECTIVE: Lending/business development position

QUALIFICATIONS

Broad banking background with strong managerial and technical expertise. Always a top producer, with the ability to establish strong, long-term customer relationships.

OBJECTIVE: Marketing/Product Management

QUALIFICATIONS

Strong background in sales and marketing management. Consistently increase revenue, market share, and profit margin. Develop excellent, long-term relationships with key accounts, leading to better long-range planning and revenue streams.

Longer Qualifications Statements with More Points

Sometimes it takes several paragraphs to do justice to your background. The following person could have identified two or three key strengths to emphasize in one or two short paragraphs, but it seemed right to provide more information. This is another example of how important it is to determine what will best work for *you*.

QUALIFICATIONS

- Strong leadership qualities with a solid sales and marketing track record. Consistent award winner for sales and operational excellence. Six-time *President's Award* winner.
- Broad experience in operations with full P&L responsibility, including sales development, forecasting, budgeting, process improvement, and quality control.
- Develop market strategies that increase market share and return on investment far above the industry norm. Most recent strategic plan resulted in a 46% revenue increase over the past two years with a 285% increase in ROI.
- Track record of successfully benchmarking and driving improvement on best practices throughout large geographic areas.
- Recognized for ability to establish long-term customer relationships and increase service to unprecedented levels. Won Costco's Top Vendor Certification Award in 2006, 2007, and 2008.

Qualifications Statements Without Supporting Data

It is always helpful to provide supporting evidence or further information to back up any claims you make in a resume. It's helpful, but not necessary. When you make statements about yourself it is because you are convinced they are true. With that in mind you must be prepared to sell that quality in an interview. In fact, any statement in your resume can result in an interview question, so you must be ready to back it up.

Let's look at two Qualifications statements from two different people. Each is effective and each contains only true statements about the person. The first was written by Sandra to help her move from office work to sales.

> Strong sales personality. Effectively market programs and sell ideas to key people. High-energy person with the initiative to "make things happen." Skilled at assessing needs and following up to resolve problems.

Sandra has held administrative positions but wants to move into sales. She has no outside sales experience but she has sales friends who think she would be great. She has the desire, personality, and drive to make it in sales. Because none of her jobs involved sales, she is using the opportunity in the Qualifications statement to show her potential. A sales manager who needs someone with five years of sales experience will not give her a second look. Fortunately, some sales managers actually prefer to train their sales reps. They are willing to take a rookie with obvious energy and drive and mold that person into a professional. That is the type of sales manager who will have the vision to see the potential in Sandra.

Notice that Sandra has provided no real supporting evidence for any of her statements. She says she can market programs and sell ideas. She claims she takes initiative. While there could certainly be a question mark in the reader's mind, it is clear by the tone that Sandra absolutely believes that these statements are true and accurate. As long as Sandra's job narratives show a pattern of success, with some reference to her initiative, these statements will be credible until Sandra demonstrates otherwise at an interview.

In the next example, Darryl provides a short description of his real estate and land development background.

> Broad background in all phases of real estate development and investment including acquisitions, design, approvals, construction, finance, marketing, and property management. Consistently bring projects in ahead of schedule and under budget.

Darryl has a ton of experience and wants the reader to move right into the heart of his last two positions, but first he wants to create an impression. His goal with this statement is to quickly show the breadth of his experience. He also wants the reader to know that he has a history of completing projects ahead of schedule and under budget—absolutely critical abilities for a project manager in any industry.

Backing Up Statements with Numbers

Using numbers and statistics to provide supporting evidence of your claims can be very effective. Since you will already have written your job narratives, ask yourself whether any of those numbers are appropriate. Often it is valuable to put together numbers that the employer would not have picked up on without your assistance. For example, the district manager for a grocery chain (page 12) mentioned that she had managed the grand openings of 13 stores throughout her career. Here are some additional Qualifications statements that have effectively used numbers to provide proof. The first is for a human resources manager:

> Broad management background with strong human resources experience gained through the complete development of an HR department. Introduced systems that have increased productivity, significantly reduced turnover, and have saved more than $120,000 per year in medical insurance, unemployment compensation, and training costs.

The entire statement is well written and convinces the reader that he is a very capable and versatile human resources manager. Every business would like an HR manager who can play a major role in increasing productivity, reducing turnover, and saving beaucoup dollars. Nearly every interviewer he met was eager to learn how he had saved so much money for a relatively small, 90-employee company.

Another two examples will reinforce the value of numbers in Qualifications statements. The first is a small business owner who wants to move into management in a larger company. The second is a pharmacy manager who has a knack for attracting and keeping customers, thus increasing sales each year.

> Strong management and sales experience. Build excellent relationships with customers and provide outstanding customer service. Built Kraft Windows into one of the top dealers in the Southwest by increasing sales 18% annually.

> Broad pharmacy background. Recognized for strong technical knowledge and ability to effectively monitor and prevent potential adverse drug interactions. Introduced numerous cost-saving measures that increased quality and productivity standards. Have increased sales volume at each store at least 15% per year.

In both cases the numbers help convince the reader that each is a highly capable person who deserves an interview.

To write effective Qualifications statements, study several examples. Analyze them to determine what makes them effective. When you're through writing your own, compare it to some of these examples. If you're not pleased, set it aside for a day. You'll return to it later with a fresh perspective. Don't give up and simply use this section as filler. It's the first opportunity the reader will have to begin assessing you. Make it count!

A Last Resort Option

Some people just find it impossible to come up with a good Qualifications section—period! One good exercise is to put yourself in the place of the reader and review the rest of the resume. Make notes of what makes you valuable. Be as objective as possible, even to the point of changing your name on the resume as you try this exercise. It probably won't take very long to come up with a usable list of assets and achievements you can use as Qualifications.

If you are still unable to create an acceptable Qualifications section, wrap it up with a short summary of 10 to 25 words without trying to make any hard-hitting statements. Here's an example.

OBJECTIVE: Programmer/Analyst
QUALIFICATIONS

Excellent background in information technology gained during eight years in programming and systems analysis.

Even though this Qualifications section lacks punch when compared to previous examples, it does have value. It defines the person as a serious and seasoned professional with almost a decade of experience. There is enough to encourage the reader to continue and seek more.

Take the Time to Make It Right

> *I apologize for the length of this letter. I didn't*
> *have time to make it shorter* — BLAISE PASCAL

As we have discussed, the Qualifications statement is typically one of the hardest parts of the resume to write; something short and powerful always takes time. When you read a great ad that has perhaps only ten words, you can bet that the copywriter spent many hours to make it perfect.

Be patient with yourself. Remind yourself that, like the copywriter, you are creating an ad that may determine the success of your own sales campaign. Devote whatever time it takes to make it right. It will be worth the effort.

Areas of Experience

You can present the scope of your experience in a variety of ways. Usually, a strong Qualifications section will fit the bill. For others a Qualifications section with an Areas of Experience section presents a person's experience and the sum total of their strengths better than Qualifications alone. The use of an Areas of Experience section can also help you get your *key words* into your resume more easily.

Areas of Experience come in assorted flavors. In the first example, the writer, a program manager in the technical world, has presented 18 items in this section. Combined with her education, it presents a picture of a highly educated, trained, and accomplished candidate.

AREAS OF EXPERIENCE

- Program Management
- Product Management
- Systems/Business Analysis
- System Integrator
- Statistical Analysis
- Quantitative Analysis
- Needs Analysis
- Technical Support
- Workflow Analysis

- Technical Writing
- Documentation
- Financial Analysis
- System Development
- Testing/Implementation
- Database Design
- Project Management
- Management Presentations
- Training

EDUCATION

MBA – Organizational Development, University of Washington
Specialized Coursework: MIS, Statistical Analysis, and Quality Systems
Special Honor: *Outstanding Graduate in Management Information Systems*

BA – Management, University of Puget Sound

Here is a similar example. This time the writer is a marketing manager in the nutrition/food industry. Once again, her education nicely complements the experience.

EDUCATION

M.S. in Nutrition, Ohio State University
B.S. in Food and Nutrition, Illinois State University

AREAS OF EXPERIENCE

Marketing Management	Consumer-Driven Industry	Leadership Skills
New Business Development	Regulatory Standards	Training Programs, Materials
Strategic Planning	Ingredient Review, Selection	Vendor, Supplier Relations
Account Management	FDA/FTC Compliance	Distribution Channels
Clinical Trials	Strong Communications	Quality Improvement
Budget Management	Brand Identity Development	Executive Interface
Promotional Efforts	Product Specifications	Organizational Abilities

The next example is the manager of a dental practice. She has grouped the experiences into three specific areas that demonstrate her administrative strengths, followed by her credentials as a former dental assistant.

AREAS OF EXPERIENCE

<u>Patient Services</u>: Services Coordination, Patient Schedule, Recall, Post-Op Instruction
<u>Office</u>: Supply Ordering, Cost Control, Accounts Payable/Receivable, Payroll, Human Resources, Vendor Management, Special Events
<u>Assisting</u>: Endo, Ortho, Perio & Oral Surgery, Graphing, Hygiene, Sterilization

A Boeing mechanic included the following section:

AREAS OF EXPERIENCE

• Electrical Safety	• Safety Coaching
• Fall Protection	• TQM Team Member
• Ergonomics	• Advanced Hydraulics
• Chemical Use	• Hazardous Waste Disposal
• Numerical Controls	• Overhead Crane Inspection
• Information Protection	• First Responder Experience

Note also how using an Areas of Experience section is a great tool for getting "key words" into your resume. For more on the importance of key words in "electronic resumes," see pages 147 to 151.

Education

In most resumes the Education section follows your Qualifications.

Your education can be a compelling part of your qualifications. Having a specific degree or a certificate might be a prerequisite for the position you are seeking. In that case, mentioning it is a no-brainer.

Even if you did not complete a degree or certificate program, but have substantial hours of study in the field, your education section can help sell you.

Unless there is a compelling reason not to, education usually belongs up front. It serves to *unfurl* your background as you lead up to your professional history. Another reason is that in occupations where academic credentials are important, this information is usually expected to be near the beginning, and its absence could be misconstrued as hiding or burying something.

If you did not complete high school, yet have completed a few basic classes at a community or technical college, list those and ditch the high school information.

Specialized training and continuing education classes can also trump the lack of a formal degree. Workshops, seminars, and in-house company training sessions reflect professional and personal development.

Sometimes, overwhelming experience and a long career will enable the writer to completely eliminate the education section, particularly if the person lacks the standard education that most peers possess.

As with each entry in the resume, the education piece must be easy to read. Look at sample resumes to see various ways to effectively show education.

HOW TO BEST DISPLAY YOUR EDUCATION

The following section reveals the best way to present your education. Highlight or place a mark by the scenario that best matches your background.

High School Graduate, No College

EDUCATION

Diploma - Roosevelt High School, Chicago, Illinois (1999)

Some College, No Degree

As previously stated, if you have attended college, there is rarely a reason to include your high school.

EDUCATION

Business Studies – University of Nevada – Las Vegas, 136 credits (2000–2003)

The above example demonstrates that the writer completed the lion's share of graduation credits. Specifying the major indicates focus. If you did not declare a formal major but have a substantial cluster of credits in one or more study areas, go ahead and present one or both as your major; choose whichever one is more valuable in selling you.

Certificate from a Technical School

Certificate - Welding Technology, Davis Technical School (2006)

or

EDUCATION

Certificate - Computer Programming, Lake Washington Technical College (2001)

No Degree, Attended Several Colleges

Some people acquire credits at several schools. It is not necessary to list every school attended, but do include all of your credits.

EDUCATION

Business Studies – Cheboit Junior College, Castlerock Community College, Riverside Community College, 98 credits.

The person in the above example actually attended three other colleges, which are not mentioned because they only yielded a few credits. The total number of credits from all six schools is included, but as they were earned over an extended period such as ten years, the range of dates is best left out.

No Degree, Two Colleges Attended

EDUCATION

Theater Studies – Northeastern Illinois University, 70 credits (2001–2003)
English Studies – University of Illinois, Circle Campus, 30 credits (1999)

No Degree, Minimal College

EDUCATION

Total Quality Management, Dreyfuss & Assoc., 24 hours (2008)
Implementing Just in Time, Bob Huston & Assoc., 40 hours (2007)
The Problem Employee, Dreyfuss & Assoc., 8 hours (2006)
Principles of Management, University of Texas, 5 credits (2004)
Motivating Employees, Dreyfuss & Assoc., 16 hours (2002)
Introduction to Marketing, University of Texas, 5 credits (2001)

This individual has been attending professional development seminars and college classes for years. The combination of the two in a single section demonstrates an ongoing commitment to learning and growth.

Degree, One or More Colleges Attended

The most important college to list is the one from which you graduated. If you received a two-year degree from a community college, but then graduated from a four-year college, the associate degree is not included unless it adds something valuable. This might include a specific field of study or a geographic connection. The only date required is the year of graduation from the school that gave you your diploma.

EDUCATION

B.S. – Physics, Rhode Island University (2006)

Will Soon Graduate

If you will graduate in just a few months you might show education like this:

B.A. – Political Science, University of Arizona (June 2009)

In the above example the assumption is that the resume has been written in the fall or winter 2008, and you are scheduled to graduate in June 2009.

If you expect to graduate in the coming year but don't know which quarter, you might express it this way:

B.A. Program – Chemistry, University of Toronto (expected 2009)

Bachelor's Degree Plus Graduate Studies, But No Graduate Degree

EDUCATION

Graduate Studies – Public Administration, University of Georgia (2001–2002)
B.A. – Political Science, University of Georgia (1998)

Graduate Degree(s)

If your thesis is impressive or relevant, present it. A more elaborate description of the thesis can be very effective. It could be described right after the thesis title, or an entire section could be devoted to it called *Thesis*.

EDUCATION

M.A. – Counseling, UCLA (1974)
B.A. – Psychology, Oregon State University (1970)

EDUCATION

Ph.D. – Industrial Psychology, Stanford University (1977)
M.A. – Psychology, Northwestern University (1973)
B.A. – Sociology, Northern Illinois University (1971)

EDUCATION

Ph.D. – Physics, University of Washington (1995)
      Thesis: Interlinear Regression Analysis of Wave Length Dichotomy
M.S. – Physics, University of Washington (1989)
B.S. – Physics, University of Manitoba (1985)

In addition to listing the title of your thesis, it may be useful to provide a brief description. This is especially true if you think that even people in your own field may not fully understand what the title of your thesis means. Even if they will likely understand the terms, they won't fully appreciate the value of your thesis or research without a short description.

EDUCATION

Ph.D. – Physics, University of Nebraska (2002)
      Major: Theoretical Solid State Physics and Mathematical Physics
      Thesis: Analytical Solutions for Flux Phase Analysis
            Research obtained the first analytical solutions for the flux phase,
            which was derived from high-temperature superconductivity
            models. Proved assertions from early numerical calculations.
M.S. – Physics, University of Nebraska (1999)
B.S. – Physics, University of Science and Technology of China (1997)

You can also create a *Projects* section, which would incorporate a description of your thesis as well as other projects you've worked on where you can usually devote more space to the description than you could in the above example.

All But Dissertation

If you have completed all requirements for a graduate degree except for the dissertation or thesis, the education entry might read:

> Doctoral Program, Physics, Iowa State University, completed all but dissertation (2005)

or

> Doctoral Program, Physics, Iowa State University, completed all coursework (2005)

TIPS FOR STRENGTHENING YOUR EDUCATION SECTION

The following tips will help you put the finishing touches on your education section.

Listing Major and Minor

You may want to list both your major and minor if you believe the minor will help to sell you. In the case below, the person wanted to become a labor relations negotiator and felt the economics minor strengthened her credentials.

> **EDUCATION**
>
> **B.A.** – Major: Industrial Relations. Minor: Economics. Syracuse University (1998)

Degrees and Abbreviations

B.A., B.S., M.A., M.S., and Ph.D. degrees are common and readily recognizable. Others are less so. Degrees such as B.F.A. (Bachelor of Fine Arts), M.P.S. (Master of Professional Studies), and A.T.A. (Associate of Technical Arts) are usually better spelled out.

When to Use GPA (Grade Point Average)

Generally GPA is listed only if it is over 3.2. It is usually dropped from your resume after you've been out of school long enough to have established an employment track record. It's interesting to note that most follow-up studies have revealed little correlation between a high college GPA and success on the job. If your overall GPA was unimpressive, but your GPA in your major was above 3.5, you might want to list it this way:

> **B.A.** – Geography, 3.7 in major, University of Oregon (2006)

When to List Honors

If you graduated with honors or with a title such as *Cum Laude* or *Summa Cum Laude*, you could include it like this:

EDUCATION

B.A. – *Cum Laude*, History, Brigham Young University (2005)
B.A. – *with honors*, English Literature, George Washington University (2004)

Location of School

The city and state in which your college is located are usually not included in your resume. This is particularly true if your college is well known in the region in which you are conducting your job search. If you think employers might be curious, however, include the city and state:

B.A. – Business, Griffith College, Austin, Texas (1989)

Order of Schools

Normally schools are listed in reverse chronological order, beginning with your most recent school. Typically this would also mean that your highest-level degree would appear first.

Whether to List Major

People should usually include their majors, even if that major did not directly prepare them for the field they are now in. There are CEOs of *Fortune* 500 companies who graduated with degrees in history or literature. Again, if you have a compelling reason for excluding the major, go ahead. We suggest keeping your major in, but if you feel strongly about removing it, it might look like this:

B.S. – University of Calgary (1992)

Don't Claim Education or Degrees You Don't Have

Confirming an applicant's education is one of the easiest parts of the resume to check and any misrepresentations will sooner or later come back to bite you.

Including Coursework Can Add Impact

Adding coursework, especially for newbies and career changers, can be particularly useful in documenting subject knowledge. Degrees and programs differ from school to school and it is often beneficial to reassure the reader that you have studied the requisite material. List the courses in order of their importance to your stated objective. If you create groups of courses (math, statistics, and physics for example), list courses in order of importance in each category.

EDUCATION

B.A. – Journalism/Advertising, University of Hawaii - 3.39 GPA (2006)
<u>Specialized Coursework</u>: Advertising Copywriting, Public Relations Writing, Media Planning, Media Representation, Production Graphics, Advertising Layout and Design, Media Aesthetics, Principles of Design, Principles of Color

Professional Training

Listing your professional training offers one of the best opportunities to demonstrate that you are up-to-date in your field. Or, if you lack the standard education or degrees typical to the profession, a Training section can demonstrate your ongoing commitment to updating your skills.

It is generally best to separate education from training. Training usually includes seminars and workshops, but can also include specific college courses taken to help you perform better in your field but that are not part of a degree program. Seminars include those sponsored by your employer and those offered by outside consulting firms. For example:

EDUCATION

B.A. – Business, University of Colorado (2003)

PROFESSIONAL TRAINING

Total Quality Control, Rainier Group (24 hours) 2008
Terminating Employees, Human Resources Inc. (8 hours) 2006
Supervising Difficult Employees, Townsend & Assoc. (10 hours) 2004

Listing workshops and seminars can help demonstrate your professional growth. But as valuable as seminars are, be selective about those you choose to include—be sure they are relevant. If you took a course in estate planning, but that knowledge will be of little or no value for the job you're seeking (restaurant management, say), it's better to leave it out.

State the seminar title, the name of the facilitating organization, and the year you attended. If the duration was a day or longer, include the number of hours (days/weeks). If your company sent you to seminars in different cities, it can be beneficial to list the locations. It demonstrates that your employer thought highly enough of you to make that sort of investment.

Some seminars have trendy and marketing-driven titles that don't describe their content. If "Make the Most of Yourself" was really about time management, call it: "Time Management." Review the following:

MANAGEMENT SEMINARS

Managing People, Harvard Business Workshop, four days (2008)
Motivating Employees, Bob Collins & Associates, two days (2006)
Management and Human Relations, California Institute of Technology,
     124 hours (2005)

SEMINARS

Financial Management for Closely Held Businesses, 40 hours,
     Bank of America (2007)
Construction Cost Improvement, 20 hours, Nevett & Associates (2006)
Scheduling, CPM, 20 hours, Nevett & Associates (2005)
Real Estate Syndication, 10 hours, NW Professionals (2004)
Construction Estimating, 30 hours, Lake Washington Technical College (2003)
Closing the Sale, 12 hours, Roff & Associates (2003)
Goal Setting/Richer Life, 18 hours, Zig Ziglar (2001)

Normally, training would be listed directly after education. The two just go together. If the information is lengthy, however, it might be better to move both sections to the second page to assure sufficient room on page one for your most important employment information. An alternative is to keep education on page one and have training on page two.

Some candidates have monster-sized training sections they wish to include. In these cases we recommend creating an additional page or *Addendum* that can be attached when appropriate and omitted when not.

Another strategy for demonstrating substantial outside training is simply describing the types of programs you have attended and the approximate number of hours. This is especially useful for attorneys, CPAs, nurses, and other professionals who require continuing education in order to maintain their licenses. The section can be called Professional Training or Continuing Education

Professional Training

Over 250 hours of classes and seminars in interviewing, hiring/firing, supervision, employee motivation, performance appraisal, interpersonal communications, COBRA administration, project management (list available by request)

Another approach is to present the information in categories:

PROFESSIONAL TRAINING

Computers/Programming

Microsoft Access, Catapult, Inc., 32 hours (2008)
Microsoft Visual Basic, University of Washington, 30 hours (2007)
Intro to C Programming, Everett Community College, 60 hours (2006)
HP Basic Programming, Hewlett-Packard Education, 20 hours (2005)

Communication Skills

Presentation Skills, Decker Communications, 16 hours (2007)
Developing Effective People Skills, Jenkins & Associates, 8 hours (2003)

Employment

Every job is a self-portrait of the person who did it. — UNKNOWN

Your Employment section is the core of the empowered resume. This is where the rubber meets the road. Everything before and after this is supporting material.

The job narrative represents your key opportunity to sell yourself, enabling you to demonstrate the breadth and width of your experience and to showcase your results. It is not just a recitation of duties and responsibilities. It is a statement of *value*.

Employment has four main purposes:

1. It reveals your career progress
2. It describes duties and responsibilities
3. It describes results and accomplishments
4. It accounts for where you've been and for whom you've worked.

You have a definite goal in mind: you want employers to sense your future worth to their organizations. Everything in your resume should demonstrate your ability to master the type of job you are seeking. Include whatever information will create that sense of value; exclude the information that will not.

> Each job narrative should be presented not simply as a patchwork of recycled job descriptions but as an individual success story, replete with duties, results, and accomplishments.

Describing results and accomplishments in your previous positions will do more to reveal your capabilities than anything else. Each job narrative should consist of concisely described duties and at least one real accomplishment. The

Employment section should begin with your most recent position and move backward in reverse chronological order.

Start with a *job sketch*!

USING JOB SKETCHES TO STRENGTHEN YOUR RESUME

If I had eight hours to chop down a tree, I'd spend the first six sharpening my ax. — ABRAHAM LINCOLN

A job sketch represents the time it takes to sharpen your ax. It's an investment of time that pays huge dividends.

The job sketch is what high-tech people refer to as a *brain dump* or *data dump*.

It is a stream-of-consciousness-like review of everything you can recall from each job and an analysis of the results you achieved. Creating an effective job sketch is not difficult, but it does require time and concentration. Our use of job sketches since the 1980s has led to dramatic improvements in the resumes our clients write. Produce a job sketch for each job you intend to include in your resume.

To get a sense of what a job sketch is, review Example 1, on page 36. You'll see how a person simply recalls duties, projects, and results. Notice the impact the results have in the job narrative appearing after the job sketch.

The key to a good job sketch is to simply write whatever pops into your mind. Don't worry about grammar or spelling, just get your thoughts on paper. Go for volume. Write quickly. Don't filter out or neglect to put something down because you think it is insignificant. Only a small portion of your job sketch will end up in the resume, but you will need plenty of data to work with. Don't forget those minor duties that you rarely perform. Some of those minor duties could demonstrate just enough exposure or experience to get you invited to an interview.

After you've listed duties, get to work on any projects you managed or contributed to. Then write a brief description of each, including results and outcomes. A project is anything that has a definite beginning and end.

For instance, bookkeeping, as a job, has ongoing daily, weekly, monthly, quarterly, and yearly activities. Bookkeeping projects can include analyzing the current system to identify areas of improvement, implementing a new software package, or designing a new compensation formula for sales reps.

The true value of the job sketch lies in compelling you to confront your successes, to recall them, relive them, and value them all over again. Once you begin writing, the floodgates will open. Using job sketches will also reduce or eliminate the writer's block that so many experience.

TIP

Even if you are intending to simply add one job to your existing resume, use this as an opportunity to strengthen your resume top to bottom. If your resume contains only duties with few or no results, a complete rewrite is probably in order.

Most of us live in the present. We are concerned with our current jobs, duties, bosses, customers, and a lot more. We can barely remember what we did last week, let alone two or three jobs ago. Recalling previous accomplishments, even duties, can be challenging.

The job sketch is your ticket back in time.

Begin with your current or most recent job. There are two ways to start.

The first method is to simply list your most important responsibilities. What do you do on a daily basis? Weekly? Monthly? Don't worry about grammar, spelling, or listing each function in order of importance. Go for volume. If you have a formal job description—use it as a starting point—then pitch it. Jobs have a way of evolving faster than the published job description.

The other method is to recall if there was a particular mission you were hired or recruited to complete. Turn around a sales program? Improve productivity? Redesign a department? Reclaim lost business? If so, recreate your success. What did you do first? Next? What were your obstacles? Your incremental successes?

Whichever method you choose, you will be surprised at how much information pours forth—like opening a floodgate.

Again, don't skimp. The more you recall, the more you will have to choose from when you actually write the resume. Include everything you can remember, regardless of how unimportant some activities might seem in the grand scheme of things. Be sure to include anything you have done that is related to your current objective, even if it only amounted to a fraction of your actual responsibilities. It still demonstrates exposure to the job you are looking at.

When you have squeezed out every drop of juice from your ongoing duties and responsibilities, dig into your projects. Treat them as mini job sketches. Projects include any task that had a definable beginning, middle, and end. See the project in the senior technician's job sketch below.

As you read the sample job sketches, and the job narratives that resulted from them, notice the impact that the results had. After reading the polished versions of the following job narratives, you will have the definite sense that these three people are very good at what they do.

This first job sketch is thorough and detailed. It took all of 30 minutes to write. Yours may take longer, especially those further back in time. The subsequent job narrative in the actual resume practically wrote itself.

The electronics technician below caught mistakes, solved problems, and constantly identified better ways to do things for a medical equipment manufacturer. Notice how those qualities come through loud and clear. Note how you get a strong sense of what this person is about. Emulate this in your own job sketches.

Example 1

SENIOR TECHNICIAN

Test-printed circuit boards, end items, and systems according to test procedures set by engineering. Troubleshoot down to component level.

Confer with clinical personnel if problems occur with functionality of units, kits, etc. Identify problems and suggest solutions.

Interface with design and R&D engineering regarding fit, form, or functional flaws or problems. Suggest solutions. On the Y235 scanner, suggested solutions that reduced time to produce prototype by four months. On the U454 scanner, identified a problem that would have cost more than $200,000 to fix in the production phase.

Work closely with production, test, and assembly personnel to ensure a proper production flow.

Work with Quality Control on functional as well as cosmetic problems. Fix if necessary or show why QC documents are wrong or why specifications should be changed. Changes in specifications typically speeded up production by 10–15%.

Work with Material Control to ensure parts are available when needed. Expedite shipments when necessary.

Assist engineering in setting up preclinical trials for prototype products.

Check out functional test procedures for Test Engineering to ensure they are correct, practical, and understandable.

Review printed circuit-board schematics and assembly drawings and make corrections where necessary.

Project: Developed a process for storing and maintaining all new product test procedures, drawings, specifications, and parts lists. Many old drawings are still kept on paper or polyester film, but 80% are now electronically stored. Researched numerous software packages that could handle the volume and complexity of drawings and documents that we deal with. Learned the software and trained employees in its usage. This hard copy filing system and the electronic system have improved access and use of all data and save approximately 400 man-hours per year. Previously engineers and technicians often did not seek out older data that we had stored because it could take an hour or more to find some physical files and the electronically stored data was often just as time consuming to find.

Notice how points in the final job narrative were taken right from the job sketch, often with only minor revisions.

SENIOR TECHNICIAN – 3/97 to Present. As Senior Technician for this manufacturer of CAT scanners, test printed circuit boards, end items, and systems, troubleshooting down to component level. Rework failed equipment. Work closely with clinical personnel and design engineers to identify problems and suggest solutions.

Identified and resolved a problem with one product that would have cost more than $200,000 to fix in the production stage. Interface with Quality Control and frequently recommend changes in QC specifications. Recommendations typically speed up production by 10–15%. Played a key role in reducing the time to produce the Y235 scanner prototype by four months.

Assist Engineering in setting up preclinical trials for prototype products. Review test procedures established by Test Engineering to ensure tests are understandable and workable. Review PC schematics, assembly drawings, and parts lists, and make corrections where necessary. Developed and currently maintain an electronic file of all test procedures, drawings, parts lists, and specifications, which has significantly improved access and use of the data, saving approximately 400 hours per year.

So, now that you understand how a job sketch works, read Examples 2 and 3.

Example 2

In the following job sketch, the writer emphasizes some great successes in the tourism industry. Once he identified his successes in the job sketch, writing the job narrative was a cinch.

EXECUTIVE DIRECTOR

Managed and administered a statewide nonprofit association developing and promoting tourism in Idaho.

I conducted tourism seminars statewide for members of the private sector and performed lobbying duties in the state legislature on tourism issues.

I managed a staff of three, plus an intern, and reported to an elected board of directors from throughout the state.

I was the chief advocate for the private sector in tourism promotion and marketing. It required strong people skills to work with the private sector, plus gain the support of several state agencies and of the state legislature.

Played a key role in the increase in tourism revenue, which increased an average of 18% for each of the three years, versus 8–10% increases each of the five previous years. Many resort and tourism areas set records for revenue.

Our association received a $150,000 federal grant to further tourism, in recognition of the high quality of our efforts the two previous years.

Project: Increased dues-paying membership approximately 20% each year because of our success in increasing tourism. Everyone wanted to be a part of what we were doing. Called or visited hundreds of hotels, resorts, and tourist spots to promote our efforts at increasing tourism. After two years of increased tourism throughout the region, owners of hotels, restaurants, and tourist attractions saw the impact we were having and were (usually) happy to pay our very reasonable dues. These dues were critical for advertising and also to provide consulting assistance to key tourist attractions.

In his job narrative, he does a nice job of combining his duties with his results.

Idaho Hospitality & Visitors Association, Boise, ID 1998–2001

EXECUTIVE DIRECTOR – Administered this statewide nonprofit association in promoting tourism to and within the State of Idaho. Lobbied the state legislature and had a solid impact in both protecting and enhancing the interests of the tourism industry. Established local groups to follow up with legislators on specific issues.

Obtained a key federal grant for the Regional Tourism Project in recognition of the overall effectiveness of the program. Played a key role in increasing state tourism revenue an average of 18% annually versus 8-10% annual increases in the previous five years.

Conducted highly regarded seminars for the private sector which enabled them to strengthen their marketing and promotional activities. Increased dues-paying membership approximately 20% per year and played a key role in increasing tourism dollars throughout the state. Supervised a staff of three.

Example 3

DIRECTOR, INTRAMURAL SPORTS

After being a volunteer coach and referee for the intramural program, I interviewed for and got the Director of Intramural Sports position as a work-study job.

Planned the intramural program and increased co-ed sports from three to six. Created teams in each sport and provided them with coaches.

The prior year I heard rumblings from the women that the co-ed intramural sports were not fun because the guys were too rough and too competitive in softball, flag football, table tennis, and volleyball. At the start of the school year I wrote an article that was published in the school newspaper explaining co-ed sports were designed to have fun and provide opportunities to meet and have fun with those of the opposite sex. Students got similar information as they signed up for intramural teams.

I emailed women and men who had participated in the past and let them know the new policies and expectations. Referees were instructed to take guys aside if they were getting too rough. Swearing and making sexist comments were "outlawed." I sent out email surveys which were returned by 80% of the women and 65% of the men. More than 90% of the men and women who responded indicated they would turn out for additional co-ed sports.

Reached out to those who had coached and refereed the year before and assured them that we would have a great year. Most of the coaches and referees returned. I brought in high school coaches and referees to provide clinics. The clinics were very well attended. Because of the quality of volunteers and the clinics, there were far fewer complaints about referees than in the past. Part of that was because participants were more interested in having fun and not worrying about a bad call.

Through a lot of publicity and talking with lots of past participants, the co-ed program started off completely different. There was a totally new attitude. Even the guys had more fun. After games the teams typically went out for pizza, something that rarely occurred before. Referees were invited to join them and got their food paid for.

Participation in all intramural programs increased from 24% to 55% for women and from 54% to 64% for men. Most of the increases occurred in the co-ed programs.

Recruited two assistants who were nearly as committed to intramural sports as I was. They were a huge asset.

Being on a tight budget I had to really negotiate with our equipment suppliers. I had excellent relationships with the suppliers. I was even able to get some hand-me-down equipment from the varsity programs.

> **Director of Intramural Sports** – Planned, staffed, and organized the intramural sports program. Working with a tight budget, assessed equipment needs, received bids from sporting goods suppliers, and purchased sports equipment. Supervised two assistants and recruited and supervised dozens of volunteers. Developed a new concept in women's athletics and actively promoted the program. Participation by women grew from 24% in previous years to 55%. Participation by men increased from 54% to 64%. Developed successful refereeing clinics along with new sportsmanship rules that dramatically reduced fights and complaints regarding calls by referees.

While the data and information you produce for your job sketch are important and useful, the very process of writing the job sketch serves other valuable functions. It compels you to recall *all* the duties and functions of the job and allows you to choose the most important ones for your resume. It also enables you to relive the experiences, making them more vivid. What's more, it helps you recall your accomplishments and results. In addition, the very act of remembering, sorting through, and writing down all of your duties, accomplishments, and experiences prepares you for interviews.

As you write your job sketches, it is important that you make the most out of each one of your accomplishments.

Save all of your job sketches and begin keeping track of what you're doing on your current job. Look for ways to produce hard data on your successes and look for opportunities to improve things at work.

ACCOMPLISHMENTS

Every job ever created has built-in criteria for success. A sales rep sells, a manager manages, a teacher teaches, and so on. If you are not fired the first day of your new job and go on to maintain even minimum tenure, you probably have succeeded in doing what you are supposed to be doing.

There's an old baseball axiom "We're never as good as we think . . . nor as bad." Even the biggest employment disasters have elements of success. Projects that have gone awry have had parts that were completed successfully.

To the resume reader, accomplishments separate real achievers from mere *job holders*. Duties alone cannot do this. Consider two people, each with ten years of experience and identical job titles. Applicant A has not had an original idea in three years. The drive and initiative that propelled A upward is gone.

Applicant B, however, has demonstrated significant accomplishments each year and still exhibits great enthusiasm. Only their accomplishments will distinguish over-the-hill applicant A from full-of-potential applicant B.

Accomplishments define you. They create strong impressions. This is an *emotional*—not an *intellectual*—exercise.

Stressing accomplishments in a resume is important for everyone, but it is absolutely critical for the person who is changing careers, because those accomplishments will prove your potential for success in the new career.

Employers make hiring decisions based on perceived potential. Experience is merely an indication, not a predictor, of this potential. It is certainly an advantage to be able to come in and be able to do the job from day one but that is not a guarantee of future success.

Accomplishments do not have to be big, knock-your-socks-off types of events. They are contributions you made to the organization. They demonstrate successes you have had in either performing the functions of your job, accomplishing projects, or going above and beyond the call of duty.

An employer who clearly sees how your past contributions stack up will sense your future value. Now, *that's* potential!

Describe your accomplishments concisely and concretely so that they'll have impact. Employers seek people who can increase profits, decrease costs, solve problems, or reduce the stress and pressure they face.

QUANTIFYING AND QUALIFYING

Statements of success in some jobs can easily be conveyed by such terms as *increased*, *decreased*, and their numerous derivatives (improved, expanded, reduced, etc.)

Specific information such as percentages and dollar figures make accomplishments more tangible and impressive. Compare these two statements:

"Implemented new personnel policies, which increased morale" and "Implemented new personnel policies that reduced absenteeism by 27% and reduced turnover by 24%." Which is more effective?

Of course, each result must be reasonable, believable, and presented in good faith. And, as is the case with any claim, they must be able to be backed up. Backup does not mean you must have a former boss, coworker, or customer who will confirm each claim, although that can certainly help. Instead, what we mean by backup is that during an interview you are prepared to tell the story of how you obtained your results. You need not produce absolute proof, nor do employers expect it.

Numbers do not have to be gleaned verbatim from company records. If available, they are solid evidence of your claims. Quite often, though, this information is not available. In these cases, it is essential to be able to describe, if necessary, how you arrived at the final number.

Each claim you make about yourself in every section of the resume will be received solely due to the credibility you elicit in the reader. This is also true when you articulate these claims at the interview.

Calculating percentages or dollar figures when you have no verifying figures can require creative thinking and, sometimes, creative guessing.

The following example illustrates how this can be done.

Saving Money in Alaska

Roger wanted to leave Alaska, where he had repaired heavy construction machinery. He knew he was a top-level mechanic but could think of no *hard* evidence to prove it. In preparing his job sketch, he recalled that he had constantly designed new tools for difficult projects that reduced the time of certain repairs. One particular tool enabled him to install a $900 part on the first try. Previously, there was no way to ensure perfect alignment, with the required reliability to function under extreme pressure. On occasion, the new part would be damaged, requiring another replacement. As the part cost $900, Roger estimated he had saved the company several thousands of dollars in immediate replacement costs as well as in longer-term damage created by faulty alignment. Noting his success, his fellow mechanics copied the tool, similarly reducing damage, downtime, and replacement costs. Roger selected $20,000 in annual cost savings as a reasonable amount he felt he could comfortably defend at the interview. Not a single interviewer disputed the numbers.

Ideas for Identifying Accomplishments, Achievements, and Results

Terms such as *accomplishments* and *results* are often used interchangeably. For our purposes, we will define results as the actual *benefit* of a given accomplishment.

So, the first step toward the result is in identifying the accomplishments.

What exactly is an accomplishment? Simply put, an accomplishment is any experience in which you:

- Did something well
- Were complimented for it
- Got satisfaction from it
- Were proud of it.

If you responded positively to any or all of these descriptions, you have defined an accomplishment. Generate as many as you can. You will be surprised and amazed at how many you come up with. Of course, not all accomplishments will end up in the resume, but it's nice to have a bunch from which to pick and choose.

- Did you create, reorganize, or establish any effective procedures or systems?
- Did you simplify or streamline a process that increased productivity?
- Did you oversee or participate in a special project that had a positive outcome?
- Have you done anything that saved money, or solved a problem?
- Did you make something work better?
- Are you a good supervisor or trainer whose people get promoted faster and farther than your fellow supervisors?
- Did you receive any awards or special recognition from a boss, the company, a customer, or an industry association?

For an extensive "trigger your brain" list of successes you may have, go to Appendix 1.

Accomplishments are not restricted to employment. Volunteer work, community service, and outside projects are fertile grounds for demonstrating value. You can determine later if these items are appropriate for your resume.

- Did you compete in marathons or other races?
- Raise money for charity?
- Coach a youth soccer team that learned team work and sportsmanship?
- Receive an achievement award from an organization you belong to?

Using Results to Create Impact

It's great when you've got company printouts or documents to prove what you are claiming, but few people have access to those types of records. In such cases it will be necessary to *guesstimate*. This is a very acceptable practice. When estimating, it is best to be a little on the conservative side so you can say in an interview that the results were probably greater than stated in the resume. You will never be expected to provide official records to an interviewer, so what you are actually selling is your credibility. Just be prepared to describe how you came up with your results and, as usual, do not misrepresent.

Accomplishments that cannot be translated into dollars or percentages can still have impact. Statements such as "Selected as employee of the month" or "Brought the product to market five months ahead of schedule" can have a powerful effect on employers.

In the following job narratives, notice how accomplishments are described very briefly, serving to generate interest on the part of the reader. Elaboration is saved for the interview.

In the Memory Academy example below, notice the quality of the contributions, despite the complete *absence* of numbers. You will quickly recognize that she is responsible, creative, hard-working, and an excellent supervisor and trainer. She is the type of person who is always looking for ways to improve programs and systems.

Memory Academy, Dallas, Texas 2002 to 2005

OFFICE MANAGER/EXECUTIVE INSTRUCTOR – Office manager of a 14-person office with direct responsibility for ten. Developed and wrote detailed manuals for each position and created a smooth functioning office. In 2003 redesigned the teaching techniques of the memory course. Instructors immediately experienced better results and received enthusiastic ratings from clients.

Accomplishments are stuffed to the gills with powerful information. One 15-word accomplishment can say more and have more impact than a hundred words in a job narrative. Look at the following two examples and notice the impact (italics added) of the accomplishments. Imagine what the impact would be without them.

Des Moines Trust & Savings, Des Moines, Iowa, 9/94 to Present

BRANCH OPERATIONS MANAGER – Managed operations at three branches and supervised 26 employees. *Overcame serious morale problems* by working closely with the branch staffs and providing better training and supervision. Within the branches *absenteeism was reduced 42% and turnover 48%.* Customer service and marketing of bank services were measurably improved. Based on customer surveys, the *customer service rating improved from 74% good or excellent to 92%.*

∽

Central Mortgage, 5/96 to Present

DIVISION MANAGER, Missoula, Montana, 8/98 to Present. Opened the Missoula office and set up all bookkeeping and office systems. Within ten months became the number-one home mortgage lender in the Missoula area and obtained 31% of the mortgage market and 44% of all construction loans. During five years have averaged 48% profit on gross income, the highest in the company among 33 offices.

The following example vividly illustrates the need for accomplishments. The first version lacks both accomplishments and impact. The revision ultimately sold the person into a good position.

Before

SALES REPRESENTATIVE – 2/02 to Present. Develop and service established accounts as well as new accounts. Set pricing structures after determining the market. Responsible for the district's western Orange County territory. Sales have increased each year.

After

SALES REPRESENTATIVE – 2/02 to Present. In the first three years moved the territory from last in the district to first among ten territories. Aggressively went after new accounts and have significantly increased market share in the territory. By 2005 became the number one sales rep in total profits and have maintained that position. Profits have increased an average of 12% annually.

Is there any question which resume would more likely result in an interview?

Notice that the impression you get of the person is much stronger in the second version, yet it required just two more lines than the first. This powerful effect can be created by presenting *how well* you've done in jobs, rather than just what you did. Accomplishments speak for themselves and you rarely need to go into detail regarding all the things you did to get your results. Save the details for an interview.

Sometimes you will want to allude to what was done without providing details. The bank branch operations manager presented earlier provides a perfect example. She said, "Overcame serious morale problems by working closely with the branch staffs and providing better training and supervision. Within the branches, absenteeism was reduced 42% and turnover 70%." How she got her results is merely implied. An employer who wants to know more of how she did it will have to interview her.

In the resume below, a bank controller's job narrative does not do him justice. Because this was his most recent and most responsible position, more detail is required to show his potential. Although the second job narrative is longer, it is well written and concise. It does not contain any unnecessary words. Everything mentioned is designed to sell him and give an employer a full view of his experience.

Before

Controller – Managed accounting department, seven-person staff; prepared financial statements and filed various reports with state and federal agencies; assisted and advised senior management concerning regulatory accounting and tax ramifications of decisions and policies; worked with savings and loan divisions on operational and systems design; served as primary liaison with computer service bureau in Los Angeles.

After

Controller – Managed a seven-person accounting department and significantly increased productivity by simplifying procedures, cross-training staff, and improving morale. Prepared financial statements and advised senior management on regulatory, accounting, and tax ramifications of new policies and programs under consideration. Heavily involved in the research and planning of an investment "swap" program that resulted in a $5.3 million tax refund. Successfully directed the bank's response when the refund resulted in an IRS audit.

As financial division representative, worked closely with both the savings and loan divisions to increase interdivision cooperation related to new systems, operations, and customer service. Significantly improved communications with the bank's service bureau and implemented modifications in the general ledger system that streamlined operations and saved more than $40,000 per year.

The accomplishments he included were his increase in productivity, finding a unique approach for justifying a large tax credit and then defending it before the IRS, increasing cooperation among divisions in the bank, improving relations with the computer service bureau, and saving money on computer services. These accomplishments cannot help but pique the interest of a targeted employer.

Results Sell People

Below are additional statements that effectively convey accomplishments. Read them and see how you might apply the ideas to your own situation. Quantified results are those that use numbers, such as percentages. Qualified results use only words to describe the result.

Quantified:

Developed a new production technique that increased productivity by 7%.

Through more effective recruiting techniques, reduced terminations company-wide by 30% and turnover by 23%.

Edited a newsletter for an architectural association, with readership increasing 28% in one year.

Organized a citizen task force that successfully wrote a statewide initiative, adopted with a 69% favorable vote.

As chairperson for fund-raising, developed a strategy that increased funds raised by 26% while reducing promotional costs.

Set a record of 46 days without a system failure.

Qualified:

Awarded *Medal of Merit* for contributions to the community.

Established a voluntary labor-management forum that significantly reduced tension between labor and management.

Developed a self-managed quality program that substantially reduced noncompliant parts.

The advertising tie-in with *Toy Story* was credited with building strong name recognition for our new toy line.

Received a letter of appreciation from the chairperson of the Ballard Community Council for bringing together 20 local businesses that provided seed money for a community center.

Played a key role on a task force that recommended over 20 ways to improve plant safety. Not only have injuries been significantly reduced, but morale has also improved as production personnel recognized that the company valued and respected them.

Which/Which Resulted In

Accomplishments and results are powerful. Everything you've done in your jobs has had a result. When the result is positive *and* significant, it belongs in the resume. Train yourself to look for results. You don't need company documents to lend credence to your claims. Your own honest estimate is sufficient. If asked about it during an interview, just describe how you arrived at the figure and then go into more detail concerning how you accomplished it. The credibility you've built during the interview and your good-faith estimation will cause employers to more fully appreciate your value.

Here's a surefire method for identifying accomplishments.

As you list each duty or project, tack on the words *which*, or *which resulted in*, and then follow it where it leads.

For example, "Wrote an office procedures manual" becomes, "Wrote an office procedures manual, *which* decreased training time and billing errors." Now, give the results some results and see how it becomes:

"Wrote an office procedures manual, which decreased training time of new employees by 25% and reduced billing errors more than 30%."

When numbers aren't available, results still can be expressed. "Automated the accounting system" becomes "Automated the accounting system, which (dramatically/substantially/significantly) improved efficiency and accuracy."

When you think you have completed your job sketches, take a deep breath and have another run at it. Check each entry for something you might have missed.

Where Are You in the Pecking Order?

If others in your office, group, or organization perform similar functions, is there a way to compare your performance to theirs? A salesperson, for example, might ask, "How am I doing in comparison to the other salespeople in my district in terms of revenue generation or new accounts obtained?" A machine operator might ask, "How am I doing compared to the other machine operators regarding production, quality, and the ability to produce complex parts?"

When describing an accomplishment, include concrete information about its effect. Don't stop short. People often write in a way they think demonstrates a solid result, but they fail to show its true benefit. For example, one individual wrote, "Developed a new system to better schedule production and reduce late deliveries." Through the use of the word "to" the person is merely implying that the *goal* was to improve scheduling and decrease late shipments. The statement does not tell us for sure that it actually worked! Look what happens when we add *which*: "Developed a system *which* improved production scheduling and nearly eliminated late deliveries." There is now no doubt that the new system accomplished its goal and had a positive impact on the operation.

Don't assume, just because a result does not come to mind immediately, that it does not exist. People are often amazed when they go over their job sketches a second time, or when a friend helps out, to find that there were many more results than were initially visible.

All projects that have successful conclusions contain one or more results you can use. Some duties, however, do not lend themselves to obvious results. So you did your job . . . big deal. But here's the thing: every job has built-in success criteria. Consistently doing your job well is, in itself, an achievement. That's why you are being paid. So what is your track record? Have you been dependable? Conscientious? Thorough? Accurate? Helpful to others? These are all real accomplishments.

Recall your duties from previous jobs and ask yourself whether there could be a result hiding in there that you might have missed. The more you find, the more empowering your resume will become—along with the subsequent interviews you will be invited to.

Identifying Results Within an Accomplishment

People often decide their mission is complete after defining a single result from an activity. Many times, however, others are actually lurking in the shadows, just waiting to be discovered. Each one is important. Even if not all of your results get into your resume, they can become highly valuable in letters, interviews, and in your general sense of marketability.

TO VERSUS *THAT*:
DID IT OR DIDN'T IT?

Remember the guy a few paragraphs back who "developed a system that improved production scheduling and nearly eliminated late deliveries?" His is a case that proves that when you are presenting results, good intentions are not enough.

For instance:

- "Developed new procedures to increase office productivity" is a noble effort. But to say "to" only indicates intent, leaving the reader hanging, wondering if it worked out.
- "Developed new procedures *that* increased office productivity" is a real accomplishment. It happened!

TIP

In many of the examples in this section, and in the sample resumes you'll notice that one or more results are included in each job narrative. This is necessary to give you good examples. Don't be discouraged if your results don't fully match the ones in these resumes. Simply spend the time to identify your personal accomplishments. If you're not satisfied with your past results, look for ways to obtain results in your current job or in your next job. Also, take it as a cue that you were working for the wrong organization, or are working in a job that does not fully utilize your strengths or which does not motivate you.

CALCULATING RESULTS/GUESSTIMATING

One reason we don't see more statistics in resumes, such as percentage increases, is that people are not always sure of or comfortable in calculating their results.

In fact, most of us are not all that comfortable in saying nice things about ourselves to begin with.

Calculating results normally takes a bit of simple arithmetic, basic division, a dose of logic, and a little *guesstimating*.

NUMERATE NOW!

In the process of calculating results, the first step is to identify all the benefits, whether these were something improved, increased, or decreased. Start with the assumption that if you can identify it you can quantify it. Quantifying results may require some guesstimating, but here's how you can do it.

Review your job sketches to see what clues they might give you. Were there any functions that were left off the sketches that you now think might be valuable? Were there any projects that were not mentioned? If a project achieved its goal, it almost assuredly had a slew of usable results. Even if you think a particular result was too small or insignificant to mention in the resume, spend some time developing it because it might be a useful addition to an interview.

Remember, your resume will contain only a fraction of the information you will be generating. You will need additional and supporting information to present at interviews. This is the place to build your arguments and develop the evidence to back them up.

Suppose you know that an action you took improved something—sales, profits, productivity, turnover—but you don't have the company's records to prove it.

Let's look at turnover. When you took over the department, there was a chronic morale problem. People were regularly leaving out of frustration. Of the 16 people who had been employed the previous year, five quit and one was fired, for a total of six and a 38% turnover rate.

With a turnover rate that high, productivity was bound to be low because people did not stay around long enough to adequately learn their jobs nor were they sufficiently motivated to perform them well. In addition, the supervisor was probably devoting an inordinate amount of time training new people and cleaning up mistakes. So that supervisor was fired and you were thrown into the hornet's nest.

Having identified the failings of your predecessor, you developed a corrective plan. You worked closely with the core group until they were adequately trained and reasonably proficient in their jobs. This took a lot of overtime on your part, which you probably did not get paid for, but you made sure they knew what they were doing. You gave them strokes and they appreciated that.

During your first year as manager, four people left, the next year only two, and the next year, two again. Your turnover rate for the first year was 25%. The second and third years it was 12%. There is no doubt things had stabilized.

Now you need to determine the percentage by which you reduced turnover, and what other benefits accrued as a result. The turnover rate has been reduced from 38% to 12%. Just an approximation will tell you that the reduction is about two-thirds, or 67%. The actual reduction is 68% and it is what we would call a hard number since the manager knew the actual turnover rate each year.

As valuable as reducing turnover is, that is only the tip of the iceberg. Because the staff was now better trained, they made fewer mistakes, got more done, and provided better customer service.

Were there previous measures of productivity (such as number of widgets produced) or quality (error rate, customer complaints)? If so, the result can be presented as:

- Developed an effective training program that increased productivity 14%, and reduced customer complaints 75%.

Or

- Effectively improved morale, resulting in a 68% reduction in turnover in just two years.

Or

- Effectively improved morale resulting in reducing annual turnover rate from 38% to 12%. (You can make this even stronger if you can determine whether your result brought the turnover below the industry standard.)

From here, measure the improvements in quality, productivity, and customer service. The resume might read:

Developed an effective training program that reduced turnover from 38% to 12%. As a result of the program, productivity increased more than 14%, and customer complaints were reduced 75%.

You are going to impress yourself with that statement.

> **Tom:** We're not saying that all of your results and benefits can be quantified. We are saying that many can be and you owe it to yourself to look for ways to quantify them. When you simply cannot quantify a result, work hard to write about it in such a way that the reader will sense that something was better because of your efforts.

Calculating Results

Calculating results is not difficult, but some folks are challenged so we're going to show you how to calculate your results *and* how to get a website to magically do the calculation for you. The website is www.csgnetwork.com/percentchangecalc.html. When you go to this URL the screen will look like this.

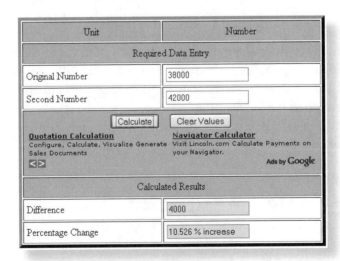

Simply key in both your numbers and hit calculate. **Do not use commas such as 1,245,621.** The system will not calculate it if there are commas. The site does not tell you this, but trust us, it will not work.

Increases

Let's look at a simple example and we'll give you easy formulas for calculating increases and decreases. Here's a scenario. As a kid you took over a paper route with 50 customers. At least one day a month you would knock on a few doors to sell subscriptions. Over a two year period you built your route to 60 customers. By what percentage did you increase your customers?

The formula is $\dfrac{b-a}{a} = x$

a (the original number) is 50   b (the second number) is 60

So, $\dfrac{60-50}{50} = \dfrac{10}{50} = .2$ which is 20% Customers were increased by 20%.

Whether you increased something from 10 to 14 (40%) or from 126,000 to 148,000 (17%), the formula always works.

Decreases

Let's say you were responsible for reducing overdue accounts for a small business. You developed a better way to contact people and to discuss their overdue accounts more effectively. When you started the program your company had 1200 overdue accounts. A year later you had reduced the number to 500. By what percentage did you decrease overdue accounts?

The formula is $\dfrac{a-b}{a} = x$

a (the original number) is 1200   b (the second number) is 500

So, $\dfrac{1200-500}{1200} = \dfrac{700}{1200} = .583$ or 58% Overdue accounts were reduced by 58%.

Provide Proof of Results When Possible

The value of including results, especially quantified results, has already been established. In addition to including a quantified result, it is very helpful to provide documentation if possible. This might include figures published by your company, numbers that you produced but that were confirmed by your boss, or figures produced by an informed third party.

Many companies want to know their market share and will regularly retain research firms to provide it. If you are a sales manager and have access to data documenting that market share increased significantly on your watch, don't hesitate to use it. Such proof can be presented in several ways. Achievement awards, bonuses, and merit raises are always useful in demonstrating your successes. Below you'll see a couple of examples.

> **Mechanical Engineer** – For this $45 million manufacturer of latex surgical gloves, designed a total quality management program that has saved $1.5 million in the first year as documented by an internal management audit.

Or

> **Operations Manager** – Designed a cost-saving program in the areas of shipping, warehousing, material flow, and just-in-time purchasing. Received the *Corporate Gold Medal Award* for one of the top-five cost-saving programs among the 25 plants nationwide.

TAKE THE CREDIT YOU DESERVE

Most group activities consist of leaders, workers, and shuckers. The leaders and workers make things happen, the shuckers go along for the ride. The reasons why the shuckers are in the group include being assigned against their wills or volunteering in order to get out of doing their own jobs.

If you were a leader or worker . . . do not be afraid to take the credit due your efforts. If you were the moving force who initiated everything and led the department or division in implementation, you are justified in taking full credit:

* Designed and implemented a cost-saving inventory program that . . .

    Or

* Led the team that . . .

    If you were one of two or three leaders, who deserve credit, share it:

* Co-led the initiative that . . . .

    Perhaps you were in charge of various parts of a project:

* Led key processes in the project that . . .

Or you were an important worker who made solid contributions to the success:

- Played a key role in . . .
- Actively contributed to . . .
- Credited as a major factor in the success . . .

AVOID *ASSISTED/HELPED IN*

Using the phrase *assisted in,* nearly always dilutes your actual contribution. Select examples from above to better describe your actual role.

WHEN NUMBERS ARE NOT AVAILABLE

When actual numbers for your results are just not available, and you don't feel comfortable estimating, use terms such as *substantial, dramatic, significant, solid, or strong.*

In these cases, you still want to accurately present your contributions with the right impact.

You can have:

- *Substantial* sales increases
- *Dramatic* reductions in turnover
- *Significant* improvements in customer satisfaction rankings
- *Solid* growth in satisfied customers
- *Strong* improvement in quality.

QUALIFYING YOUR RESULTS

Not every achievement is quantifiable or neatly folded into specific dollars or percentages. How do you measure morale increases? Or your reputation among your peers? What about your track record as the *go-to person?*

Every time you are commended by your boss, a customer, a co-worker, or anyone else, for that matter, for doing something on the job, it is a statement of value. It can be a written commendation, letter of appreciation, or pat on the back. You have made an impression.

Perhaps you are the *subject matter expert* in legal issues or policy. Or, you are the one who always seems to be handed escalated problems. Do customers ask specifically for you to service their accounts or resolve their problems? Do you get a lot of referrals from previous customers? Are you regularly selected by your supervisor for special or difficult assignments?

Do you have a track record for completing your work on time with a high rate of accuracy? Have you been recognized for coming in early, staying late, or coming in weekends to assure deadlines are met?

There is a place in the resume for all these commendations, pats-on-the-back, and "we couldn't do it without you" statements. They do not have to be formal personnel-file type of acclaim, just as a salesperson's numbers may not be published or available. It is a matter of credibility and how you present the information.

- Consistently commended by clients for providing timely and customized service.
- Regularly selected by management for special projects and assignments.
- Track record for accurately completing all assignments on time.
- Recognized as the branch's primary resource on customer service policies.

THERE IS SUCCESS IN FAILURE

Most of our job functions are components of a larger organization. Despite our personal performances and those of our peers, the company might be on a downward spiral. Or a project we have contributed to has been defunded. Or the overall revenue figures of our region's sales team are down while yours are on track.

> Don't tar yourself with the brush of failure. If your contributions were positive, present them as such!

WRITING YOUR JOB NARRATIVES

Job narratives are the heart of the resume. Everything else is just supporting material.

The job narratives are a series of success stories that provide the reader an unbroken string of value, achievement, and contribution. This is where, as they say in law, you make your argument.

Who is this *"Employer?"*

We speak the term *"Employer"* as if it were bold, italicized, and in an extra-large font. Just who is this *"Employer?"*

Well, guess what? The *"Employer"* is just a person. Like you and me. Male, female, father, mother, son, daughter, nephew, niece . . . etc. There is no single prototype of the *"Employer."* So, don't try to create something directed at this monolithic mythical beast. You are the expert in what you need to present.

If you have a reasonably focused vocational direction, a good place to start the first draft of the resume is with your objective. That will help keep you on track in selecting those pieces of your background that specifically relate to it.

Thus, you will choose the duties, experiences, and achievements that best demonstrate your qualifications for that type of work. If you have substantial direct experience, the selection process becomes one of determining which information best sells you.

Those without a true objective have a somewhat different mandate. In this case, you want to select those experiences that represent you more generally to the reader. The beauty of the narrative format is its ability to demonstrate your skills in diverse enterprises and settings.

In reviewing the job sketch you created for your current or most recent position, identify the most important things an employer should know about the experience. Don't worry about length; you can tighten the writing and eliminate less important duties later.

The empowered resume will present your best attributes to the reader: Diligence . . . Initiative . . . Efficiency . . . Cooperation . . . Effectiveness . . . Teamwork. Your duties must be adequately covered so that the employer will understand and appreciate the full range of your experience. The types of positions you will be seeking will determine which duties should be highlighted the most. Duties unrelated to your objective can be dispensed with briefly or omitted entirely. By focusing on the related activities along with accomplishments, the reader can sense your potential.

The examples below demonstrate these points. Read the job narratives as originally written; then read the revisions. Notice how the revisions were made and how they heightened the overall impact.

In the following example, notice how the first version is concise, but lacks valuable detail. The second version provides a fuller, more vivid picture of her experiences.

Also, as you study the revised job narrative, ask yourself what you know about the person that you didn't before. The revised job narrative is somewhat longer, but the extra detail and value it provides, more than justifies the extra few lines.

Version 1

EMPLOYMENT

Employer	Wiggins Sportswear 2007 to Present
Position	Marketing Coordinator
Responsibilities	Coordinate the entire clothing program
	Creating and utilizing Excel spreadsheets for marketing, production, and finance projections
	Market research
	Coordinating advertising with publications
	Work with outside contractors on special projects
	Fabric and notion research/purchasing
	Calculated preliminary and final costing of garment
	Approved bills relating to the clothing program
Employer	Broadway Department Store 2006 to 2007
Position	Salesperson
Responsibilities	Sales and interior layout and display
	Opening and closing the department
	Handling customer complaints and problems

Version 2

EMPLOYMENT

Wiggins Sportswear, San Diego, California 2007 to present

Marketing Coordinator - Coordinate the production and marketing functions for a new line of active sportswear. Came into the project when it was two months behind schedule and over budget. Worked with the designer to select colors, designs, and fabrics.

Purchased fabric and accessories. Negotiated with two garment manufacturers to produce small lots, thus reducing the required unit sales to reach a break-even point. Worked out schedule arrangements with manufacturers and authorized any changes in specifications. Line was introduced on schedule with final costs 10% lower than originally projected.

Coordinated the production of the annual sales catalog. Designed order forms, verified prices, and consulted with graphic artists and printers. Had authority to make all necessary changes.

Set up the company's first computerized systems, using Excel and other software to provide the first accurate year-to-date sales figures, as well as highly useful marketing, financial, and manufacturing projections.

Broadway Department Stores, San Diego, California 2006 to 2007

Salesperson - Sold women's clothing and had interior layout and display responsibilities. Selected as Employee of the Month for December in this store of approximately 190 employees. Selected on the basis of sales, favorable comments from customers, and taking on added responsibilities.

The revised version is longer than the original, but because it provides more background, you get a clearer picture of her capabilities. By mentioning a project that was behind schedule and over budget, her ability to complete it on schedule and under budget makes the accomplishment especially meaningful. Her original resume contains only a brief list of duties and provides no information regarding whether she had been successful. The revised job narrative conveys her talent and potential. It shows that she was given a lot of responsibility and that she handled it well. It suggests to the reader that she has some very interesting stories to tell about her experiences at Wiggins; but hearing them will require an interview.

The experience at Broadway did not receive as much space because she has no intention of returning to retail work. The experience does, however, demonstrate valuable background which pertains directly to her career in marketing. It is important that she was able to demonstrate success even in a short-term job. Simply listing her duties provides no clues about the quality of her work and could be construed that she left early as a result of poor performance. Mentioning that she was employee-of-the-month proves she was valuable. By mentioning the basis for the award—sales, comments from customers, and taking on added responsibility—she demonstrated she excelled in each category and was recognized for it.

As you write your job narratives, look for ways to tell your story that convey your value and your successes. Even if you were fired from a job it is possible to demonstrate value. Stress what you did well and ignore the other stuff.

The next job narrative was created by a youth counselor. One of his earlier positions was as supervisor for a municipal parks department. Version 1 provides nothing but a dull list of duties. He was a very interesting person with an excellent background, but you couldn't tell from this. The entire narrative is one long sentence set off with semicolons. This style is extremely hard to read, but unfortunately, not uncommon. Mark Twain described this type of sentence as one "in which you can ride all day without have to change cars!"

Version 1

Supervisor — Portland Park Department, Portland, Oregon. Overall responsibility for staff, facility, and program at a neighborhood community center; supervising, hiring, training, and recruitment; program planning, implementation, and evaluation; record keeping, budgeting, grant writing, and analyses; work with schools, local, state, and federal agencies in a variety of capacities; direct service including teaching, training, and work with adults and youth in social, educational, cultural and athletic programs; community and business presentations.

The revised narrative will pretty much make you want to meet this guy. There's a personal element here sorely lacking in the earlier attempt.

Version 2

Portland Parks Department, Portland, Oregon

Supervisor – Developed and promoted social, educational, cultural, and athletic programs for the community. Contracted with consultants, instructors, and coaches to provide instruction in dozens of subjects and activities at the Browser Community Center. Interviewed and hired instructors and conducted follow-up assessments to ensure top-quality instruction. Personally taught several courses and coached athletic teams. In three years tripled participation at the Center and took it from a $1,400 deficit to a $12,000 profit.

The revised narrative presents a person with goals and ideals. It is clear that he really cared about his job: he got involved, he took action, and he got results. This picture is created by using action verbs such as *developed* and *promoted*. You feel the action. The programs that the community really wanted did not exist so he *developed* them. Since people don't come flocking to programs they don't know about, he *promoted* them. And he not only planned programs, he taught some, and even coached several athletic teams. This has the added benefit of demonstrating he is an action-oriented and physically fit individual. The ultimate result of his efforts was the tripling of participation, yet his original job narrative did not even mention it.

Writing the empowering resume takes time. From these examples you can see why. Describing oneself in positive terms is difficult for most people, yet it is necessary. Write and revise your job narratives until they approach the examples you find in this book. Everyone can do it, but it will take time and thought. Taking the time will pay off in interviews and job offers. And you can take that to the bank.

THE RIGHT EMPLOYMENT FORMAT FOR YOU

The format you choose for your employment section can make a big difference in the visual appeal and readability of your resume. Our clients have reported that the following format (and its variations) has been consistently well received by their targeted employers.

EMPLOYMENT

Balboa's Steak House, 7/99 to Present

General Manager, Miami, Florida, 10/01 to Present. Took over a troubled restaurant, which had had six managers in two years and had incurred losses each month during that time. Resolved serious morale problems, instituted an effective training program, and redesigned the menu. During the first nine months increased lunch revenue 38% and dinner 29%. Losses were eliminated within two months and a consistent profit margin of 14% has been maintained.

Assistant Manager, Ft. Lauderdale, Florida, 7/99 to 10/01. Redesigned the menu and helped introduce wine sales. Provided extensive staff training that enabled the restaurant to become number one in wine sales in the chain of 20 restaurants. Purchased all food and supplies.

Saga, Inc., Tallahassee, Florida, 9/97 to 7/99

Student Manager – For this college cafeteria, prepared food, scheduled part-time workers, purchased supplies, and oversaw lunch and dinner lines.

Following are sample treatments of various types of work histories. One of them should be similar to your own.

Same Company, Three Positions, All in the Same City

EMPLOYMENT

Douglas Bolt Company, St. Louis, Missouri, 8/89 to Present

V. P. Purchasing, 7/99 to Present. . . . .
. . . .

Director of Purchasing, 5/94 to 7/99 . . . .
. . . .

Manager, Stock Parts Purchasing, 8/89 to 5/94 . . . .
. . . .

Same Company, Three Positions, Three Different Cities

EMPLOYMENT

Horizon Gear, 8/92 to Present

Regional Sales Manager, Houston, Texas, 7/03 to Present . . . .
. . . .

District Sales Manager, Atlanta, Georgia, 3/99 to 7/03. . . . .
. . . .

Sales Representative, Little Rock, Arkansas, 8/92 to 3/99. . . . .
. . . .

In a situation like this you might want to indicate where the headquarters is located. In that case you would show it as: Horizon Gear, Chicago, Illinois, 8/92 to Present.

One Position With Each Company

EMPLOYMENT

Shannon Electric, Garden City, Michigan, 5/95 to Present

Installer – . . . .
. . . .

Preston Electric, Detroit, Michigan, 6/88 to 5/95

Installer – . . . .
. . . .

Work for a Subsidiary or Division of a Major Company

EMPLOYMENT

Antac, Inc., Subsidiary of A&R Industries, Buffalo, New York, 5/03 to Present

It is seldom necessary to specify the parent company. If you choose to, however, this is the easiest way to do it.

PRIOR EMPLOYMENT

A prior employment section is particularly useful if you are trying to shorten your resume or de-emphasize your earlier jobs. A prior employment section is an effective way to explain how you've gotten to where you are without making the reader wade through early and dated experience. Other titles for this section include *Previous Employment, Prior Experience,* or *Additional Experience.*

The example below shows the most commonly used format for the Prior Employment section. This person, currently VP of Purchasing, held the position of Assistant Purchasing Manager, four jobs and 15 years earlier.

Assistant Purchasing Manager – 3/90–5/93. Set up and developed an inventory control program to reduce inventory and operating costs. Over the next year reduced inventory by 20%.

PRIOR EMPLOYMENT

Parts Manager, Zenith Electronics, Los Angeles, CA, 3/88–3/90
Expediter, Hughes Aircraft, Los Angeles, CA, 5/84–3/88
Parts Manager, High Lift Equipment, Long Beach, CA, 4/82–5/84

In the above example, the job title, name of company, city and state, and dates were all included. In the remaining examples you will see how personal taste varies. It is generally wise to include the city and state, but if it seems like unnecessary detail for some distant jobs, feel free to discard them. An example of this is below.

Example (starting with the fourth position on a two-page resume for this person who is currently a district sales manager with responsibility for five electronics stores):

National Computer Stores, Spokane, WA, 5/97-6/99
Sales Representative – Sold hardware and software for the largest independent computer retailer in Spokane. Consistently exceeded monthly sales goals.

PRIOR EXPERIENCE

Food Service Specialist, Johnson Nursing Home (5/95-5/97); Cook, Boyd's Restaurant (6/92-5/95); Cook, Iron Pig Restaurant (6/90-6/92)

In the following example the individual created a bare bones summary of prior positions within a specific timeframe.

Example (starting with the person's sixth position on a two-page resume):

Xytelin Electronics, Mountain View, California, 1980 to 1984

> **Internal Auditor** – Discovered weaknesses in the parts inventory control procedures and recommended remedial action. Responsible for quarterly and yearly audits.

Prior Experience, 1970 to 1980: Airline Internal Auditor, Cost Clerk, Production Scheduler.

Below, the dates are listed, but not the employers' names.

Example (starting with fifth position on a two-page resume)

Department of Social Services, Winston-Salem, North Carolina, 3/94 to 4/96

> **Eligibility Specialist** – Assisted families in obtaining all of the Medicaid benefits they were legally entitled to. Provided psychological and social support services.

Previous Experience:

> Cashier/Hostess, 1/92 to 3/94; Sales Clerk, 6/90 to 1/92; Long Distance Operator, 7/88 to 6/90.

The remaining examples provide additional options.

PRIOR EMPLOYMENT

> **Cashier** - Pay Less Drugs, Elgin, Illinois, 1994–1998
> **Cashier** - Don's Rexall, Carbondale, Illinois, 1992–1994
> **Stocker** - Jewel Foodstores, Peoria, Illinois, 1990–1992

Previous Employment

> Truck Driver (1998–2000); Warehouseman (1997–1998); Machine Repairman (1994–1997)

Sometimes a person will choose not to describe each position with a particular company, especially for the earlier employers. The writer of the following section worked for Boeing for 17 years prior to leaving the company in 1998.

> **Production Inspector** – 3/95–4/98. Performed final interior, flight line modification, and wing line inspections on Boeing 737 aircraft. Verified that the production department installed assemblies according to specifications.

Prior Boeing positions: Assistant Production Inspector, 4/90–3/95; Tooling Inspector, 5/85–4/90; Jig Builder, 3/81–5/85.

TIPS FOR WRITING POWERFUL EMPLOYMENT HISTORIES

The Job Narrative Summary

It is often helpful to begin your job narrative with a straightforward summary, or an overview of what you did. It typically consists of a string of items and helps the reader quickly understand what exactly you did. Here are examples:

> Research databases and create surveys to analyze trends and identify opportunities for improving customer support strategies.
>
> For this sign manufacturing company, prepared financial statements and supervised payroll, billing, and accounts receivable personnel.
>
> Directly responsible for all phases of investment analyses, development, and management of properties.
>
> Coordinated all aspects of the Early Childhood Special Education Program, including hiring and training of staff and support professionals, and the design and implementation of curriculum.
>
> Supervised and trained a lending staff of four in credit and business development efforts.
>
> Interviewed, counseled, and educated patients and families preceding and following open-heart surgery.

Even before learning the details in the rest of the job narrative, the reader has a good overview of what the person did. It is fine to start off with "Responsible for . . ." but don't overuse it. Notice that only one of our examples used "responsible for . . ."

What To Call Your Employment Section

There are a variety of words and phrases you can use to head your employment section: *Employment, Employment Experience, Work Experience, Professional Experience, Professional History, Employment History, Work History,* and *Experience* are all good terms. Select the one the one that feels right for you.

If all of your work has been in one particular field, and you intend to stay in that field, use that term as your employment section heading. You could call it Healthcare Administration Experience, Automotive Experience, Engineering Experience, or Financial Administration Work History.

Dates

Dates should be used on nearly all resumes. If you have no time gaps between jobs or short gaps, you should usually use the months and years you started and ended. If you have long gaps, you can just use the years.

When to use month and year (example: 5/87–3/93):

1. No gaps in employment.
2. Short gaps of less than five months.
3. One gap of more than five months, several years ago.

Some believe that omitting months can be interpreted as hiding something. On the other hand, long gaps between jobs can raise other concerns. With this in mind, decide what is best for you. Select one and move on. Neither will be a show stopper if the experience is conveyed as valuable.

Job Location

Your resume should indicate the city and state you actually work in, not the location of your company's national headquarters. If you work out of your home, include your city as your location; if you live in a suburb, include either the name of the suburb or the more familiar name of the large city near you, which is usually the official name of the market you are serving.

Clarifying What Your Company Does

If you work for General Motors, General Electric, or Boeing, there is no need to explain the nature of your business. If your employer is Eastside Masonry Products, it is also unnecessary to elaborate because the company name explains its type of business. If you work for SLRC Corporation, though, you may want to explain what it is. Handle it this way:

SLRC, Inc., Boston, MA 1996-1999

> **Sales Rep**—For the second largest distributor of electronic components in the Northeast, increased sales over 20% each year.

Or

> **Sales Rep** for the Northeast's second largest distributor of electronic components. Increased sales over 20% each year.

Or

> **Sales Rep**—Increased sales over 20% each year for SLRC, the Northeast's second largest distributor of electronic components.

You can also use such phrases as these to explain what business your employers were in:

For this social service agency . . .
For this social service agency providing help for the homeless . . .

Or

Managed a variety of key programs for this agency responsible for eliminating chemical hazards in the work place.

Directed all financial operations for this not for profit company.
Supervised a nine-person technical team for this software development firm.

Scope Of The Job

The scope of a job includes such things as the products and services of the company, size of company in terms of gross sales, the size of your department in terms of people and dollar budget, the budget you personally work with, and the number of people supervised. Include the scope of the job to clarify your level of responsibility or any other key point. To describe the scope of a job you might say, "Managed all finance, accounting, and data processing functions for this $80 million manufacturer of outdoor equipment." Or you might say, "Supervised a staff of four supervisors and managed a department budget of $1.2 million."

How Much Detail and Space Should You Devote to Each Job?

Principles (not laws) to keep in mind:

1. Describe your current or most recent position in the greatest detail as long as it is similar to the type of job you are seeking. Each preceding job will receive slightly less detail.
2. If the job you held three positions ago is closest to what you're seeking, devote the most detail to it.
3. Early jobs and those unrelated to what you are looking for can usually be glossed over in two or three lines or handled as *Previous Employment* or *Prior Employment*. See page 60 for more on Prior Employment.

How Far Back Should Your Narratives Go?

Recent College Grads. Most college graduates drop their part-time and summer jobs within two to three years of graduating. Those who held part-time or full-time positions for several years while in college may want to keep those in the resume for a longer period. The basic principle is, include pre-graduation experience if it offers value to your candidacy. If you're not ready to completely get rid of some earlier position, using a Prior Employment section may be appropriate. If your first job out of college was very short and it does not add to your credentials, consider leaving it off.

Those With 10+ Years Experience. The resume is your marketing tool in which you present only the information you consider positive and compelling. Consider omitting early and short-term positions if they might raise questions about you, questions that are better dealt with at the interview. In doing so, however, make sure you are not leaving obvious gaps between your education and employment or between different jobs. Omitting dates of graduation might be helpful when covering a gap between education and employment. Providing only years (without months) in your dates of employment can usually provide sufficient flexibility when dealing with employment gaps.

Those with 10–20 years of experience should usually provide full job narratives going back at least ten years.

Current Job Is Less Relevant Than a Prior or Prior Jobs

Generally, it is wise to devote less space to a current, less relevant job, than a previous position more closely aligned with your employment objective.

Another option can be productive: you can separate your experience into two segments, calling one *Related Experience* and the other *Additional Experience*. Instead of Related Experience it could be given a name. For example, if a real estate agent wanted to return to the field of Training and Development, she would call the section Training and Development Experience rather than Related Experience or Relevant Experience.

The related experience section would come first and would generally have the greatest detail. Except for the fact that you have two employment sections, Related Experience and Additional Experience, it is a standard reverse chronological resume. Within each category you should list jobs in reverse chronological order and show the correct dates. Showing the information in this way makes it clear to the employer that even though you are using an atypical format, all jobs have been covered. More importantly, it means that the employer will read your relevant experience first. This strategy will be covered in detail in the chapter on the Clustered Resume.®

Avoid Long Sentences

A convincing job narrative uses a combination of short, medium, and longer sentences to make its points. A common mistake in resume writing is to cobble together all duties and responsibilities into one endless sentence separated only by a series of overworked semicolons. Check out the example below and ask yourself if it is something that would convince you to meet the writer.

> Duties: Writing all local copy for top-rated contemporary radio station involving: Dealing with a broad range of advertisers from fashion to food; supervising flow of ad materials from sales through production to on-air status; communicating with advertising agencies re: national advertisers; voicing special news reports, ski reports and various commercials; and overall, maintaining efficient station continuity and copy excellence enhancing advertiser/station relations and decreasing commercial errors.

And this comes from a professional copywriter!

Quite a mouthful, isn't it? Now review the version on the next page after a bit of editing.

Write all local ad copy for this top-rated contemporary radio station. Customers include a broad range of advertisers in the fashion and hospitality industries. Manage flow of ad materials from sale through production and broadcast. Communicate with advertising agencies regarding national advertisers. Appear as on-air talent in special news reports and perform voice over services for numerous commercials. Have significantly strengthened advertiser relations by improving copywriting, reducing on-air commercial errors, and making station operations more efficient.

Several Jobs Within One Company

It is no longer rare to have five or six changes in job title within one company in a short period of time. Frequently this is the result of promotions, lateral moves, and reorganizations. In many such cases most of the previous responsibilities were maintained, with newer ones being added with each new job title. To describe each position individually would be redundant and unnecessary. Any two jobs that were *essentially* the same, can be treated as one.

Multiple Similar Jobs

Many careers consist of a series of similar positions in which the duties and responsibilities were almost indistinguishable from each other. Real estate agent comes to mind. Writing three identical job narratives would be redundant and boring. If the experience in each agency was essentially identical, it can be combined into a single job narrative. Here are two options in handling this type of entry, both listing each agency in the header.

Both are preferable to multiple entries consisting of, "same duties as above."

McKenzie Real Estate, Seattle, WA; ReMax Real Estate, Bellevue, WA; Cole Real Estate, Redmond, WA 1996–2004

Real Estate Agent—Developed a strong real estate referral base by specializing in home listings throughout northern King County, selling homes ranging from $450,000 to $2.5 million. At each branch became either the number-one or number-two producing agent. Developed a reputation for holding deals together and getting full price for home sellers.

Or

McKenzie Real Estate, Seattle, WA
ReMax Real Estate, Bellevue, WA
Cole Real Estate, Redmond, WA

Real Estate Agent, 1996–2004—Developed a strong real estate referral base by specializing in home listings throughout northern King County, selling homes ranging from $450,000 to $2.5 million. At each branch became either the number-one or number-two producing agent. Developed a reputation for holding deals together and getting full price for home sellers.

Similar positions in similar types of organizations can, at times, be significantly different to warrant their own job narratives. In real estate that might be an agent who has sold in diverse markets to diverse customers, representing residential properties at one and commercial properties at others. Or, serving as the onsite sales/leasing agent for a property developer. In this case, the most recent job narrative can serve to showcase the generic duties, skills, and successes shared by all positions such as the marketing, networking, negotiating, staging, problem solving, *ad infinitum.* The succeeding narratives need only define the differences (market, clients, properties, etc.) and cut to the accomplishments.

Emphasizing You Were Recruited

It never hurts to stress that you were recruited whether directly by the employer or through a headhunting firm. Begin your job narrative with, "Recruited by the president of XYZ . . ." If you had a specific mission or mandate, include it. "Recruited by the president of XYZ to turn around sales and improve quality."

Including Volunteer Experience

Volunteer experience can often showcase skills you rarely or never were able to demonstrate in your paid positions. If it was substantial and relevant to your current career objective, include it in your employment history with its own job narrative. You can label it in the job title ("Volunteer Event Manager") or in the opening line of the narrative ("In a volunteer capacity . . .").

Overqualified?

Sometimes you will be attracted to a position where you sense you may be viewed as overqualified. If your title or responsibility level are significantly higher than the job you are seeking, you may want to tone down those responsibilities and be prepared to discuss it during an interview. If you appear to be overqualified the main thing you can do is convince the company that you really want the job and believe that you could do it well. For more on what to do if you are overqualified see Appendix B.

Gaps

Job seekers are typically ultra-sensitive regarding any perceived problems with their work history. This often includes concern over gaps in employment. Most gaps are non-issues and don't merit much concern or thought.

Truth be told, gaps ain't what they used to be. The past few decades have seen more and more people voluntarily take extended leaves between jobs. Paternity leave is now the norm in many companies and more and more male members of the species are opting for house husbanding.

One of our younger clients had a dream of circumnavigating the globe in a sailboat. Lo and behold, he somehow came into possession of a boat. He went to his boss and explained that he had decided to follow his dream. He did, however, offer to stay on as long as needed to find and train a replacement. He was as good as his word and the boss was so grateful by the way he had handled the situation, he provided a glowing letter of recommendation and an open offer of employment if there were an opening in the future.

Well, he never actually made it around the world, but far enough to say he had lived the dream. When he asked about how he should handle the gap when he interviewed, our advice was to share the experience with the employer. The caveat, of course, was that his dream was behind him now and it was time to get back to work. Clients with similar experiences have told us the typical responses of the interviewers was "I wish I could do that!"

Another client took nine months off work to hike the Pacific Crest trail, 2650 miles from Canada to Mexico. Hiking through the Cascade Mountains down into the Sierras is a huge undertaking. We described it briefly in the resume under the heading of *sabbatical*. His interviewers, to a person, expressed their admiration for the feat.

If you've been away from work for six months or longer, you may be asked about it with a question such as "why haven't you been hired by now?"

So, what were you doing all that time?

Some folks fill in the space with consulting services. These include management, financial, marketing, and technical offerings. The beauty of consulting is that you need not have been doing it full-time or even a lot of time! Just as a freelance writer or musician is not always working. The risky part of presenting yourself as a consultant is that you will inevitably be asked to share information on your projects. As in any situation, best to be prepared with a few good stories and results. Also, your clients might be considered as your most recent "employers" and subject to reference checks and verification. So, make sure they are on board when it comes to being contacted.

Of course, eliminating months in your employment dates and including only the years will alleviate most of your concerns.

Gaps of One Year or More

Long gaps that occurred two or more jobs back can often be ignored—they're old history. Interviewers often assume that women with gaps in their work history did so to care for their children. Those parents who were, in fact, parenting during this time can easily allude to this by including their PTA, scout leadership, and T-ball coaching activities in the Volunteer section of their resumes.

One client described his one year gap in his resume by calling it a special project. The project included major work on his house so it could be sold. He then moved from Massachusetts to Washington.

With our aging society, the care of older and infirm relatives can often take a bite out of our job search. If you have been providing such care in addition to your job search activities, feel free to list it. You may have been working at it full-time or an hour or two per day. In either case you could show that on your resume:

Home care provider for terminally ill relative 2007–2008
Full-time home care provider for a terminally ill relative 2007–2008

Other options include:

Independent travel to Asia and Africa 2006–2008
Personal travel 2004–2005
Adventure travel 2005–2006
Travels to Indonesia and Thailand 2006

Full-time parent and PTA volunteer at Robert Frost Elementary 1998–2008
Full-time parent 1995–2006
Home management 1993–2005
Family management 1997–2007

Independent study 2005–2006
Professional development 2000–2001
Personal growth and development 2001–2003
Student 1998–2004

Volunteer 2004–2006
Volunteer with Habitat for Humanity 2003–2005

Your task is to determine the best way to show that there was a reason you were not working during a certain period of time.

Temping

If you worked for a significant period of time through temporary agencies, it is generally best to simply mention the one you got the most assignments from. If you had a long-term assignment with one organization you could choose to list only that business and not the agency that placed you there.

If some of the organizations you provided temporary services for are well known, you might want to mention some of them.

Blaylock Temporary Services 2004–2007

Office and Administrative Services—Provided clerical services for local firms with assignments ranging from one to twelve weeks. Functions included project management, developing improved systems, desktop publishing, reception, bookkeeping, and collections. Worked for such firms as Merrill Lynch, IBM, Nordstrom, State Farm Insurance, Matthews & Sons, and Jones & Jones Construction. One of the most highly sought temps with Blaylock because of ability to quickly learn existing systems and procedures.

Below is a section of a resume of a person seeking permanent employment in the human resources field. Much of her HR experience was gained as a temp. As she wanted emphasis on the longer term projects that were more HR oriented, she simply omitted the shorter and non-related assignments. Note below that by calling the section *Long-Term Contract Services*, she is telling the reader that only major projects have been included.

LONG-TERM CONTRACT SERVICES 1999–2006
Projects typically ranged from 6 to 15 months. Major projects:

Regal Insurance Group—Employment Specialist

- Provided recruiting services for technical and administrative personnel, including offer letters and reference verification.
- Performed periodic EEO surveys and ensured all goals were met.
- Researched and worked with Corporate Counsel in a training awareness program for supervisors regarding the Americans with Disabilities Act.

Sun Microsystems—Employment Specialist/Recruiter

- Recruited qualified candidates for a hardware design program. Interfaced with department managers and Corporate Relocation Services. Authorized and explained appropriate relocation benefits to managers.
- Provided employee counseling and problem resolution.
- Promoted, planned, and coordinated the Software Business System personnel database, which significantly increased personnel data available to management.
- Participated in the design of a redeployment plan.
- Developed, implemented, and directed a Reward and Recognition program for a 500-person project, with the award budget totaling $150,000. Program was well received by management and employees.

Unisys—Transition Team

- Initiated and facilitated employer relocation and outplacement services for 95 engineering and manufacturing people. Provided job search training, skills assessment, career counseling, and advocacy.
- Coordinated with 45 high-tech firms to arrange employment interviews both locally and out-of-state. All employees successfully transitioned to other positions with Unisys or outside companies.

IBM—Employee Benefits Office

- Researched, interpreted, and communicated benefit-related issues to coworkers and clients. Acted as liaison between employees and insurance companies to resolve claims.
- Worked with insurance companies to effectively introduce new programs to employees. Assisted in new-hire orientation, 401(k), medical, vision, and dental programs.

BULLETS VS. NARRATIVE FORMATS

Last we heard, the proponents of bullet and narrative formats were tied in the fourth quarter.

One debate in the world of resume writing is whether job narratives are more effective using bulleted vs. paragraph formats. There are fairly strong arguments for both sides. Let's take a look at both arguments and you determine which is a better option for you.

Bullets—The primary argument used to justify bullets is that it makes the resume easier and quicker to scan. This includes the so-called common wisdom that employers devote next to no time in reviewing it prior to making the decision on whether to keep or pitch it. Using that argument, the bullet version seems the stronger format.

Paragraphs—The argument for paragraphs runs like this: If the paragraphs are kept to 3–7 lines, they are actually easier to read than bullets because most of the text we read—books and newspapers—use paragraphs rather than bullets.

In reality, both bullets and paragraphs can work well. They can even be used in combination with each other. The key is to use them to their greatest effect.

Too many short bullets can lose the reader while overly-long ones can be clumsy and actually negate the benefit of using bullets in the first place.

Bulky paragraphs with few line spaces between them will make the document imposing and difficult to read. Eye appeal is important in a resume, but neither the bullet point nor paragraph format is the automatic favorite in the eye appeal competition.

The single biggest drawback usually associated with bullet point resumes is they tend to provide too little information. Because many job seekers are still convinced that employers want short resumes that can be fully reviewed in under 30 seconds, the job narratives tend to be extremely lacking in useful information. Bullet point resumes usually focus on listing duties and tend to be devoid of results. Those results that are included are usually hanging around without context, essentially compromising their value. Thus, even if they pass the initial scan, more in-depth review will find a dearth of useful and valuable information about the candidate. It is like a sprinter who might win the first leg of a marathon but has little left in the tank for the rest of the contest.

The problem with the paragraph resume is often just the opposite; it can be verbose and bloated and not likely to be read.

All things being equal, we favor the crisply written and visually appealing paragraph format. As art is in the eye of the beholder, there are an equal number of thoughtful and experienced resume professionals out there who would disagree. We encourage that because when all is said and done, the more solid information you get, the better choice you will make in what works for you.

GARY: I prefer the narrative format. When someone throws bullets at you . . . there is a tendency to duck out of the way. When a story is told . . . you become engaged . . . you pay attention. Stories with "happy endings" are particularly memorable and emotionally gratifying. Besides, 100 years of movies and 60 years of TV have trained us to ingest information as stories each with a beginning, middle, and ending. We expect these stories to entertain, interest, enthrall us. We expect dramatic conclusions!

EXAMPLES: PARAGRAPHS VS BULLETS

Below is an example of a well-written and visually attractive paragraph-oriented job narrative. There are no unnecessary words—everything included helps demonstrate quality and experience.

> **Store Manager**—7/06-Present. For the third largest music retailer in the Midwest, maintain profitable store operations. Supervise 16 employees and execute corporate sales programs. Evaluate inventory levels and order CDs that will sell in our market. Record and track store sales and overhead costs. Maximize retail sales through effective space allocation, merchandise presentation, and signage.
>
> Recognized as a highly effective trainer and manager. Six of my trainees have been promoted to store manager. Exceeded the monthly revenue plan 23 of the last 24 months. Improved DVD sales 120% in the first year of a marketing program I developed and tested for the region. Increased store profitability by increasing sales 27% in 2007 and 24% in 2008, while at the same time decreasing labor costs 4% and reducing theft 65%.

The next example consists of the exact same content crammed into an over-large, single, imposing block of text. The above paragraph is clearly more inviting.

Store Manager—7/06–Present. For the third largest music retailer in the Midwest, maintain profitable store operations. Supervise 16 employees and execute corporate sales programs. Evaluate inventory levels and order CDs that will sell in our market. Record and track store sales, payroll, and overhead costs. Maximize retail sales through effective space allocation, merchandise presentation, and signage. Recognized as a highly effective trainer and manager. Six of my trainees have been promoted to store manager. Exceeded the monthly revenue plan 23 of the last 24 months. Improved DVD sales 120% in the first year of a marketing program I developed and tested for the region. Increased store profitability by increasing sales 27% in 2007 and 24% in 2008, while at the same time decreasing labor costs 4% and reducing theft 65%.

Now let's look at the same job narrative in a bullet point format.

Store Manager—7/06–Present.

- For the third largest music retailer in the Midwest, maintain profitable store operations.
- Supervise 16 employees and execute corporate sales programs.
- Evaluate inventory levels and order CDs that will sell in our market.
- Record and track store sales, payroll, and overhead costs.
- Maximize retail sales through effective space allocation, merchandise presentation, and signage.
- Recognized as a highly effective trainer and manager. Six of my trainees have been promoted to store manager.
- Exceeded the monthly revenue plan 23 of the last 24 months.
- Improved DVD sales 120% in the first year of a marketing program I developed and tested for the region.
- Increased store profitability by increasing sales 27% in 2007 and 24% in 2008, while at the same time decreasing labor costs 4% and reducing theft 65%.

The above bulleted example looks good and is easy to read. It provides valuable information with each bullet point being the right length to convey its message.

The following example includes most of the same information, but has been intentionally shortened to reflect how a typical bullet point resume reads. The job narrative is too short and simply does not give the reader enough useful information even though the key results have been maintained. It reads like a company job description, devoid of any personality.

Store Manager—7/06–Present.

- Maintain profitable store operations
- Supervise 16 employees
- Execute corporate sales programs
- Evaluate inventory levels and order CDs
- Record and track store sales and overhead costs
- Maximize retail sales
- Recognized as a highly effective trainer and manager
- Exceeded the monthly revenue plan 23 of the last 24 months
- Improved DVD sales 120%
- Increased profitability by increasing sales 27% in 2007 and 24% in 2008

Now let's look at the store manager narrative in a bullet format that many prefer. It begins with a paragraph of several lines that provides an overview of the position. Then it reverts to bullets. One of the benefits of this form of bullets is that it breaks up the left margin that otherwise would consist of nothing but bullets. See what you think, and then go to pages 209, 214, 218, 239 for an entire resume that uses this format.

Store Manager—7/06–Present.

For the third largest music retailer in the Midwest, maintain profitable store operations. Supervise 16 employees and execute corporate sales programs. Evaluate inventory levels and order CDs that will sell in our market. Record and track store sales, payroll, and overhead costs.

- Maximize retail sales through effective space allocation, merchandise presentation, and signage.
- Recognized as a highly effective trainer and manager. Six of my trainees have been promoted to store manager.
- Exceeded the monthly revenue plan 23 of the last 24 months.
- Improved DVD sales 120% in the first year of a marketing program I developed and tested for the region.
- Increased store profitability by increasing sales 27% in 2007 and 24% in 2008, while at the same time decreasing labor costs 4% and reducing theft 65%.

From this you can see that both the paragraph format and the bullet format can work well. The quality of preparation and presentation of your job narratives will determine the success of your resume more than which format you select.

Shifting Careers or Industries

Any time you make a career or industry shift, you face disadvantages. By definition you're lacking knowledge or experience that most of your competitors possess. Somehow you must overcome these deficits.

First, if you have not formally prepared for the transition through education or training, make the effort to thoroughly study the career field and industry. Read trade journals, magazines, and even textbooks. Do Internet searches and follow the appropriate links to informative sites.

Next, talk people in the field. They are the experts. and your potential network. Share your background to determine if it is a reasonable transition. Which organizations can best accommodate you? How do they see the industry? Expanding? Contracting?

When you are ready to make the move, get working on your resume. Your research has enabled you to identify those pieces of your background that will be best valued in the new industry. Learn the jargon. If a specific function in the new industry has a label different from what you have called it in the past . . . adapt.

As in any presentation, emphasize your strengths. Look for areas where your universal assets can be included such as problem-solving, initiative, decision-making, technical acuity, etc. Select the most compelling of these for the cover letters. You are presenting a package of strengths, not simply isolated job-specific qualifications. Many employers prefer quality people they can train, especially if you are at an entry point, as many career changers are.

Sometimes it works well to have a section labeled *Highlights*, where you can present key projects or experiences which used critical skills needed in your new field. Or you might want to consider alternative resume formats such as Functional (pages 117, 120, 121) or Clustered (pages 129–139) that might better illustrate this experience.

Important to Read

Resume Empower is unique in numerous ways, including its use of the printed page and the Internet. We've sought to provide our readers with valuale insight and information. Some resume issues, however, are very important to small numbers of people. We've tried to cover those points on our website. Go to Appendix B to see what we're currently offering. We've listed numerous topics where you'll find in-depth information. The number of topics will grow as readers ask about such topics or as we come to realize that information on a certain topic would be valuable. So, don't rely solely on Appendix B. Go to www.careerempowering.com and click on "Books and articles by Tom Washington and Gary Kanter." Once on that page you'll quickly find topics not currently listed in Appendix B. If you have a topic that you believe should be addressed, email either of us (Gary at gkanter@yahoo.com and Tom at tomw@careerempowering.com) and we'll seek to provide a response. Unfortunately we cannot promise to provide extensive answers to all questions, especially those which are more personal and may be unique to just one individual.

Special Projects/Activities/Awards

A Special Projects section can be especially effective for a person with valuable experiences that did not occur on a job.

Outstanding people have one thing in common: an absolute sense of mission.

Career changers, recent college graduates, and parents re-entering the work force can benefit from including a section on special projects. The section can also be labeled *Selected Projects, Accomplishments, Achievements, Activities, Projects, Noteworthy Projects, Selected Accomplishments,* or *Noteworthy Accomplishments.* Volunteer experiences with clubs and associations, as well as special projects performed as part of a course, can be presented in this section.

Use these examples as guides to determine whether a Special Projects section will strengthen your resume.

In the example below, the person had been at home rearing children since 1999. Her Special Projects section helps make it obvious that she is very capable and energetic.

SPECIAL PROJECTS

As President of PTA, increased parent participation 26% and funds raised 34% over the previous year. (2008)

As a United Way fundraising team leader, exceeded the quota by 22%. Honored at banquet as Team Leader of the Year. (2006)

A project or accomplishment seldom requires over 45 words—20 to 30 words is usually best. Do not try to describe the project in detail—concentrate on results. When writing out each accomplishment in the first draft, feel free to describe it in 50 to 70 words. Then rewrite it by concentrating on results and include just enough detail so that the reader will understand what you did. Save all other details for an interview. List the projects and accomplishments in reverse chronological order and include the year.

The following person had been active in community affairs for several years and was seeking the directorship of a city-run agency for youth. On its own, his employment experience would not even have gotten him an interview.

SELECTED PROJECTS

Wrote news articles and special features for *Troy Herald*, *Outdoor News*, and *College Forum*. (2006–2008)

Lobbied for and obtained Troy city council support for three community parks. Played a key role on the planning committee and helped obtain matching federal funds for this model project. (2005)

Participated as a guest expert on disadvantaged youth for a public affairs radio talk show. (2003)

Organized a basketball camp for disadvantaged youth in Troy and obtained $55,000 in corporate and city funding. Got four coaches and seven college players from three surrounding colleges to donate one week to the program. (2001)

Below is a special projects section used by a 40-year-old woman re-entering the workforce after completing an MBA. She had held just one part-time research position ten years earlier.

SPECIAL PROJECTS

Developed and coordinated budgets for YWCA and Big Sisters Program, Newark, 2001–2008.

Developed highly successful parenting, exercise, and personal growth programs for the Newark YWCA, 2000–2003.

Planned and coordinated programs for the League of Women Voters, Newark, 1998–2006.

Chaired The Mayor's Conference on Aging, Newark, 1999.

The following example was written by a teacher who was seeking a position in private business and needed to demonstrate non-classroom abilities.

SPECIAL PROJECTS

Interned for Omaha National Bank during the summer of 2008. Received assignments working with retail credit, corporate loans, and trust departments. Developed and completed a survey that determined customer needs. (2008)

Supervised the senior class store that sells school supplies, tickets, jackets, and sweaters. The store maintained a profit each year under my management, something it had never done previously. (1998–2005)

Supervised the research and publication of the Omaha "Volunteer Directory," which helped draw new volunteers into dozens of agencies. (2004)

Developed an intern program to allow students to work in nursing homes and schools for the disabled. Dozens of students gained new skills and several now work in geriatrics. (1997–2001)

Organized record-breaking blood drives and won trophies each year from 1997 to 2001. No other school came close to matching the high percentage of students who donated blood. (1997–2001)

Sometimes other section titles such as Honors and Awards, Publications, or Activities will work better than Special Projects. This recently graduated college student had only one special project to describe so she combined it with an award and called the section Awards and Publications.

AWARDS AND PUBLICATIONS

Chairperson, Task Force on Teaching Quality. Investigated teaching evaluation methods at Reed College and published position paper that helped initiate change in tenure decision policies. (2008)

Senior Class Inspirational Person-of-the-Year Award. (2004)

Licenses/Certificates

A ny licenses you hold that are necessary or valuable in the field you are seeking should be listed. Be selective, though. Only list certificates and licenses that are relevant to the new position. Mentioning a real estate license when you want to be a purchasing agent for a tool manufacturer would not add to your qualifications and might cause the employer to wonder whether your preferred career was selling real estate or purchasing.

LICENSES

First Class FCC Radio Telephone Operator (2004)
Commercial Instrument Pilot rating (2002) 840 hours flight time
Private Pilot (1996)

(Electronics technologist and sales rep who flies to see customers)

LICENSES

General Electrical Administrator Certificate – California (1997)
Journeyman Electrician License - California, Nevada, Arizona (1990)
Commercial Instrument Pilot's License (1990)

(Electrician who would like to do some flying for his employer)

LICENSES

FCC, 1989

(Broadcast journalist who needs a Federal Communications Commission license to operate on the air)

LICENSES

CPA – New York, New Jersey, California

LICENSES

Professional Engineer, Mechanical Engineering – Colorado (1990)

CERTIFICATION

Standard Elementary and Secondary, Idaho (Lifetime 1989)
(Teacher)

CERTIFICATE

Personal Coaching, The Coaching Institute (2002)

CERTIFICATE

Human Resources Management, Continuing Education, University of Washington (1997)

Associations/Memberships/ Professional Affiliations

Including associations and memberships can demonstrate that you are keeping up to date in your profession and that you have developed useful contacts. For the person making a career change, listing memberships can demonstrate you are serious in making a shift in career direction. Use these categories only if they are relevant and will help you. An engineer might use the following:

PROFESSIONAL AFFILIATIONS

American Chemical Society (1989–Present)
American Institute of Chemical Engineers (1986–Present)

Belonging to associations and professional organizations may mean only that you paid the annual dues, or it could mean that you are active in the organization. List every office held. If you want a one-page resume and you are three lines over, affiliations can be sacrificed. The section provides interesting, but not usually crucial, information. The examples below can be used as guides. Do not list an affiliation unless you believe its adds credibility or value to your resume. Organizations you are no longer a member of or no longer active in are usually not mentioned, unless you held an office.

Use the examples below as guides for presenting information regarding affiliations.

MEMBERSHIPS

Pacific Northwest Personnel Managers Association (1989–present)
American Society for Personnel Administration (1987–present)

ASSOCIATIONS

Homebuilders Association, member 1994–present
    Officer 2004–present
    Associate of the Year 2000
Board of Realtors, member 1989–present
    Chairperson, Legislative Committee 2002–2006

Chairperson, Political Affairs and Education 1995–1999

ASSOCIATIONS

Southeast Community Alcohol Center
    President, Board of Directors (2006)
    Member of Board (1999–Present)
Northwest Nurses Society on Chemical Dependency
    Treasurer (2003–2006)
    Member (1993–Present)

You should rarely mention associations that indicate religious affiliation, political identification, ethnicity, or race. Bias and prejudice are alive and well in the United States and Canada. Don't give people excuses for not meeting you. When we meet people in person we are often able to overcome stereotypes—do everything possible to get that interview.

If you want the reader to know your politics, religion, ethnic background, or race, then by all means indicate the association. You would do so, however, only if you are quite sure that by including that information you have increased the likelihood of obtaining an interview. Don't do it with the rationale that you don't want to work for them if they don't like that part of you. Everyone is biased, much of it on a subconscious level. Get the interview, get the job offer, and then decide if you want to join that organization.

Being active in an association often provides opportunities to demonstrate leadership, program management, and project-management skills. As an officer or as a committee chair or co-chair, you may have gotten some excellent results in that capacity. As Program Chair, perhaps you brought in the best speakers in the past several years and, as a result, attendance at meetings picked up significantly. You may have, for example, recruited minority mechanical engineers and thus increased membership and the diversity of your organization. You may have coordinated a highly successful conference.

If you've been an officer or a committee chair, ask yourself what you accomplished. How did the organization benefit from your participation? Even if you later choose not to put that in your resume, you have just added stories you can share in interviews.

Once you've identified what your results were, or those results you were at least partially responsible for, determine if mentioning those results will help sell you. If yes, just begin writing.

Memberships

Association of Mechanical Engineers, member — 1995–present
    Board Member — 2000–2006
    President — 2006

As president, developed a recruiting program that increased minority membership from less than two percent of total membership to over ten percent.

Treasurer — 1999–2003

Recommended selling booth space for the first time at the 2002 state convention and recruited over 45 vendors. This brought in $15,000 in additional revenue, equal to 10% of total association revenue for the year. The number of vendors and revenue have grown significantly each year since.

This section works well for this engineer. His job descriptions do a nice job of selling his technical skills, but he is now seeking to move from senior engineer where he oversees projects and guides younger engineers, to a true management position. The fact that he was an effective president and treasurer helps an employer picture him in a management role.

Volunteer Experience

Volunteer experience can be used effectively to emphasize certain skills and results that don't show up in your work experience. Keep in mind that listing volunteer experience is never a requirement. Include it only when you believe that a potential employer will see desirable strengths or experience that will help you obtain an interview. When most people include volunteer experience it is only to list a title, the organization, and the year or years it took place. Providing only that information rarely grabs an employer enough to elicit a call.

Write about your volunteer experience in the same way you would write about a job you've had. Include your duties and successes.

In the example below, Julie wants to work for a nonprofit and wants to showcase her serious volunteer experience and commitment to help the less fortunate.

VOLUNTEER EXPERIENCE

Sojourner Domestic Violence Shelter, Oakland, CA 2005–Present

Kitchen worker three days a month for a 95-bed residential facility. Prepare and serve food, including meals ready to serve and cooking from scratch. Stocked and inventoried donated food.

Center Against Sexual Abuse Rape Crisis Hotline, Oakland, CA 2002–2005

Answered rape crisis hotline phone calls. Provided emergency counseling and referrals for more than 200 victims of sexual assault. Received numerous thank-you notes from victims I assisted.

Sally was out of the workforce for several years and wants to demonstrate her very impressive results. She clearly is a person who makes things happen.

VOLUNTEER EXPERIENCE

President, Volunteer Bureau of Eugene, Oregon 2004–Present. The organization recruits, trains, and places individuals into volunteer agencies and also establishes programs that serve the needs of the local community.

• Instituted the first all-volunteer Respite Care Program in the country. This

program became a model program for the healthcare reform initiative of 2005, due to its high success rate and low cost.
- Obtained a $200,000 grant from the Kellogg Foundation for expansion of the program.
- Developed Senior Transportation Services for the elderly and infirm to assist these individuals in maintaining their independence with daily activities. The program provides more than 5,000 rides annually to seniors, by volunteer drivers.
- Created "Single Parents Network" for those in need of socialization. Fifty or more people attend most meetings and socials.
- Established youth programs for junior and senior high school students that provide safe environments for teen activities on Friday and Saturday nights. The activities are well attended by teens and the program has been highly recommended by the police department and several school districts.
- Presented a community education series focusing on "Women's Issues."

School Board Member, Eugene, Oregon 2000–2003. Instrumental in strengthening the district through the recruitment of a new superintendent.

Sam wants to demonstrate his organizational and project management abilities. He is clearly a person who makes things happen.

VOLUNTEER PROJECTS

Christmas House – 2004–Present. Planned and organized Snohomish County Fire Protection District 17 Christmas House for the past 4 years. Project provides children from families in need with gifts for the holiday. Solicited donations, advertised event, and organized purchase and distribution of toys. Result: Last year over 320 children were provided with new toys and gifts. Over the past 4 years, approximately 1100 children have benefited from the project.

Stevens Falls School District – 1995–1999. Participated as a citizen on the Strategic Planning Committee for establishing the School District's first mission, vision, values, and goals statements. Played a key role in the development of the strategic plan. Result: The mission, vision and values that were established are still in use now, ten years later.

Jason wants to demonstrate that he gets things done and can motivate people to take action.

VOLUNTEER WORK

Member of United Way Community Employment and Literacy Panel. The panel is responsible for the annual review of six member agencies that receive semiannual distributions of United Way funds. Review five to ten grantee applications annually, resulting in the award of two to three additional grants each year. These more recently funded agencies have continued to receive funding based on the quality of their programs. 2003–Present

Volunteer for the Minneapolis Crime Prevention Program. Coordinated outreach efforts of social workers and met with community leaders and neighborhoods.

Formed more than 60 neighborhood block-watch groups and participated in block-watch meetings to inform and educate residents how to protect their homes and neighborhoods. National studies demonstrated that statistics for crime in those neighborhoods, as well as surrounding neighborhoods, showed drops that were much greater than the drop in crime of similarly sized cities. 1996–2001

For more examples of Volunteer experience, see Appendix B

Publications

A list or description of publications can be used to demonstrate expertise in a particular field. Listing publications can also demonstrate your abilities in researching, interviewing, and writing. If you are widely published, include only your most relevant articles.

Publications include articles in newspapers, magazines, trade journals, professional journals, school papers, anthologies, or just about anything in printed form with a circulation larger than 50. If you have many publications, but are including only some of them, call the section *Selected Publications*.

PUBLICATIONS

"The Arts in Seattle," *The Weekly*, July 27, 2008
"Marketing a Symphony," *The Conductor*, April 2007
"Will Bach Be Back?" *Symphony News*, November 2003

PUBLICATIONS

"The Dismantling of Student Loans," *University of Kentucky Daily*, 2007
"Tenureship Under Attack," *University of Kentucky Daily*, 2007
"An Hour With G. Gordon Liddy," *University of Kentucky Daily*, 2006

PUBLICATIONS

"Robots and Production," *Chrysler Employees Newsletter*, 2008
"Automation and Its Impact on Blue Collar Workers," paper presented at the annual Industrial Psychologists Symposium, 2004

If you are going to use a special projects section and have only one publication, you could include the publication with your projects. For example:

ACTIVITIES

Volunteer Probation Counselor, King County – 1999 to Present
Authored an environmental article published in *Ecojournal* – 2005

Personal Information

Using a Personal Data section has become outdated. During the 1970s and '80s resumes moved from almost always having a Personal Data section, which included such information as age, marital status, height and weight, and health status, to the almost total extinction of such a section. Women began excluding it from their resumes about 30 years ago and men followed suit. Equal Employment Opportunity legislation also helped hasten the trend. It was never a very helpful section, but it was traditional to include it.

In the 1930s and '40s it was traditional to include religion and the national origin of parents in a Personal Data section. It was assumed that employers wanted to know and therefore it should be included. Actually, including this information merely gave employers greater opportunity to discriminate.

Our recommendation is to exclude it as a section. Sometimes, however, it is useful to use a section called "Personal." It can be used to cover bonding, security clearances, citizenship, willingness to relocate or travel, and any other aspects that might not fit in other categories of a resume.

Include personal information only if you believe the points covered will help sell you.

With that in mind, do not include the older types of personal data information such as age, height, weight, marital status, and health status. Also, do not include information that reveals age, religion, political affiliation, or ethnicity.

BONDING

Mention you are bondable if your type of work requires it. Essentially, anyone who does not have a prison record is bondable. Bonding is a type of insurance employers take out on employees who handle large amounts of money. If an employee heads to Mexico with thousands of dollars, the employer collects from the bonding company.

SECURITY CLEARANCE

Many people in the military, and civilians working on military projects, have been given security clearances, typically "Secret" or "Top Secret." After leaving the military, these quickly lapse and a new investigation is conducted before reestablishing a security clearance. By including your security clearance, however, you're really saying, "My honesty and integrity were verified by a very thorough investigation; you, too, can trust me." If you held a security clearance within the last ten years, it may be helpful to mention it. Indicate the years it was active. An alternative is to mention your security clearance in your military job description.

CITIZENSHIP

Include this information only if you believe an employer might question your citizenship, or if you especially want to let an employer know that you are a U.S. or Canadian citizen. If you are not a U.S. citizen, you may want to state "Permanent Resident" or indicate your status. There is no need to specify "Naturalized U.S. Citizen;" simply say "U.S. Citizen," or possibly "U.S. Citizen since 1988." Other terms could be "Canadian Citizen since 1979," or "Valid Green Card."

HEALTH

We suggest not listing your health status. Everyone always states "Excellent Health" anyway, so it really has no purpose.

RELOCATION

If you are willing to relocate and you are contacting national or regional firms, state this in the Personal section or merely state at the bottom of the resume, "Willing to relocate." Do not include a statement in the resume or cover letter that you are unwilling to relocate. Save that for the interview or after you get the job offer.

TRAVEL

If the job is likely to require extensive overnight travel, and you're willing to do so, consider stating that in a Personal section, or in the cover letter. If you are unwilling or unable to travel, or if you could travel only one night a month, say nothing in the resume or cover letter about travel. Be prepared to discuss it in the interview, however.

FOREIGN LANGUAGES

If you want to sell your language skills you can create a category called foriegn Languages, or you can include it within a Personal section. It would typically look like this:

FOREIGN LANGUAGES

Fluent in reading and writing French
Conversational in Spanish
Able to translate and interpret in Russian

See below how languages can be incorporated into a personal section.

ACTIVITIES

List only those activities that you are heavily involved in and knowledgeable about. More than one person has lost a job opportunity because an employer who truly was active in that endeavor simply asked a few questions to compare experiences, only to discover the person knew almost nothing about it. As small as it seems, none of those people were able to recover in the interview. All credibility had simply been lost.

PERSONAL
Languages: French (12 years of study); Spanish (2 years of study)
Hobbies: Reading literature and business subjects, piano, horseback riding
Willing to relocate

Whether you should include activities or interests is open to debate. Some insist that anything not demonstrating work-related skills or background should be excluded. Others feel a discussion of activities can become an interesting topic of conversation and helps the candidate to be remembered. Both sides make good points. We sometimes include activities because it can make a person seem more real. Select your interests and activities carefully; use only those in which you really are active. Jogging is an excellent activity to include, but don't list it if you run only occasionally. Physical activities can help indicate high energy and excellent health.

With each activity you select, ask yourself what impact it will have on an employer. Unless you believe most employers will view it positively, do not include the activity.

Give a consistent picture of yourself. Decide what image you want to convey and then select the appropriate activities. Office workers are wise to state interests that indicate a highly energetic personality.

ACTIVITIES

Strong involvement in marathon running, skiing, and scuba diving.

ACTIVITIES

Actively involved in golf, jogging, and camping.

INTERESTS

Enjoy making exotic breads, creating stained glass windows, and dance exercise activities.

Saying It with Impact

Producing impact through your words is crucial in a resume. Knowing which action verbs, adjectives, and adverbs to use and how to use them will significantly strengthen your resume. This section will cover all of these points and show you how to bring it together in your resume.

ACTION WORDS

A resume should sound alive and vigorous. Using action verbs helps achieve that feeling. "I changed the filing system" lacks punch and doesn't really indicate if the system was improved. "I *reorganized* and *simplified* the filing system" sounds much better and provides more accurate information.

Review the sentences below to get a feel for action words. Then quickly scan the words in the following list and check any you think you might want to use in your resume. Don't try to force them in; use them when they feel right.

Conducted long-range master planning for the Portland water supply system.

Monitored enemy radio transmissions, analyzed information, and identified enemy strategic and tactical capabilities.

Planned, staffed, and organized the intramural sports program for this 1,200-student college.

Produced daily reports for each trial and made sure documents and evidence were handled properly.

Presented seminars to entry-level secretaries and worked to increase the professionalism of secretaries in the county system.

Improved the coordination, imagination, and pantomime techniques of adults through mime and dance training.

Allocated and dispensed federal moneys to nine counties as board member of the JTPA Advisory Board.

For a more complete list of effective verbs see Appendix B

ACTION VERBS

accelerated	constructed	equipped	interpreted	prioritized	serviced
accomplished	consulted	established	invented	processed	settled
accumulated	contributed	exceeded	investigated	procured	(disputes)
achieved	controlled	executed	launched	produced	shaped
acquired	converted	expanded	led	programmed	simplified
acted (as)	convinced	expedited	lifted	projected	sold
activated	cooperated	explored	lobbied	promoted	solidified
adapted	coordinated	expressed	lowered	proposed	solved
adjusted	counseled	extended	maintained	proved	sparked
administered	created	fabricated	managed	provided	spearheaded
advised	culminated in	facilitated	marketed	purchased	specified
advocated	cultivated	finalized	mastered	quadrupled	stabilized
aligned	customized	focused	maximized	raised	standardized
analyzed	cut	followed up	mediated	realigned	stimulated
applied	decreased	forged	mentored	received	streamlined
appointed	delegated	forecasted	minimized	recognized	strengthened
approved	delivered	formed	mobilized	recommended	structured
arbitrated	demonstrated	fostered	moderated	reconciled	succeeded
arranged	designed	founded	modified	recruited	supervised
assessed	detailed	fulfilled	monitored	redesigned	supplemented
assisted	determined	galvanized	motivated	reduced	supplied
attained	developed	generated	negotiated	reevaluated	supported
authorized	devised	grew	nurtured	refined	surpassed
automated	diagnosed	guided	observed	regulated	taught
awarded	directed	halved	obtained	rehabilitated	tested
boosted	discovered	handled	offered	reinforced	took over
broadened	distributed	headed	opened	rejuvenated	tracked
built	documented	helped	operated	remedied	trained
carried out	doubled	identified	optimized	renewed	transferred
centralized	drove	implemented	orchestrated	reported	transformed
championed	earned	improved	organized	represented	tripled
clarified	effected	improvised	originated	researched	troubleshot
coached	eliminated	increased	overcame	resolved	turned around
collaborated	employed	influenced	overhauled	responded	uncovered
communicated	empowered	informed	oversaw	restored	unified
compiled	enabled	initiated	perfected	restructured	united
completed	enacted	innovated	pinpointed	resulted in	updated
conceived	encouraged	inspired	pioneered	revamped	upgraded
concentrated	endorsed	installed	planned	revised	utilized
conceptualized	enforced	instilled	positioned	revitalized	validated
concluded	enhanced	instituted	prepared	revived	verified
conducted	enlarged	instructed	presented	safeguarded	won over
consolidated	ensured	integrated	prevented	saved	wrote

DESCRIBING RESULTS WITH KEY ACTION VERBS

The typical resume merely lists duties and does little else to sell the person. One of the best ways to sell yourself is to describe accomplishments in terms of *results*. While duties are often represented by phrases such as "Responsible for . . .," results are frequently conveyed by using the verb *developed*. For example, one might say, "Developed a manual for administrative assistants that explained hundreds of procedures and significantly reduced clerical errors." This person's duties were typing, filing, and answering phones, so to show that she stood above the rest she demonstrated results.

When describing projects and results, one of the best words to use is *develop*. More than any other word, it seems to be both useful and effective, and it clearly expresses what a person wants to convey. But while *develop* is an excellent word, when used three or four times in a resume it becomes overworked and loses impact. You'll need substitutes. The most useful are:

built	implemented
created	instituted
designed	introduced
established	set up

Other verbs that may be appropriate substitutes for develop in certain circumstances would be:

composed	enhanced	installed	prepared
constructed	fabricated	organized	produced
coordinated	fashioned	originated	refined
cultivated	formed	perfected	revamped
devised	formulated	pioneered	
elaborated	generated	planned	

Here are examples that demonstrate how to describe results in various situations. In parentheses are words that could have been used instead of *develop*.

Developed (devised, prepared, produced) a creative financing/purchasing package to obtain 1900 acres of prime California farmland.

Pioneered a mime program for gifted children aged 8–12.

Developed (designed, established) training programs for new and experienced employees and supervised the new employee orientation program.

Set up apprenticeship programs for five skilled trades at the Physical Plant Department.

<u>Developed</u> and <u>implemented</u> an information and referral service for consumer complaints and human rights issues.

<u>Coordinated</u> the company marketing effort, including advertising and promotions.

Another set of action verbs is particularly useful when you are describing a result and plan to quantify it:

achieved	produced
cut	reduced
doubled	saved
eliminated	tripled
increased	

VERB TENSES

Describe your current job in the present tense. For all previous jobs, write in the past tense. You may need to describe an event in your current job, such as a project, that has already been completed. In that case, use the past tense to describe the project while using the present tense in the remaining portions of your current job.

Example:

STORE MANAGER – 6/99–Present. Oversee total operation of the store, supervise and schedule employees, and complete monthly profit and loss statements. Designed a new inventory system, which has saved over $10,000.

Since the inventory system was designed over a year ago, it must be described in the past tense.

USING ADJECTIVES AND ADVERBS

Adjectives and adverbs are words that describe things and actions. Used appropriately, they can enliven a resume and more accurately describe what you did. While adjectives and adverbs can add sparkle to a resume, if overused, they can actually weaken a phrase. Notice how they change the tone of the sentences below. In each example the second sentence has more impact.

1. Worked with industrial engineers.
   Worked <u>closely and effectively</u> with industrial engineers.

2. Initiate and develop working relations with local, state, and federal agencies.
   Initiate and develop <u>outstanding</u> working relations with local, state, and federal agencies.

3. Establish rapport with customers.
   <u>Quickly</u> establish rapport with customers.

Here are more examples of how to use adjectives and adverbs effectively:

Dealt <u>tactfully</u> and <u>effectively</u> with <u>difficult</u> customers.

Presented technical material in <u>objective</u> and <u>easily understood</u> terms.

<u>Consistently</u> maintained <u>high</u> profit margins on projects.

<u>Significantly</u> improved communications between nursing administration and staff.

<u>Continually</u> streamlined policies and procedures to create a more reasonable work schedule.

A list of adjectives and adverbs is given below. Review the list and check the ones you think may be useful to you. Try to include them but don't force it. Don't use a word or phrase unless it really fits your personality and strengthens your resume. After writing each draft, go back through the list to see if still another word or two might be useful.

ADJECTIVES AND ADVERBS

accurate/accurately
active/actively
adept/adeptly
advantageously
aggressive/aggressively
all-inclusive/all-inclusively
ambitious/ambitiously
appreciable/appreciably
astute/astutely
attractive/attractively
authoritative/
authoritatively
avid/avidly
aware
beneficial/beneficially
broad/broadly
capable/capably
challenging
cohesive/cohesively
competent/competently
complete/completely
comprehensive/
comprehensively
conclusive/conclusively
consistent/consistently
constructive/constructively
contagious
continuous/continuously
contributed toward
decidedly
decisive/decisively
deft/deftly
demonstrably
dependable/dependably
diligent/diligently
diplomatic/diplomatically
distinctive/distinctively
diverse/diversified
driving
easily
effective/effectively
effectually
efficient/efficiently

effortless/effortlessly
enthusiastic/
enthusiastically
entire/entirely
especially
exceptional/exceptionally
exciting/excitingly
exhaustive/exhaustively
experienced
expert/expertly
extensive/extensively
extreme/extremely
familiar with
familiarity with
firm/firmly
functional/functionally
handy/handily
high/highly
highest
high-level
honest/honestly
imaginative/imaginatively
immediate/immediately
impressive/impressively
incisive/incisively
in-depth
industrious/industriously
inherent/inherently
innovative/innovatively
instructive/instructively
instrumental/instrumentally
integral
intensive/intensively
intimate/intimately
leading
masterful/masterfully
meaningful/meaningfully
natural/naturally
new and improved
notable/notably
objective/objectively
open-minded
original/originally

outstanding/outstandingly
particularly
penetrating/penetratingly
perceptive/perceptively
pioneering
practical/practically
professional/professionally
proficient/proficiently
profitable/profitably
progressive/progressively
quick/quickly
rare/rarely
readily
relentless/relentlessly
reliability
reliable/reliably
remarkable/remarkably
responsible/responsibly
rigorous/rigorously
routine/routinely
secure/securely
sensitive/sensitively
significant/significantly
skillful/skillfully
solid/solidly
sophisticated
strategic/strategically
strong/strongly
substantial/substantially
successful/successfully
tactful/tactfully
thorough/thoroughly
uncommon/uncommonly
unique/uniquely
unusual/unusually
urgent/urgently
varied
vigorous/vigorously
virtual/virtually
vital/vitally
wide/widely

Résumé Tips

Here are some important points to help you *empower* your resume.

MAKE IT READABLE

Since resumes are often skimmed the first time through, it must be easy for the reader to pick up key pieces of information quickly. Using long paragraphs of over ten lines or heavy blocks of text can be a real disincentive to read it.

HONESTY

If you tell the truth you don't need to remember anything. —MARK TWAIN

Be honest and accurate. Whatever is stated should be true—but that doesn't mean you have to tell everything. The resume is your marketing tool, not an application. Present what you consider the strongest information.

> Never attempt to present yourself better than you are; the key is to demonstrate how good you are!

Thou Shall Not:

- Claim to have a college degree if you don't have one. Neither should you claim a degree from a college other than the one you received it from. This is the easiest information for employers to check. One person we know who was just 20 credits short of a degree figured he was "close enough" and indicated he had graduated. He received an offer for a very good position, but it was rescinded when the lie was discovered. He also burned the bridge with the executive who had originally recommended him for the job.

- Claim responsibilities that were not yours, nor job titles that would inflate your actual level of responsibility.
- Exaggerate your accomplishments. Results do not have to be stupendous or earth shattering. Modest results effectively presented are sufficient. (e.g., improving a procedure or process). The *action* involved in the accomplishment can be just as compelling as the result. It demonstrates your ability to make things more efficient, regardless of the scale, which is always valuable to an employer.
- Hijack another's accomplishments. If you were part of a team, describe your contributions and how they led to the overall results. Of course, managers and supervisors can claim credit for individual and group results . . . and usually do!

Studies by search firms and reference checkers indicate that as much as one-third of applicants lie on their resumes or job application. To counter this trend, many firms are going to great lengths to verify the information provided by their top candidates. Don't become a finalist only to be eliminated because you stretched the truth. It isn't worth it.

Oh, what a tangled web we weave,
When first we practice to deceive!

WHAT TO CALL IT

It's not necessary to type *Resume, Qualifications Brief, Profile,* or any other such title at the top of your resume. Everyone will know it's a resume just by glancing at it.

COLOR AND TYPE OF PAPER

While paper is available in a variety of colors, textures, weights, and sizes, there are some standard guidelines to follow. The color of paper you choose can definitely make a difference in the number of interviews you get. White is always a safe color, but studies reveal that buff or off-white paper provide even better results. (Keep in mind that if you believe the resume will be scanned it should be white or a very light off-white.)

The finest resume paper is the 20- or 24-pound off-white or light gray classic linen made by several paper manufacturers. White can also work well. Many people also like classic laid. Both classic linen and classic laid have a texture that implies quality without overdoing it. If you prefer a paper without a textured surface, choose one with a "rag" or cotton fiber content of at least 25%. For those seeking management positions a light gray can be effective. Blues and greens have not tested well. Color should have a positive effect; this will nearly always mean you should use light shades. Dark grays and browns or bright colors are not recommended.

Twenty-pound paper is always a safe standard. A slightly heavier paper is fine, but avoid heavy stocks. Monarch size paper (7 x 10") is fine for thank-you notes, but stick with 8½ x 11" for your resume. Good papers often have a watermark, so make sure it is right side up if you print it or copy it yourself. Copy shops usually check for this, but it's wise to double-check this yourself.

You can buy all types of fancy papers with borders and other nifty stuff. Such overkill is typically a distraction from your message and often counterproductive.

AVOID OVERUSING WORD PROCESSING FEATURES

One drawback of using today's feature-laden word processing programs is the temptation to cram the document with all manner of special graphics and effects. Too much of a good thing, however, can make the final result appear busy, over-produced, and annoying. These include different fonts, bolding, underlining, and italics. The example following is exaggerated to make the point. See if your eyes go all over the place, trying to concentrate on the content.

General Motors, Detroit, Michigan 10/97–Present

<u>SENIOR ENGINEER</u> – As part of a team of **Software Quality Assurance Engineers,** evaluate <u>CAD/CAM</u> software and make recommendations for improvements before software is made available to users within the company. Review functional specifications to *ensure* all portions are testable and fully meet user needs. REDUCED time necessary to fully evaluate software from **45 days** to **18 days**.

Keep it simple.

HONEY, I SHRUNK THE FONT

Three font sizes are typically used for resumes: 12-point, 11-point, and 10-point. For serif fonts such as Times New Roman, Garamond, and Bookman, we typically recommend 12-point, 11-point, and 10-point. The larger 12- and 11-point sizes are preferred because they are easier to read, especially for the older eyes among our population.

For sans-serif fonts such as Arial, Tahoma, and Century Gothic, we generally recommend 11-point and 10-point as the most readable.

If you are using 12-point and your resume is running long, you can adjust the font downward (most software packages allow fractional changes such as 11.5), or consider playing with the margins. While the standard margin is usually one inch on each side, slight reductions to 0.9", 0.8", or even 0.75" are also acceptable for top, bottom, and side margins.

Another way to get more on a page is to reduce the space between paragraphs. If you are using a 12-point font, every space between lines will be that size. After you've finished the resume, you can reduce those spaces to 8-point or even 6-point. There will still be sufficient white space between paragraphs.

TIP

If you want to try this with Word, here's how to do it. Highlight the first paragraph symbol ¶ you want to reduce in size. There will be paragraph symbols throughout your resume if you are using that function. If you don't see the paragraph symbol, go up to the toolbar and click on the paragraph symbol. Instantly your resume will be filled with paragraph symbols and there will be a dot between each word. With the paragraph symbol highlighted, find the font size control on the toolbar and click on it. Click on the font you want. Sizes below 8 as well as fractions (e.g., 8.5), require manual entry using the number keys. Hit the enter key and the space will be reduced. Move the cursor to the next paragraph symbol and hit the F4 key (the repeat key). Repeat as desired.

If you suspect your resume might be scanned into an employer's databank, use 11- or 12-point. With 10-point, the scanner and OCR software are more likely to misread the content and obscure some of your valuable information. Writing in 10-point is also getting down to the very edge of legibility, especially for older readers . . . like us. Use it only as a last resort. For more on scanning see pages 144, 146–150.

PHOTOGRAPHS

Photographs should rarely be submitted with resumes. They are fairly standard, however, for such careers as models, performers, and media personalities. Many organizations are leery of receiving photographs with resumes because it increases the likelihood of age and race discrimination charges. Employers are nearly unanimous in preferring not to receive photographs.

GARY: One client told me he had been sending out photos with each resume. He was a man in his late fifties who looked like Yankees owner George Steinbrenner. He said he did it to show the employers how robust and healthy he was in appearance. I asked him how he would feel if he opened an envelope and a picture of George Steinbrenner spilled out onto his desk. He grimaced, nodded, and discontinued the practice.

CONFIDENTIALITY

Employers who receive your resume will rarely inform your current boss. Even if they know your boss, they understand the importance of confidentiality. If, however, your current boss or company is known for firing people for "disloyalty," consider the steps listed below.

1. Type "Confidential" at the top of your resume.
2. At the bottom of the resume type and underline, "Please do not contact employer at this time."
3. Replace the name of your present employer (and possibly your next to last employer) with a description such as, "A major manufacturer of automotive parts," "A Fortune 500 Corporation," or "A National Retail Chain."
4. Utilize an executive recruiter (headhunter) who can sell you over the phone without revealing your name and will send your resume only if the employer is particularly interested.

If your boss suspects you are looking but considers you a valuable employee, you are more likely to get a raise than a pink slip. In one sense, everyone is looking for another job—some are just more active than others. When headhunters call regarding truly great jobs, everyone is willing to talk. A good piece of advice, though, based on others' experiences: Don't tell even trusted friends at work that you are looking. Even your most discreet pals can inadvertently slip up and spill the beans.

SALARY

Salary history and salary requirements do not belong on the resume.

Classified ads frequently ask for such information. We normally recommend ignoring the request. In this country what we earn is our own business not to be easily shared with strangers. Besides, this very information is usually the basis of your salary negotiations down the pike. Don't tip your hand.

If you feel compelled to acknowledge the request, you might simply write in your cover letter, "Salary is negotiable." Another option when asked for desired salary is to indicate a large range. For someone seeking $40,000 it might state, "Seeking $37,000–47,000 depending on responsibilities." For someone seeking $100,000 or above, a larger range might be used, especially if there are bonuses and other perks to consider. HR managers confirm that highly rated candidates who do not include salary history or desired salary are still given strong consideration.

RELOCATION

Positions with national companies often require relocation. A simple statement under a "Personal" or "Additional Information" heading stating "Willing to relocate" will provide an additional qualification often overlooked by your competition. If you don't feel it deserves its own section, simply enter it in at the end of the resume.

REASON FOR LEAVING

Everyone has a reason for leaving a job, but the only time to present it is when it can be of value. Anything negative or complicated should be saved for the interview. Trying to deal with these issues in a resume or cover letter only causes confusion and distracts from the positives you are trying to convey.

Promotions and recruitments are always appropriate and can be cited either in the description of the job you were promoted/recruited into or the job you were recruited from. Other useful reasons include relocation of your company or department, especially if you were offered the opportunity to be relocated.

Lead, Order Entry Department — Responsible for scheduling, training, and supervising four employees. Delegated work load, resolved customer problems, and coordinated with other departments. Developed procedures that increased order entry accuracy by 35%. Left due to a merger with NOP Industries when the order entry department was moved to Chicago. Received option for relocation and a position in the new enterprise.

Downsizing and reorganization have become facts of life in the modern world. Few have escaped it. Usually, there is no need to include the reason for leaving in the resume. It is usually best dealt with at an interview. If you do wish to address it, make sure that you point out the loss of your position was not an indication of your performance but a structural change in the company.

Left when the company downsized and position was eliminated.
Company went out of business in 2002.

ABBREVIATIONS

Avoid abbreviations that may cause confusion to readers who are not familiar with them. As a rule of thumb, use an abbreviation only if you are certain that *everyone*, from the HR screener to the hiring manager, will recognize it. Keep in mind, however, that words are more visually attractive when spelled out. For this reason we generally recommend spelling out the names of states, particularly in the address at the top of a resume. The trend, however, is to use the two-letter abbreviation for states used by the Postal Service. In essence you can't go wrong with either option. The key is to be consistent throughout the resume. Some abbreviations such as "B.A.," "M.A.", and "Ph.D." are preferred over the extended versions.

If you are going to use an abbreviation more that once, spell it out the first time followed by the short form in parentheses. An example would be: Introduced a Total Quality Management (TQM) program that reduced rejected parts by 22%.

CREATIVE LICENSE

Remember, this is a marketing process. Don't be afraid to be creative. What can you do to separate yourself from the crowd without going overboard and looking ridiculous? Always put yourself in the place of the reader. How would you respond if it came across your desk? If you can come up with something that you are reasonably certain won't backfire, give it a shot. Otherwise, it is better to stick with the more standard presentational strategies.

We have all heard stories such as the one about the guy who wrote his resume in crayon and was invited in for the interview. That is always used as "proof" by people who denigrate the importance of a quality resume in the job search. What never gets resolved in this story, however, is whether or not the crayon-guy was actually offered a position or merely brought in so the folks could see what kind of moron writes resumes in crayon!

Before you get too creative, remember this: Hiring a person is a serious business and employers are not looking to entrust their organizations and livelihoods to *characters*!

SELECTING A FORMAT

The format is essentially the layout of the resume. Many of the sample resumes included in *Resume Empower!* use the layout that has served our clients well for nearly three decades. It is easy to scan and it makes excellent use of space. Throughout the resume there is a balance of white space and text.

There are dozens of formats with dozens of variations within each format. Flip through the resume section from page 172 to page 245 and you'll probably find one you like. If you've found a format in the past that you like, and feel it would do a good job of presenting your background, by all means use it. If you do not have a preferred model, you cannot go wrong if you adapt one of our sample resumes. They are time tested and well accepted.

SHOWING YOUR NAME, ADDRESS, PHONE, CELL PHONE, E-MAIL ADDRESS, AND WEB SITE

A reader's eye invariably starts at the top of the resume. For this reason, the very first impression of you is created by the appearance of your name and contact information.

Check out the heading below:

Rob Thomas

23654 Savoy Lane
Houston, Texas 77058
(713) 483-0098 (h) (713) 483-5555 (c)
rthomas@mind.com

Everything is centered and the name is 2 to 3 point sizes larger than the rest of the text. In this case the text is 11-point and the name is 14-point. The bolded name stands out, but it is not so much larger that it visually blasts the reader.

Since so many people now carry cell phones, it is not unusual to see these listed along with the home phone.

GARY: I caution my clients not to include a cell phone number unless it is their only phone. Cell calls usually come in at the wrong time—in the middle of traffic, for instance, while you are trying to steer with one hand and suck down your latte with the other, while listening to your stereo. By the time you have answered the call you have bumped into the car ahead of you, spilled your latte in your lap, and, instead of hitting the off-button of the stereo, accidentally changed the channel and are now blaring *Black Sabbath's Greatest Hits*!

The real downside, though, is that while you are driving or away from your desk or home, you don't have access to the notes you made about the job, the company, and the name of any contacts that would be calling. Very rarely is there a *hiring emergency* that can't wait until you have checked the messages on your home phone. Yes, your cell phone has a voice mail feature, but how many of us have the will power not to answer, afraid we will miss out on something immediate?

> **TOM:** The answer is simple: Include your cell number on your resume and then just don't answer your cell phone while driving or when you don't have access to information on the positions you've applied for. It's not that hard to do. If someone is seriously trying to reach you they can leave a message or e-mail you. Besides, if they don't leave a message, you can usually tell who has called you. No big deal. Include your cell number.

E-mail addresses have become as common as street addresses and phone numbers. If you don't have one, we advise getting one, as it is now the norm and conspicuous if absent. If you have created an online portfolio, include the Web address, usually on the same line as your e-mail.

Below are some variations. We've used 12 point for the name and 10 point for the rest.

Rob Thomas	**ROB THOMAS**	**ROB THOMAS**
23654 Savoy Lane	23654 Savoy Lane	23654 Savoy Lane
Houston, TX 77058	Houston, TX 77058	Houston, TX 77058
(713) 483-0098	713-483-0098	713/483-0098
rthomas@mind.com	rthomas@mind.com	rthomas@mind.com

> **TOM:** Show your name at the top the way you want to be called. I'm Thomas Fuller Washington, but I go by Tom and few know my middle name. No one ever called me Thomas, not even my mother when she was angry with me. If your resume says Robert you'll be called Robert even if you prefer Rob or Bob. If you write Elizabeth but prefer Liz, write Liz. There is no reason to include your middle name or middle initial. Employers will be looking at the resume more than the cover letter so they will call you whatever you have at the top of your resume. I don't want to have to tell an interviewer to call me Tom, not Thomas, when I can get that result simply by putting Tom on my resume.

> **GARY:** The resume is a quasi-formal or business document. As such, you should use your full name, including middle initial. It is the resume equivalent of dressing up for the interview. You can always sign your cover letter "Bob" or "Liz" just as you can similarly introduce yourself at the interview ("Call me Al").

All of the examples in this section had everything centered. That is the most common way to present your name and address, but there are other ways as well. For additional ways to create a heading review the sample resumes.

There is more than just an aesthetic reason the name should appear at the top. Electronic scanners usually assume automatically that the top line is the name and process it accordingly. Yes, another example of technology limiting, rather than expanding, our options.

SHOWING WORK NUMBERS ON YOUR RESUME

It is rarely appropriate to include your work number on the resume. While privacy might be an issue, it is often considered unethical to use an employer's time and resources for job hunting. With that said, the choice is yours.

JUSTIFIED LEFT AND RIGHT OR RAGGED RIGHT?

Books and magazines are invariably printed using justified right and left margins (called full justified). This means all of the type starts in a straight line on the left and all type ends at the same spot on the right. This paragraph is justified left and right.

Most word-processing software enables you to select either a justified right or "ragged" right format. With ragged right, the lines do not end at the same spot. This is normal in letter writing. It is easy to pop your paragraphs into either format with a single click of your mouse on the appropriate icon and then decide which one better represents you. By the way, this paragraph uses ragged right. See pages 176 and 177 for ragged right and pages 180 and 182 for justified left and right resumes.

SIMPLE TRICKS TO USE WITH YOUR WORD PROCESSOR

Word processing is a wonderful tool, particularly for those of us ancient enough to remember typewriters, whiteout, and carbon paper. There are two particularly helpful tricks that you can do with a word processor: You can use the cut and paste features, and you can manipulate both the font size and margin settings to get your resume to the right number of pages, as discussed above.

Copy and Paste. You can use this feature to quickly tailor your resume for different positions. First, create a generic "copy and paste" folder. This is where you will store items you can add to or delete from your resume as needed. Every time you delete or add an item in the resume, park it in this file for future use. After awhile, you will probably have all the items you will ever need for your resumes and adding them to a new document becomes a matter of cut and paste . . . just like the name of the folder.

DON'T RELY ON THE SPELL-CHECKER TO BE YOUR PROOFREADER

As great as spell-checker is, it is no substitute for good old-fashioned proofreading. The spell-checker will catch typos and misspellings, but it is not perfect. It cannot determine if the properly spelled word you used is truly the correct word. The sentence "I went to there home on Saturday and then returned for a short visit their on Sunday" would not be flagged by the spell-checker, despite the fact that *there* and *their* were used incorrectly. Frequent examples of this include *waste* and *waist, two, to* and *too,* as well as just plain misspellings such as *at* for *as* or *it* for *is.*

Two of the most frequent, if not *the* most frequent errors that get by the spell-checker in resumes are *mange* for manage, and *manger* for manager.

Always use the spell-checker. It is great for picking up misspellings and words that have reversed letters like *worte* instead of *wrote,* missing letters like *lttle* for *little,* or too many letters like *tellling* instead of *telling.* Mistakes like these are often difficult for proofreaders to pick up.

NO TYPOS, NO ERRORS

Whether or not you use the spell-checker, you must produce a resume with zero errors and typos. This usually requires at least three careful readings by you and one other person who is versed in spelling and grammar. Those with a lot of technical entries should have a fellow *techie* check for accuracy and spelling. These suggestions are valid for cover letters as well.

When asking for such assistance, make sure the helpers understand that proofing is all you want them to do. Too many times a request for proofreading or technical checking is taken as a license to critique the entire resume, format, fonts, number of paragraphs, use of bullets, and on and on. If they do offer that advice, unsolicited as it might be, accept it with good cheer, consider it their fee for the proofreading, and let them know you will take it under advisement.

PUT YOUR NAME AT THE TOP OF PAGE TWO

Pages sometimes get separated, so add your name at the upper left corner of the second and any additional pages along with the appropriate page number.

Joe Stephens
Page Two

If space is tight you can save a line like this:

Joe Stephens – Page Two

If you absolutely have no room, feel free to use the header/footer feature of your software. That will set the information in the upper margin and not intrude into the body of the document.

SKIP THE ART SHOW

Unless you're Picasso, no art! We've seen a few small logos that people have created for themselves that looked okay, but the vast majority of art simply detracts from the message.

LEARN THE LINGO

Every occupation has its own special language, jargon, nomenclature, and buzzwords. Learn the jargon and make sure you use the terms correctly. Then look for ways to get these into your resume and cover letters. This can be valuable in a key word search and when a real live person reads it. Using the right buzzwords creates the impression that "you're one of us." Without it you come off as an outsider. Make sure you use the jargon in appropriate places and don't force it.

UNLEARN THE LINGO

Some professions, companies, and organizations have specialized vocabularies that do not translate well to the outside world. The military and government agencies, for instance, have a tendency toward bureaucratese and alphabet soup–type abbreviations. Companies often have pet names for many of their processes, which can be completely incomprehensible to someone in another organization doing the exact same thing. So, as you go through your job sketches, flag any terms you think might be too *in-house* for the type of audience you are trying to reach.

USE SIMPLE WORDS

Some people believe that a four-syllable word is always superior to its two-syllable cousin. They believe that longer words demonstrate intelligence and a strong vocabulary. Actually, good writing consists of using just *the right word*, not the longest or the shortest. Keep your writing simple and straightforward. A common problem writers face when using long or unfamiliar words is that they frequently use them incorrectly. Your resume is not the place to experiment with new words. If used incorrectly, just one word can make you look ridiculous and disqualify you from consideration.

GET YOUR KEY INFORMATION ON PAGE ONE

Qualifications, education, and your most relevant jobs usually belong on page one. If the employer scans your resume and is not sufficiently hooked by the end of the first page, it's unlikely the rest will be read. If your most important or valuable experience took place earlier in your career, see Clustered Resume on pages 129–139 on how to get it to the forefront.

HOW TO CREATE A TWO-PAGE RESUME WITH THREE PAGES

We like to keep a resume to two pages. It is the format we believe can best tell a person's story without boring the reader.

A third page can be somewhat intimidating, causing a reader to balk. However, if the resume is well-written, informative, and—above all—interesting, and you believe the additional information supplied is critical, three pages can work nicely.

In some cases, if there is useful supporting information the writer wishes to include, we recommend the creation of an *addendum*.

Here's how it works.

If you have several categories to include on the page, such as Training, Presentations, and Publications, simply create a generic Addendum title for the page and include each group under its own title.

Extremely lengthy Training sections can be disruptive to the flow of the resume. The first order of business is to limit the section to a manageable number that effectively represent the breadth of training received. Sometimes, however, the entire list of courses is important. In that case, creating a page header called "Training Addendum" adds the information. With this wording you have just created a two-page resume with a one-page addendum. To the reader it is still a non-threatening two-page resume.

CLAIMING IT DOESN'T MAKE IT SO

Just because you say something or claim something doesn't mean the employer will automatically accept it or be impressed. Back up your claims with evidence whenever possible. Evidence or proof is not always necessary to bring a person to accept or believe a point you are making, but it sure helps. See pages 12, 16, and 19 for more on providing evidence.

A USEFUL FONT

The section header above is in a font style known as *small caps*. It provides another format for listing employer names or job titles.

Exeter Manufacturing   EXETER MANUFACTURING   **EXETER MANUFACTURING**

The middle version uses the small caps in bold. Notice that the first letter E in EXETER is a full-sized capital letter. The remaining letters in EXETER are also capitals, but they are slightly smaller. It's just a nice touch that can be used. Check your software tutorial to access this feature.

MULTIPLE RESUMES

If you are considering more than one type of job, you may need two or more resumes. In this case you may want to write only one resume, yet give it more flexibility by using more than one objective, leaving everything else the same. This is easy to do with word processing.

An example will help. Jim is a very good computer salesperson with no desire to leave sales, but we created three different objectives for him to use in three different versions of his resume: "OBJECTIVE: Computer Sales;" "OBJECTIVE: Electronics Sales;" and "OBJECTIVE: Sales." Nothing else in the resume was changed. Computer companies got one resume, electronics companies got another, and if Jim saw something interesting outside those two industries, he sent the one that said "Sales."

Changing the objective, however, may not be adequate if the types of jobs you are seeking are considerably different from each other. Writing a new or modified Qualifications section for each objective will often do the trick. Far less frequently, you may need to make small changes in the employment section. Typically that consists of adding an area of experience that was a very small part of your job, but that will help sell you with that particular objective. You would also look for ways to get the right buzzwords in. And, of course, make sure you dip into your *cut and paste* file.

USING COVER LETTERS FOR FLEXIBILITY

A cover letter should accompany each resume you submit unless specifically prohibited by the employer. Another exception is for those resumes you personally hand out to hiring managers. The cover letter provides an excellent opportunity to highlight or elaborate on points you know are important to that particular employer, which may or may not be fully showcased in the resume.

ANSWERING CLASSIFIED ADS

When an ad provides specific job requirements, there are a number of ways to respond. You can:

- Send your resume with a custom-written cover letter discussing key points mentioned in the ad; or
- Customize your resume to hit all the important points in the ad *and* write a creative cover letter.

The latter approach is more likely to provide the best results, and it really doesn't take much more time.

As you customize your resume, you may find that the job narratives require few if any changes, while the qualifications section might require substantial changes. The entire process of rewriting might take one to two hours. Time is your working capital, so consider it an investment. Taking time to redo the resume will not guarantee an interview, but it can *seriously enhance* your chances. If you lack certain desired skills or experience that were mentioned in the ad, simply ignore those points and really sell what you do have.

MAILING

Traditionally resumes are folded in thirds and sent in a standard number ten business envelope. That is still perfectly acceptable, but consider spending a little more and sending the resume in a 9 x 12" envelope so the resume does not need to be folded. It's not a big thing, but if it is not folded it will look nicer in the stack. To keep the costs down, the latter option is best confined to your most important employers.

For a really hot job, consider having it delivered by an overnight delivery service. For a super hot local job, consider having a messenger service deliver it. The extra effort is one way of saying you want the job. Priority mail also works well. While two- or three-day service is not guaranteed, most letters do get delivered in the U.S. within three days.

READ THOSE REJECT LETTERS, THEN TOSS THEM

Most reject letters are form letters that tell you that though "you have a fine background, we had many excellent candidates, and have selected those for interviews who have just the right experience." Of course, your resume will be kept on file (for 90 days/six months/one year) in case something comes up more suited to your profile. Go ahead and read such letters and then toss them.

Make a note on your sheet that contains the clipped-out ad you responded to and simply write "No" or "Reject." Then move on.

Occasionally you'll get a reject letter that indicates that the recruiter liked you, but you simply didn't have the credentials or experience that some others had. Such statements are rarely made just to make you feel better. It indicates that this is an organization you should stay in touch with. Send the recruiter a polite thank-you note. Follow this up in the near future and ask for advice on more effectively presenting yourself or classes you might take to make yourself a better candidate.

WHEN THE RECRUITER CALLS

When a headhunter, corporate recruiter, or hiring manager calls you to set up an interview, listen attentively and take detailed notes. After agreeing to an interview, ask for more details about the position. The more you can learn about the position, the better prepared you will be for the interview itself. Questions you could ask include:

> Could you tell me a little more about the position?
> You indicated that the person would do (a duty), could you elaborate a little on that?
> Who does the position report to?

Sometimes the headhunter will be calling you without having seen your resume. Perhaps you were referred by a third party. After a few initial questions, the recruiter will, hopefully, ask you to send a resume. By gaining additional information about the job, you can then tailor your resume and cover letter to fit the exact requirements of the position.

MAINTAIN A FILE FOR EACH AD YOU RESPOND TO

When an employer calls regarding an ad to which you have responded, you should be able to quickly locate it and refer to it as you speak. After applying for numerous positions, this type of refresher can be critical to your presentation.

IF YOU DON'T HAVE YOUR OWN COMPUTER OR INTERNET ACCESS

Some people do not own a computer or have Internet access. While not usually a precondition of employment, an Internet address is becoming a standard part of an individual's contact information. Even though most employers won't contact you by e-mail unless you have applied for the position in that manner, it is just expected these days.

If you do not have or want a computer in your home, most libraries offer computer and Internet access. There is usually a posted time limit of an hour or so but that is often sufficient to write a letter or check email. If no one is waiting to use the computer after you, the time limits are often waived. You can also print out your tailored resume and cover letter at the library.

In addition to libraries, your state Job Service will have computers available. Certain nonprofit agencies, particularly those designed to help targeted populations, will also have computers available. If you don't know how to use a keyboard, or access the Internet, the library or agency may provide assistance or direct you to the available training resources.

Friends are often willing to help out by sharing their computers and teaching you about word-processing.

FREE E-MAIL

There are dozens of free e-mail services, the most popular being:

> Google (www.gmail.com)
> Hotmail (www.hotmail.com)
> Inbox (www.inbox.com)
> Mail.com (www.mail.com)
> Yahoo (www.yahoo.com)

DON'T EXPECT RESPONSES TO YOUR RESUME

It used to be standard practice for employers to acknowledge receipt of a resume. Even if it was the standard "We'll keep it on file for six months" at least you knew the resume had been received and reviewed by *somebody*!

Well, that was then and this is now. Most organizations no longer feel that it is their responsibility to confirm receipt of your resume. It is both expensive and time consuming of company resources—that is, HR staffers. So, don't waste two seconds complaining about, or even thinking about, the resume you mailed last week. We may criticize our postal service but the happy fact is that more than 99% of all letters reach their correct destination within a reasonable time. With that in mind, assume the resume was delivered on time to the right place. You will be contacted if you are considered in the running. So don't waste time fretting about it and go on with your job search. Fretting takes time and energy and you don't want to waste either.

Jobs you feel particularly suited to, however, but haven't received responses to might require some follow-up. If you haven't heard anything in a couple of weeks, go ahead and contact the company to inquire as to whether they received your resume and where they are in the selection process. While this might not net you any information, you have lost nothing by asking. On the other hand, you might learn that your resume was received and that the selection process has not actually begun. This happens a lot; there are often lags between the recruiting and selection stages of hiring. You might even be able to wangle a connection to the hiring manager for the same information. That is a bull's-eye. That is pay dirt! You have the opportunity few others will have: personal contact with the decision maker. Make the most of it!

BEFORE YOU FAX OR E-MAIL THAT RESUME

Most faxes and e-mails arrive at the appropriate destination without a problem. Some don't. Perhaps your fax came out the other end looking smudgy, or your e-mailed version was turned to gibberish. To determine if there is a problem, and whether the problem is at your end, send some test faxes and e-mails to friends. If they came out pristine, you are ready to roll. If there were problems, try using other faxes or e-mail servers. The quickest way to check the quality of an e-mail is to send it directly to yourself.

MATCHING ENVELOPES ARE FINE BUT NOT NECESSARY

When you buy a nice quality paper for your resume, you can also buy matching envelopes. The truth is, the envelope is unlikely to be seen by anyone of hiring consequence and is an unnecessary expense. Some folks even go to the trouble of using special edition postage stamps. That's only a requirement when you are trying to impress the mail clerk who receives the envelope.

AVOID COMMON FAUX PAS

Copying your resume at work is not recommended. Aside from the ethics of using company resources for such a personal activity, people have been known to remove their copies and leave the originals in the copier. Or have the resume on the computer screen when the boss walks by. This is similar to the inadvisable practice of receiving job-related correspondence on shared office fax machines. Not a great idea.

YOU CAN'T PLEASE EVERYONE!

No matter how hard you try, you can't please everyone. For every hundred people you talk to about resumes, you'll find a hundred different opinions.

Write the resume as if you were the hiring manager who was going to read it. What would you need to know about the candidate? Skills . . . Experience . . .

Achievements . . . Education . . . Training . . . and more. When it is complete, read it carefully. Does it make you feel like meeting the person described? If so, find someone you trust to proofread it. With that accomplished, read it again. If you still like the person you are reading about, smile. You have yourself a resume!

To show you how little control you have over who reads your resume and how they evaluate it, here's a true story about the process used by one HR manager. When narrowing the list from 30 applicants to six finalists, she frequently found two or three tied for that sixth spot. So how did she decide? She took a ruler, measured the borders of each resume, and selected the one that had margins that came closest to exactly one inch on all sides.

Résumé Formats

Historically, there have been four types of resumes—reverse chronological, functional, qualifications/chronological, and hybrid, a combination of the qualifications, functional, and chronological resumes. Chronological and functional resumes have both advantages and disadvantages, while the qualifications/chronological and hybrid resumes offer the advantages of the chronological and functional resumes with none of the disadvantages. The *clustered resume®*, as we will see in the next chapter, adds a valuable and flexible tool for marketing yourself more effectively.

REVERSE CHRONOLOGICAL RESUME

The standard reverse chronological resumes describe the candidate's work experience in reverse order, with the current or most recent position appearing first. Traditionally these present employers, dates, job titles, duties, and results. The primary advantage of the chronological resume is that employers are used to reading it. They know how to scan it quickly and get what they need from it. Its major disadvantage is that it is often difficult to present valuable experience that was achieved earlier in the career without adding excessive verbiage, pages, and tedium.

FUNCTIONAL RESUME

The functional resume, on the other hand, is expressly designed to showcase specific experience or functional areas of experience. The job seeker identifies key areas of experience, or "functions," and labels each entry with headings such as Management, Design, Project Management, and Technical Skills. The sections are then filled in with the candidate's most impressive experience and results. Major drawbacks of the functional resume are that it is more difficult to read, and that the employer typically does not know when or where the experience being described took place. For this reason it can be confusing. It is hard to find a hiring manager who prefers to read this type of resume above the other formats.

QUALIFICATIONS/CHRONOLOGICAL RESUME

The qualifications/chronological resume is essentially a chronological resume with an extended qualifications section at the beginning. It utilizes the most effective attributes of both the reverse chronological and functional formats. The qualifications section of this resume is usually shorter than the functional portion of a functional resume, but it covers the most crucial areas of experience and provides a quick introduction to the candidate's core strengths. The job narrative section, the other main part of the resume, provides the context for the experience, a critical element normally lacking in the traditional functional resume. Most of the resumes you'll see in *Resume Empower!* are of this type.

HYBRID RESUME

The hybrid resume typically includes functional *and* chronological sections, and often a qualifications section as well.

On the next six pages you will see examples of each of these resume formats followed by a more in-depth description of the functional resume, how to write it, how to determine whether you should use it, and additional samples.

Reverse Chronological   **Verdana**

Juan Lozano
19301 Whispering Road
Phoenix Arizona 85044
(602) 555-2809
jlozano@hotmail.com

OBJECTIVE: Restaurant Management

EDUCATION

AA – Liberal Arts, Frost Community College (1999)

RESTAURANT MANAGEMENT TRAINING

Restaurant Management Training School, 300 class hours, Gaucho Restaurants
(2004–2006)

EMPLOYMENT

Gaucho Restaurants, Phoenix, AZ 2003–Present

GENERAL MANAGER – 2006–Present. Took over a troubled restaurant in the chain
that was experiencing high employee turnover, poor service, and a loss in the
customer base. Within nine months stabilized the operation. Resolved serious
morale problems, instituted an effective training program, and developed
a strong support staff for consistent service. During the first nine months
increased sales 18% and reduced staff turnover 50% and labor costs 10%.
Provided excellent wine training for the staff and significantly increased wine
sales.

In 2007 increased sales 15% and profits 21%. In 2008 increased sales 14%
and profits 18%. Named 2007 Regional Manager of the Year in a region of 21
fine dining restaurants.

ASSISTANT MANAGER – 2003–2006. As assistant manager oversaw one of the
highest volume restaurants in the chain and was responsible for reducing
turnover and regaining customer confidence through training and development
of floor staff. With stronger training and better marketing, increased sales
11%, achieved tighter budgets, and produced a level of service that brought
strong compliments from customers.

La Casa Restaurant, Phoenix, AZ 1999–2003

ASSOCIATE MANAGER – 2001–2003. For this well-established restaurant,
responsible for maintaining high standards related to service, food quality,
personnel training, cost control, and sales. Introduced a method of analyzing
previous sales figures that better predicted staffing needs, cut labor costs, and
increased food and beverage sales.

MANAGEMENT TRAINEE – 1999–2001. Learned all aspects of the restaurant
industry with assignments in purchasing, food preparation, wait staff, and
hosting.

SUZANNE HALL

18852 52nd SE
Bothell, Washington 98011
(206) 555-2756
suzannehall@msn.com

OBJECTIVE: Personnel Management

QUALIFICATIONS

Personnel Management – Six years experience in personnel, with three years as Personnel Manager of a store with 230 employees. Supervise and train a staff of four. Significantly increased morale among store personnel and successfully fought off a unionizing effort.

Recruiting, Interviewing, Hiring – Very effective interviewer. Screen and hire all sales, supervisory, clerical, and support personnel. Over 80% of all people hired have remained with the store at least one year. Turnover has been reduced 22% by careful screening and by implementing other improvements throughout the store.

EEO - Perform periodic surveys and ensure all goals are met as required.

Wage and Salary Administration – Identified unfair wage differentials between recent hires and those with longer service. Removed pay scale discrepancies and nearly eliminated turnover among more experienced staff.

Promotions – Work closely with supervisors to determine those ready for promotions. Write all final recommendations for promotions.

Terminations – Arbitrate in all firing situations and participate in all firing interviews. Conduct exit interviews and identify causes for termination. By taking quick action, several terminations have been averted.

Manpower Planning – Predict staffing needs for Christmas and major sales and hire necessary personnel.

Career Counseling – Provide extensive career path counseling to store employees.

Training and Development – Developed and conducted a 16-hour training program emphasizing customer service and job training. Turnover and customer complaints have been reduced substantially since the program was increased from 8 to 16 hours. Supervise additional training during the probationary period.

EMPLOYMENT

Briggins Department Stores, Seattle, Washington (1993 to Present)
Personnel Manager (2003–Present)
Assistant Personnel Manager (2001–2003)
Schedule Coordinator (1998–2001)
Credit Manager (1995–1998)
Credit Adjustment Processor (1993–1995)

EDUCATION

Business Studies – Bellevue Community College (35 credits)

Functional   **Arial**

JASON RYERSON
14568 NE 9th Street
Redmond, Washington 98053
(425) 555-7594
jvrye@comcast.net

OBJECTIVE: Facilities Management

QUALIFICATIONS

Over 20 years of exceptional management experience. Proven ability to successfully complete projects cost effectively and on schedule. Received numerous awards for completion of high-quality projects.

Implemented comprehensive programs that dramatically improved productivity and efficiency of personnel.

PROFESSIONAL EXPERIENCE

ENGINEERING MANAGEMENT – Eight years of demanding and successful hands-on engineering management and plant management responsibilities. Coordinated hundreds of repair jobs conducted by both own workforce and outside contractors. In one instance increased overall plant reliability by 220%. While providing repair support for 12 naval ships over a three-year period, reduced equipment downtime by 50%.

FACILITIES MANAGEMENT – As Chief Engineer and Material Manager, directly responsible for operation, maintenance, and repair of steam and diesel electric power plants. Associated equipment included heating, ventilation, and air conditioning systems; firefighting and sprinkler systems; and various emergency equipment. Charged also with infrastructure repair and modifications. Supported numerous office and work station relocations in minimal time and without loss of productivity.

CONTRACT ADMINISTRATION – Broad experience in working with prime and subcontractors in overseeing scheduled and emergency repairs. Represented the U.S. Government in the management of an $18 million resupply contract for 76 remote sites in the Pacific.

TROUBLESHOOTING – Volunteered to rebuild a faltering yet critical department of 95 personnel. Within 45 days identified all major problem areas and initiated a corrective action plan that included a comprehensive training program for 900 people. The revitalized training program improved morale and decreased absenteeism over 60%. Received a special commendation for the project.

EMPLOYMENT

United States Navy 1985 to 2008. Completed Naval service with rank of Commander.

EDUCATION

MA – Political Science, Naval Postgraduate School (1990)
BA – International Studies, University of Washington (1984)

ROBERTA JENNINGS

1121 Peach Drive
Atlanta, Georgia 30601
(404) 574-8769
ra_jennings@aol.com

OBJECTIVE: Airline Management

QUALIFICATIONS

Excellent management and supervisory capabilities. Highly respected by subordinates and able to obtain high performance levels from employees. Established one of the best on-time performance records in the airline industry.

EDUCATION

B.A. - Business, University of Southern California (1996)

EMPLOYMENT

Air Florida 2002 to Present

Customer/Ramp Service Supervisor, Atlanta, Georgia, 2005 to present. Opened the Atlanta airport facility for Air Florida and have created one of its most efficient and effective operations. Supervise and train 30 Customer Service Agents and Ramp personnel. Responsible for all day-to-day operations decisions and handle all crises related to weather, passenger deaths and illnesses, bomb threats, and hijackings.

Established one of the top records in the industry by successfully loading planes and preparing them for departure in twenty minutes or less, 97% of the time. Effective planning and scheduling permit up to four planes to be serviced simultaneously. Lost time due to illness has been reduced by 68% and industrial accidents by 71%.

Customer Service Agent, Miami, Florida, 2002 to 2005. Functioned as Ticket Sales Agent, Boarding Agent, and Customer Service Representative. Provided the type of service and concern for customers that made Air Florida one of the fastest growing airlines in the U.S. Became adept at solving problems and satisfying customers' complaints. Consistently maintained monthly sales in the top 10%.

Alaska Airlines, San Francisco, California 1997 to 2002

Customer Service Agent - Worked closely with customers to provide the best connecting flights and make each flight an enjoyable experience.

Hybrid   Tahoma

PAUL R. SHUPBACH

2917 S. E. 112th
Pittsburgh, Pennsylvania 15203
(412) 555-0002
prshup@pennet.com

QUALIFICATIONS

Technical Expertise – Hands-on person. Capable of operating and troubleshooting almost any piece of equipment. Understand the problems faced by machine operators and utilize engineering knowledge to effectively solve those problems.

Proposals, Contracts, and Negotiations – Have written and developed dozens of proposals and negotiated over 40 major contracts. Heavily experienced in all types of contracts, including DCAS, ASPR, and DAR. Consistently negotiate the most favorable terms for Cost Plus, Cost Sharing, Cost Plus Incentive Fixed, and R&D Contracts.

Cost Management, Cost Analysis, Cost Control – Over 15 years of cost management experience with all types of products and components, including processing equipment, fiberglass, and sheet metal parts. Establish program financial controls that pinpoint manufacturing problems and prevent cost overruns. Expert in Value Engineering.

Cost Estimating – Experience covers all facets of manufacturing, including machined parts, sheet metal, plastics, fiberglass, and software. Highly experienced in all methods of estimating including parametric estimating.

Vendor Selection – Inspect and analyze vendor facilities, equipment, capabilities, and quality. Recommendations to use a vendor have always been adopted.

EDUCATION

B.A. Industrial Management, University of Pennsylvania (1991)
B.S. Industrial Engineering, University of Pittsburgh (1989)

EMPLOYMENT HISTORY

Davenport Engineering & Consulting, Pittsburgh, Pennsylvania 2005 to Present

Industrial Engineering Consultant – Work on assignments ranging in length from 3 to 12 months in the areas of Bidding, Estimating, Selecting Vendors, Cost Management, and Manufacturing Planning. Enabled one manufacturer to obtain their first-ever contract with U.S. Steel and to expand production from $40,000 to $140,000 per month with no increase in personnel. Researched and adapted a new technology which allowed the firm to consistently underbid all competitors.

Pennsylvania Division of Purchasing, Scranton, Pennsylvania 2001 to 2005

Specification Analyst – Developed quality standards, specifications, and test procedures for many raw, semi-processed, and processed materials. The capabilities and sophistication of the Division were substantially increased through these efforts.

U.S. Steel, Pittsburgh, Pennsylvania 1991 to 2001

Cost Analyst – Estimated and analyzed costs of machined parts, hydraulic components, and mechanical systems supplied by vendors. Negotiated prices and engineering changes.

Hybrid   **Cambria**

DAVID L. GOLDMAN
2430 Stoneway North
Little Rock, Arkansas 72202
(501) 254-3242
dlg202@razorback.com

OBJECTIVE: Project Management

QUALIFICATIONS

Supervising. Took over a district with high turnover and low morale and created one of the top teams in the company. Work closely with individuals to enable both company and personal needs to be satisfied.

Negotiating. Negotiate contracts that are fair, workable, and satisfactory to customer and manufacturer. Work hard to get the best for both.

Coordinating/Planning. Installations have always been completed on schedule. Maintain close contact with customers, manufacturing, and field engineering to deal with all problems as they arise. Able to get commitments and support from those not directly responsible to me.

Computers. Excellent training and broad work experience installing and maintaining computer systems.

EMPLOYMENT

Data Systems, 1994 to Present

Senior Project Manager, Little Rock, Arkansas, 2003 to Present. Negotiate contracts, schedule deliveries, and troubleshoot all phases of computer installations. Work closely with customers to determine their needs, then gain contractual commitments from manufacturing and field engineering to install systems by specific dates. Monitor factory schedules and software support schedules to ensure delivery schedules are met. Despite many difficulties, all deliveries and installations have been completed on schedule.

District Manager, Field Engineering, Los Angeles, California, 1999 to 2003. Supervised and scheduled the work of 18 field engineers installing and maintaining computer systems. Took over a district with high turnover, low morale, and a poor reputation for customer service. Within one year turnover was reduced from 35% to 8% annually. Response time to down systems was reduced from six hours to two hours. Functioned as Project Manager for the installation of a branch online system for Security Western Bank (180 branches). All installations were completed on time.

Field Engineer, Washington, D. C., 1994 to 1999. Installed and maintained systems for banks, hotels and airlines. Customers were kept very satisfied because of extremely low downtimes.

U.S. Air Force, 1988 to 1992

Computer Tech – Maintained and serviced on-board aircraft computer systems. Supervised a five-member team.

EDUCATION

Computers
Field Engineering, Data Systems Manufacturing School – 6 months, 1994
Computer Repair, Computer Learning Institute – 6 months, 1993
Electrical Engineering, Old Dominion University – 1 year, 1992–1993
Computer Tech School, U.S. Air Force – 9 months, 1988

THE FUNCTIONAL RESUME

Despite its previously described reputation, the functional resume offers some job seekers a viable format to get their stories across to employers. If your core strengths can readily be planted into definable categories, consider using a functional resume.

As you will notice in Suzanne's resume (page 120), employment was included but job descriptions were not. This is common in functional resumes, and helps employers feel more comfortable with this format. The functional section in Suzanne's resume is devoted entirely to her duties as personnel manager and assistant personnel manager. Those were the only jobs that were relevant to the position she was seeking. In a chronological resume it would have been difficult to have devoted so much space (24 lines) to just two positions. For Suzanne the functional resume was a great choice.

Jason Ryerson's resume (page 121) enabled an ex-military officer to sell his experience in basically nonmilitary terms. He began with a traditional chronological resume that overemphasized military terminology. Only with a functional resume was he able to avoid the military jargon and instead use civilian-oriented terminology. Once that was accomplished he quickly found a position with an aircraft manufacturer.

If you are considering a functional or hybrid resume, review the section below, which offers functional categories that should be useful.

Read the sample functional resumes to get a feel for how they are constructed and what makes them effective. Although the backgrounds of the people will differ from yours, you should be able to determine whether your experience is better suited to the functional format or the qualifications/chronological format illustrated and discussed throughout the book.

THE HYBRID RESUME

A hybrid resume worked well for Paul Shupbach (page 123) and David Goldman (page 124). The format enabled them to go into much more detail about their work experience than they could have done with any other format. Their job narratives also add important information.

There are hundreds of categories that can be used in hybrid and functional resumes. Begin by trying to identify the categories that will work best for you. Some might be very specific to your field or industry. An art supplies sales representative might use three primary categories called "Sales Experience," "Customer Service," and "Art Supplies Background." The first two are generic categories and the third is specific to the industry.

IS A FUNCTIONAL RESUME FOR YOU?

Functional resumes do have drawbacks. While reviewing functional resumes, readers often wonder where the experience occurred since dates, job titles, and employers are not specified for each particular area of experience. Their eyes tend to dart up and down the page looking for the answers. They often become frustrated because the information in the resume is difficult to read and interpret—the applicant is making them work too hard. They may also suspect that something is being hidden.

Keeping these considerations in mind, some still wish to use a functional resume under the following circumstances: (1) when changing careers; (2) if changing industries, with related experience but no direct experience; (3) with substantial gaps in employment; (4) when the qualifications/chronological and hybrid formats just seem unsuitable for your background; (5) when your background can readily be illustrated in *functional* categories such as Management, Supervision, Coordinating, Troubleshooter, Motivator, or Training; or (6) when you've had your current job for many years and you want to highlight different aspects of it through functions rather than one very long job narrative.

If you think a functional resume may be good for you, go ahead and write one. Test it out on friends or associates to determine if it truly sells you and is easy to read. If you get positive feedback, take it to the next level and start submitting it to employers.

Be sure to study the format of the qualifications/chronological resumes as another option. It has the advantages of the functional resume *and* the chronological resume, with none of their individual drawbacks.

> **GARY:** Although the functional resume seems like a good idea to the resume writer, I have yet to find a resume *reader* who is a fan. In the course of 20 years' anecdotal polling of individuals and groups, even those who have written them have maintained doubts of their effectiveness. The single most common issue raised when a functional resume is mentioned is "What are you trying to hide?" As soon as that specter is raised in the reader's mind your cause is lost. There are better options, such as the *qualifications/chronological resume*, and the *hybrid* resume, both presented below, or the *clustered resume*® in the following chapter.

> **Tom:** I agree with Gary that employers tend to dislike the functional resume. I rarely use it myself, but there are times that the background of the person simply does not work with other formats. Jason Ryerson's resume on page 121 is an example. His traditional reverse chronological resume, with an overemphasis on military terminology was making it difficult for him to transition into a civilian career. The functional resume gave readers a sense of the brilliant project manager that he was.

WRITING YOUR FUNCTIONAL OR HYBRID RESUME

Once your job sketches have been completed, the first step in writing an effective functional or hybrid resume is to list the duties, experiences, projects, and successes that you want to include.

Just as you did with the job sketches, write these points quickly, without concern for grammar or spelling. Once you're done, you'll begin to see how some seem to naturally fit together. Select the category headings you will use; three to six is a good range. For your highly specialized or technical categories, you might have to come up with more definitive headings but that should not be difficult.

As we have seen, some of the more commonly used category headings include: Management, Supervision, Training, Planning, Designing, Research, Coordination, Negotiating, Public Relations, Administration, Marketing, Public Speaking, Organization, Counseling, Writing and Editing, Design, and Teaching.

Next, list the category headings with sufficient space in which to add your points. Initially you wrote those points quickly; now is the time to polish them. Once all the points have been placed in each category, determine the order in which they should be presented. Usually they are listed in order of importance to the position you are targeting. Take a long break.

Review what you've written and see if you can find ways to improve it. Prepare a second draft and take another break. With each fresh review, you should be able to find ways to make each point clearer and more concise. All of the previously described general instructions for resume writing apply to the functional or hybrid formats.

The following list may contain categories that will work well in your resume. This list is provided to give you ideas so you can produce nearly ideal category names.

FUNCTIONAL CATEGORIES

Accounting
Accounts Payable
Administering
    (Programs)
Administration
Advertising
Analysis and
    Preparation
Auditing
Behavior
    Modification
Benefits
Brochure Design
Budget Controls
Budget
    Management
Business Law
Buying
Caseload
    Supervision
Client Relations
Communications
Community
    Relations
Community
    Resource
    Utilization
Company Benefits
    Programs
Computer
Computer
    Programming
Computerized
    Accounting
Conflict Resolution
Construction
Consulting
Contract Bid
    Preparation and
    Administration
Contract
    Negotiations
Cost Accounting
Cost Controls
Cost Effectiveness
Cost Effectiveness
    Studies
Cost Estimating

Cost Saving
Counseling
Creative Writing
Credit and
    Collections
Credit
    Management
Crisis Intervention
Curriculum
    Development
Customer Service
Customer Training
Data Processing
Database
    Management
Design
Display Design
Editing
Employee
    Relations
Engineering
Engineering
    Proposals
Equipment
    Acquisition
Equipment
    Repair And
    Maintenance
Environmental
    Impact
    Statements
Expediting
Facility
    Management
Finance
Financial
    Management
Financial
    Statements
Full-Charge
    Bookkeeping
Fundraising
Government
    Contracts
Grant Proposal
    Writing
Group Therapy
Growth Planning

Human Resources
Industrial Security
Initial Public
    Offerings
Internal Auditing
Inventory Control
    Management
Information
    Management
Inspection
Interviewing
    (Techniques)
Investor Relations
Invoice Processing
Job Costing
Labor Negotiations
Labor Relations
Leadership
Learning
    Disabilities
Legal
Manufacturing
Management
Management
    Consulting
Management
    Information
    Systems
Managing
    (Projects)
Market Penetration
    (Strategies)
Marketing
Material Support
Media Relations
Mediation
Merchandising
Mergers and
    Acquisitions
Negotiations
Office
    Management
Operations
Organizational
    Development
Organizational
    Theory
Payroll

Personnel
    Administration
Personnel
    Management
Planning
Policy
    Development
Presentations
Problem Solving
Procedures
    Development
Product Design
Product
    Development
Production
Program
    Coordination
Program
    Development
Project
    Engineering
Project
    Coordination
Project
    Management
Production
    Planning
Production
    Management
Progress Reports
Promoting
Public Relations
Public Speaking
Publishing
Purchasing
Quality Control
Quality Assurance
Re-engineering
Records Control
Recruitment
Repair Procedures
    Development
Research
Research And
    Design
Research And
    Development
Retail

Management
Safety
Safety/Accident
    Prevention
Safety/OSHA
    Standards
Safety Procedures
Sales
Sales/Customer
    Service
Sales Personnel
    Training
Scheduling
Security
Security
    Procedures
Shipping and
    Receiving
Staff Development
Staff Evaluating
Statistical Analysis
Strategic Planning
Supervision/
    Training
System Design
Systems Analysis
Tax Analysis
Taxes
Technical Report
    Writing
Technical Writing
Technology
    Acquisition
Technology
    Transfer
Telecommunica-
    tions
Theft Control
Training
Troubleshooting
Turnover
    Reduction
Vendor
    Negotiations
Vendor Relations
Writing

The Clustered Résumé®

For many job seekers, the traditional reverse chronological and functional resumes simply do not offer the appropriate vehicle for telling their particular stories. These include those new to a career, returning to a career, or having a non-linear path with sporadic experiences in the field.

The answer might lie in the *clustered resume*®.

As its title suggests, the clustered resume presents the bulk of the individual's relevant education, training, and work experience in clearly defined blocks or *clusters*. The document becomes in effect, a series of two or more *mini-reverse chronological resumes*, the first of which provides your most relevant experience and strengths in a clearly defined group. In this manner, the writer can present solid chunks of value, without the reader having to wade through or hop over non-related jobs and projects, or irrelevant and dated education and training.

TOM

This is Gary's section. He coined and trademarked the term *Clustered Resume*®, a very descriptive and useful term. He has taken this special type of resume further than probably any other writer today. He has experimented with many ideas over the past ten years and has pretty well found all the ways to add value using this style of resume. If you sense that the other types of resume may not fully meet your needs, study this chapter carefully.

Gary introduces the clustered resume with Donald Jones. Don's resume shows the benefit of this style. While a reverse chronological resume could be used, it would not have sold him as well. Below, Gary explains why the clustered resume made sense for Donald.

DONALD V. JONES

258 S 44th St
Philadelphia, Pennsylvania 19104
(267) 555-7667
dvjones42@aol.com

OBJECTIVE: Manufacturing Management

QUALIFICATIONS

- Ten years' successful experience in manufacturing management and supervision combined with a solid sales history.
- Record of improving systems and procedures which consistently increased productivity while reducing costs.
- Effective personnel manager and team builder recognized for increasing communication and morale while reducing turnover in a variety of highly demanding settings.
- Winner of numerous achievement awards for production and quality.
- Strong decision maker noted for the ability to turn marginal and failing operations into profit makers.

EDUCATION

BA – Business Administration, Temple University (1989)

TRAINING

"Managing for the Future"—American Management Consultants, 16 hours (2001)

"The Quality Challenge"—The Manufacturing Group, 8 hours (2000)

"Managing Diverse Employees"—American Management Consultants, 8 hours (2000)

MANUFACTURING MANAGEMENT

Northeast Dynamics & Manufacturing Inc., Philadelphia, Pennsylvania 1989 to 2005

PRODUCTION MANAGER—2001 to 2005. For this manufacturer of specialized parts for the aerospace industry, performed a variety of critical management functions. Reported directly to the Vice President of Manufacturing. Supervised three assistant managers and a workforce of 150. Developed and implemented annual goals and budgets. Facilitated regular production meetings. Designed and implemented improved training for all workers resulting in higher measured productivity and reduced turnover. Facilitated regular production meetings to generate ideas and resolve problems. Worked with engineering to expand capacity, which resulted in a 15% reduction in product delivery time. Received several merit raises and performance bonuses.

ASSISTANT PRODUCTION MANAGER—1996 to 2001. Directed manufacture of all metal components. Managed a staff of three supervisors and a 40-person crew. Created production priorities and schedules. Resolved production problems. Crew received highest productivity rating in plant two consecutive years.

Previous Positions Within Company
PRODUCTION SUPERVISOR (1994 to 1996)
LEAD WORKER (1991 to 1994)
ASSEMBLER (1988 to 1991)

SALES EXPERIENCE

REAL ESTATE AGENT, SarCar Real Estate, Philadelphia, PA (2006-to present)

BUILDING THE CLUSTERED RESUME

Career Resumers

Like our friend Donald, on the previous page, workers have been known to take detours from their formal careers and then choose to eventually return. The clustered resume can be of enormous value to these candidates. Since Donald's real career was manufacturing management, we used the Qualifications section to establish that fact right out of the chute. The forthcoming clustering of jobs under the heading of "Manufacturing Experience" provided his entire experience in that field. Thus, the reader did not have to trip over the Real Estate period of his life enroute to his relevant experience.

As a real estate agent, Donald has performed some office management functions, purchasing, and training. As these skills are all part of management he can add them to his repertoire in letters and interviews if he needs them.

Other special accomplishments, such as being a leading sales producer, also are worth mentioning. For hard-to-move properties, he had to creatively identify and contact the most likely purchasers, market/show the properties, work with the sellers, assist the buyers in obtaining financing, and close the deals. These are impressive logistical skills and achievements valuable to almost any position. Had his manufacturing experience been less impressive, we probably would have created a job narrative to describe these additional assets.

Example #1 Returning to a previous occupation

Ross Coleman, took a similar detour from his career path as Donald. He was a highly skilled and successful purchasing manager who left the corporate world to live his dream of buying, remodeling, and selling residential properties. He had a solid three-year run before tiring of self-employment and wishing to return to the corporate world.

Since his major successes were his corporate management and entrepreneurial experience, we presented them as two distinct clusters, with the more relevant purchasing experience leading off, even though it was the more dated of the two. Ross needed to demonstrate his successful purchasing career with major companies right off the bat in order to have a chance at capturing the reader's attention. The fact that the dates are less recent is a secondary consideration to the overall impact of his corporate career.

ROSS D. COLEMAN

820 Mercer Street Cherry Hill, New Jersey 08002 (856) 555-3520 coleman.r@nj.net

OBJECTIVE: Supply chain management

QUALIFICATIONS

- Strong background in corporate and supply chain management for national companies combined with successful entrepreneurial experience.
- Effective negotiator with the ability to achieve win-win outcomes.
- Track record of increasing sales, market share, and profits in all settings.
- Record of implementing successful cost containment and efficiency enhancing systems.
- Regularly selected for corporate and regional special assignments.

EDUCATION

B.A. – Human Resource Management, Temple University (1996)

CORPORATE PURCHASING EXPERIENCE

Verizon Wireless, Cherry Hill, New Jersey 1999 to 2004

MANAGER OF SUPPLY CHAIN ENTERPRISE PROCUREMENT – 2002 to 2004. Assigned by executive management to centralize and streamline national purchasing programs in such areas as commercial printing, office equipment/supplies, and fulfillment/distribution. Reviewed existing programs to identify most serious issues and developed corrective action. Designated as "super user" for SAP and PeopleSoft integrated buying systems. Trained, supervised, and developed a group of six assistant buyers.

Selected, negotiated, and administered contracts with regional and national suppliers. Reduced annual costs in commercial print by $8 million (18%), $20 million (22%) in office equipment, and $7.5 million (28%) in digital print and fulfillment.

MANAGER OF NATIONAL & DIRECT DEALER ACCOUNTS/SUPPLY CHAIN – 1999 to 2002. Selected by executive management to integrate newly acquired companies into the Verizon purchasing-management structure and distribution channel network. Visited distributors and retailers to resolve concerns. Developed customized strategies and procedures to resolve contract compliance for both national accounts and over 10,000 independent customers. Resolved critical distribution problems with the company's largest account, improving shipping from 76% to 99% compliance. Earned Executive Club award for excellence.

Trademart Drugs, Philadelphia, Pennsylvania 1997 to 1999

SENIOR BUYER – For this drug store retailer, recruited to centralize the purchasing structure of the 20-store chain. Developed and implemented an ordering procedure for over 40,000 products. Evaluated existing vendors and buying programs. Negotiated new contracts and renegotiated existing ones. Purchased $75 million in annual products, more than one-third of the chain's inventory. Developed and introduced a new film developing program which tripled revenues and provided a profit margin significantly greater than the previous vendor's program.

Special Assignment: Selected to work with First Auto Corporation to implement an automated category tracking system and train corporate users. The system improved planning and significantly increased accuracy in ordering. Served with CEO on a special Pricing Strategy Committee.

Prior Purchasing Experience: Assistant Buyer/Buyer/Senior Buyer, Dixon Manufacturing 1988 to 1997

ENTREPRENEURIAL EXPERIENCE

Coleman Properties, LLC, Cherry Hill, New Jersey, 2004 to Present

OWNER/GENERAL MANAGER – Started this small property development company to purchase, restore, and sell vintage homes. Developed financing and recruited a designer, an architect, contractors, and realtors. Identified and negotiated purchases of target properties. Worked closely with designers and architects on design. Obtained permits and purchased all materials and supplies. Implemented production schedules and timelines. Supervised all work to assure quality and progress. Managed all financing, accounting, payroll, and tax filings. Successfully restored seven properties to vintage condition resulting in successful and profitable sales.

Example #2 Using three employment clusters to seal the deal

Pamela had a diverse background including office and operations management, mortgage lending, and as a skilled healthcare provider. Her current goal was to access the medical field as an administrator or office manager.

Her management experience was the most important and relevant of the various clusters of experience. Notice how the two management positions combine to provide a solid block of management achievement despite the fact they are not consecutive.

The mortgage section adds an additional dimension of experience and skills in a structured and regulated environment.

Finally, since her education and technologist experience was early in her career, it was sufficient to merely list her positions and locations. The important point is that she spent this period of her life in the medical profession, specifically in hospital settings. Her service at such a pedigree facility as UCLA Medical Center was a major asset with no further explanation required.

Bookman Old Style

PAMELA R. DYER

112 Bellevue Way #355
Bellevue, Washington 98004
(425) 555-8740
prd004@comcast.net

QUALIFICATIONS

Successful experience in business and office management combined with solid experience as a skilled medical technologist. Proven ability to manage multiple tasks, projects, and assignments simultaneously.

Demonstrated ability to quickly learn and master new methods, systems, and procedures. Track record of regular promotions and increasing responsibilities. History of improving processes resulting in greater efficiency and productivity.

Broad experience in hospitals. Work effectively with doctors, administrators, coworkers, and patients. Understand hospital operations.

MANAGEMENT EXPERIENCE

Majestic Home Improvement, Renton, Washington 2004 to Present

OFFICE/BUSINESS MANAGER – Perform a wide range of administrative and financial functions for this prominent regional home improvement/roofing contractor. Key areas of responsibility include HR, project insurance, bonding compliance, and customer relations. Upgraded processes resulting in greater efficiency and accuracy.

Manage all day to day financial activities including A/R, A/P, and bank deposits as well as reconciling bank statements and credit card accounts. Administer customer accounts. Process contracts and prepare sales orders. Immediately resolve customer and vendor account issues. Have consistently enhanced responsibilities throughout time of service.

Andrew Stringer & Associates, Tacoma, Washington 1992 to 2001

SHOWROOM MANAGER – Directed all day-to-day operations for four showrooms for this national manufacturer's representative. Reported directly to owner. Supervised and scheduled three assistant managers and two support staff. Oversaw merchandising of over 100 product lines ranging from home décor to gifts and accessories. Worked closely with vendors on merchandising and display issues. Monitored all areas to assure optimum appeal and appearance. Assisted both customers and sales teams in order processing.

Scheduled and managed special events and shows. Coordinated all logistics ranging from catering to casual labor recruitment. Events consistently drew over 1,000 customers, generating substantial seasonal purchasing revenue. Attended national and regional tradeshows to identify and select merchandise. Received consistently excellent feedback on quality of all efforts.

SALES & CUSTOMER SERVICE EXPERIENCE

Brothers Mortgage Company, Tukwila, Washington 2001 to 2004

LOAN OFFICER – Managed all client transactions from initial contact through loan closure. Worked closely with over 100 lenders throughout the region. Achieved 100% underwriter approval.

MEDICAL EXPERIENCE

RADIOLOGICAL TECHNOLOGIST/CLINICAL INSTRUCTOR, UCLA Medical Center, Los Angeles, CA 1988 to 1992

RADIOLOGICAL TECHNOLOGIST, St. Joseph Hospital, La Jolla, CA 1982 to 1988

COMPUTER SKILLS

Word, Excel, PowerPoint, Outlook, QuickBooks, ACT! Database

EDUCATION

Certificate – Marketing, University of Washington 2002

AA – Radiology Technician, Bellevue Community College 1982

Example #3 Using multiple clusters to fully sell education, training, projects, and work experience

John was about to embark on a new career in the world of technology. His primary qualifications were his education and training combined with modest practical experience.

To get the most mileage from these assets, we basically clusterized all his education, technical training, and projects to focus the reader's attention entirely on the specialized knowledge, skill, and experience he gained in the run up to his new career.

The inclusion of his work history documented his ability to maintain employment previous to and during his technical studies. The quality and transferability of his experience were fleshed out in the Qualifications section, cover letters, and interviews.

Lucida Bright

JOHN D. DRISCOLL

2654 232nd Ave SE Sammamish, Washington 98074 (425) 555-2345 jdd74@msn.com

OBJECTIVE: IT Technician

QUALIFICATIONS

- Strong blend of current technical education, training, and certifications combined with solid practical experience and proven work ethic.
- Customer-oriented professional with a reputation for service, satisfaction, and results.
- Proven ability to manage multiple tasks, projects, and assignments simultaneously.
- Creative troubleshooter able to quickly identify and resolve problems.
- Demonstrated ability to quickly learn and utilize new methods, systems, and technologies.

EDUCATION

AA – IT Technical Support, Green River Community College (2008)

AA – General Business Management, Green River Community College (2006)

ADDITIONAL TRAINING

Cisco Network Support, North Seattle Community College (Fall 2006)

Windows 2000 Client/Server O/S, North Seattle Community College (Summer 2006)

SPECIALIZED COURSEWORK

- CPU Upgrade
- RAM Upgrade
- SCSI IDE Installation
- IDE Installation
- Optimizing BIOS Settings
- Network Card Installation

PROJECTS

<u>Computer Kit</u>: Completely built a computer in under 30 minutes, including motherboard, floppy, hard drive, CD-ROM, CPU, RAM, video & sound card, and monitor.

<u>Visual Basic</u>: Created and programmed a purchase order template that automatically calculated total costs of various products including algorithm for different state taxes.

TECHNICAL CERTIFICATION

CompTIA A+ Certification

<u>Core Hardware</u>: Installation, Configuration, Upgrading, Diagnosing &

Troubleshooting, Preventative Maintenance, Motherboard, Processors, Memory, Printers, Basic Networking

O/S Systems Technologies: O/S Fundamentals, Installation, Configuration, Upgrading, Diagnosing & Troubleshooting, Networks

PRACTICUM EXPERIENCE

LAB TECHNICIAN – Green River Community College, PC Analysis & Configuration Lab, Fall 2003. Assisted and assessed students in completing lab assignments. Maintained lab and network, tested hardware, and upgraded systems.

TECHNICAL EXPERIENCE

Rush Medical Institute, Seattle, Washington Spring–Summer 2008

INSTRUCTOR/COMPUTER LAB/NETWORK TECHNICIAN – Taught a 30-student class in basic computer skills and maintenance for this medical-technician training center. Created and added segments in complete internal and external hardware maintenance and minor repair.

ADDITIONAL EXPERIENCE

DESK CLERK, Bishop Inn, Fairfax, CA (2002–2004)

JOBSITE SUPERVISOR, Plosker Contracting, San Anselmo, CA (2000–2002)

Example #4 Using effective clusters for education, additional training, and an internship

Internships, Externships, and *Practicums* are excellent clusters for providing work experience that also bolsters education. They emphasize the systematic way the writer is transitioning into the new career, taking the reader along on the journey from education to experience.

This candidate's job history, as might be expected of a young person, is not top-heavy with examples of major league-level experience. What she does have is a solid and long-term work history, regularly performing management functions, which nicely complements her education.

The internship and market entries are designed to showcase the applicant's management-related duties. Even though the supermarket position contains reference to the checker position, description is not necessary. The reader will understand that the management role was one that was *earned* at a later date.

For Roberta's resume we will concentrate on her education, additional training, her internship, and her previous work experience.

Verdana

Roberta James
10645 W Riley   Boise, Idaho 83709
(208) 555-2121
rj206@wabash.com

OBJECTIVE: Management

MANAGEMENT EDUCATION

BA – Business Management, Boise State University (2007); graduated with honors

Specialized Coursework: Organizational Management, Ethics, HR Management, Financial Management, Management Techniques, Business Communication

MANAGEMENT TRAINING

Managing in the Global Market, Marketing Club Seminar, 4 hours (2007)

Managing Diversity, Sims Associates, 8 hours (2006)

Business Planning, Small Business Administration, 8 hours (2006)

INTERNSHIP

Northern Expeditors, Inc., Boise, Idaho Summer 2007

OPERATIONS ASSISTANT – Supported the Operations Director of this regional fulfillment company in managing warehouse, receiving, and shipping operations. Reviewed orders prior to shipment to assure completeness. Monitored labeling for postage and international customs compliance.

Quickly identified and resolved errors resulting in substantial savings. Prepared regular reports for submission to corporate management. Recommended several improvements to processes that increased efficiency and were implemented department-wide. Received an excellent evaluation upon completion of program.

RELATED EXPERIENCE

Maury's Market, Caldwell, Idaho Seasonally 2001 to 2007

CHECKER/ASSISTANT MANAGER – Worked part-time/seasonally during high school and college at this local supermarket. Performed a wide range of customer service and department management functions. Supported and filled in for the managers of the Dairy and Frozen Foods Departments. Received and inspected deliveries, refusing spoiled or incomplete orders. Trained and oriented new employees. Regularly resolved customer problems. Consistently invited back each season due to quality and reliability.

NAMING CLUSTERS

How you name a cluster will determine how an employer views you. Below, the candidate called the cluster Sales/Customer Experience. She never held a formal sales position before, but many of the salespeople she has worked with think she would be great if provided the opportunity. She had consistently demonstrated the skills and determination of successful salespeople. By calling the section Sales/Customer Service Experience, she introduced herself to the employer as sales material. Her objective stated, "Sales Opportunity" and her Qualifications statement emphasized the qualities she has that are sought after by sales managers. Her cover letter stated how much she enjoyed the sales process and working with customers. Choose your own cluster names carefully.

SALES/CUSTOMER SERVICE EXPERIENCE
Rettig Corp., Portland, Oregon 2002 to Present

CUSTOMER SERVICE LEAD – Perform a wide range of service, sales, and administrative functions for this national electronics company. Respond to and resolve escalated customer concerns. Listen intently to customers to clearly identify issues and develop solutions. Perform extensive research and consistently respond in a timely and satisfactory manner. Have established a reputation for exceptional service resulting in regularly being requested by customers to resolve their issues, renew contracts, or purchase additional items.

Rodding Industries, Beaverton, Oregon 2000 to 2002

SALES ADMINISTRATOR – Supported a team of four Key Account Managers in servicing major corporate customers of this electronics distributor. Key accounts included Boeing, Weyerhaeuser, and Genie Industries. Reviewed all documents for accuracy prior to processing. Worked closely with customer purchasing teams to immediately resolve problems and assure satisfaction. Filled in for Account Managers during their vacations and other absences and assisted customers. Developed solid relations with customers, resulting in numerous letters of commendation for providing timely and comprehensive service.

Since clusters are similar to categories used in functional resumes, refer to page 128 for additional ideas.

Writing Your Résumé

GETTING STARTED ON YOUR RESUME

The person who procrastinates is always
struggling with misfortunes. —Hesiod

Having read through this section on resumes and having completed your job sketches, it's time to start writing your resume. This is where you will discover the value of all the blood, sweat, and tears you put into preparing your job sketches.

Review your job sketches one more time. You are now ready to start.

Begin with the header: name, address, phone number, and email at the top. Next, write your objective if you have one.

Beneath the "Objective," write the "Qualifications" heading. Then skip 5–10 spaces (they'll be filled in last, after everything else is done). Since the Qualifications section is often the most difficult section to write, we leave it as the last section to write.

Next, pop in your "Experience" or "Professional History" header, and jump over that one too.

This is a good time to add in your Education, Training, Technical Skills, Professional Credentials, or other headings. It's a good way to watch the resume take shape while you get some momentum going for the employment entries to come.

Now you are ready to tackle the job narratives. With each position, carefully select what you think are the most relevant and representative pieces of the job sketches. While this version is not as free-flowing as the original job sketches, it is still too early to be overly concerned with grammatical niceties. Make sure your entries cover the spectrum of experience you are trying to convey. Then reread it. Often it helps to read aloud, so you can actually hear how the descriptions sound. If it is awkward, make adjustments.

DON'T HESITATE

Write your first draft quickly; don't worry about perfection. Concentrate on getting your thoughts on paper; you can polish the phrasing later. Once you write a phrase, read it out loud to get a feel for how it sounds. When reading, most people subvocalize; while they may not move their lips, their minds are actually saying each word almost audibly. In other words, the way a phrase sounds to you when you say it out loud is the same way it sounds when read by an employer. Read every phrase aloud four to ten times and adjust any that seem awkward.

Let the resume sit and percolate overnight. Pick it up the next day and see how you respond to it. Is it crisp? Flat? Boring? Reading with fresh eyes can help you to quickly pick up any deficiencies.

Read it over and ask yourself if all the important points are there. If not, what's missing? Where can additional information go? Decide in which section it would be most effective: Qualifications? Employment? Both? Go through the document sentence by sentence and phrase by phrase, reading and rereading aloud. Cross out extraneous phrases. Ask yourself if you can make the same point with fewer words. Use action words whenever possible. Once you've finished this process, rewrite the resume, incorporating the changes you've made. You have completed your second draft. Set it aside for at least half a day.

SPIT AND POLISH

When you pick up the resume again, take care as you go through it; this could be your final draft. As you read it aloud, it should flow. Are there any phrases or words you have used more than twice? If so, look for alternatives. Don't be afraid to use a thesaurus. Word-processing programs such as Microsoft Word have a built-in thesaurus feature accessible by highlighting the word and right clicking. If that is insufficient, free websites such as thesaurus.com can fill the bill. Are all of your sentences very long or all very short? A mixture of short, medium, and long sentences reads best. Too many short sentences make the resume seem choppy and abrupt. An abundance of lengthy sentences can cause the reader to forget the main point. A long, drawn out sentence can often be cut two into shorter ones.

Look for any troublesome phrases that sound awkward, unclear, or confusing. Your goal is to have the resume read completely and thoroughly by the employer. You don't want them to stop at any point and wonder what you meant. Just one awkwardly written, hard-to-understand sentence or phrase can substantially reduce your impact. Don't let that happen.

Of course *you* know exactly what you meant . . . so unclear sentences may be hard for you to spot. Try asking a friend to read it and watch the reaction. If there is any confusion, fix it.

Avoid big, unfamiliar words. The mark of a good writer is the ability to say exactly what is meant by using the *right* words.

Prepare the final draft and review it one last time for phrasing, spelling, and punctuation. Spelling must be perfect. It is worth it to make one quick pass through your resume, dictionary in hand, looking up words you "know" are correct. Dictionary.com is another excellent resource. You may be surprised to find that you have been misspelling a word for years. Remember, do not depend solely on your computer's spell-checker. If your misspelling is an actual word in the spell-checker, it will not be detected. Always have someone proof your work.

PUTTING IT ALL TOGETHER

Essentially, writing a resume consists of putting all of the pieces together. Most sections, such as Education, Training, Special Projects, and Employment are independent of each other. So, if each section is well written, the entire resume will be effective when you pull them all together.

The Electronic Résumé

Every day job seekers are starting new positions that they discovered online, making the Internet an essential tool for job seekers. There are hundreds of commercial sites where you can post your electronic resume, giving employers seeking someone with your background the opportunity to contact you. Employers are able to search among tens of thousands of resumes within an Internet job site, and can find your resume in less than a minute.

Thousands of employers have their own company websites. Many of them list and describe open positions. When you discover a desirable position, you can send your resume to them by email or via an interactive application on their website.

The number of job seekers posting their resumes electronically has grown so rapidly, and so many employers are now using this technology, that no solid job-search would be complete without creating an electronic resume that will sell you. Keep in mind that the U.S. Department of Labor estimates that about 70% of all available jobs are not advertised, even on the Web. While posting your electronic resume increases your chances of getting the job you want, do not rely on it as the sole method of your job search efforts but rather as one more tool to use in your job search.

In the following pages you will learn how to create plain text and scannable resumes, which can put you in the fast lane in your electronic job search.

TYPES OF RESUMES

For your job search you should have three types of resumes: formatted, plain-text, and scannable.

Formatted: The formatted resume is the resume you create with MS Word, WordPerfect, or other word processors. Those programs allow you to use italics, bold type, bullets, columns, your choice of typefaces (fonts), and other features. These are the features that let you be creative and produce an attractive looking resume to print or to send as an email attachment.

Plain-Text: Plain text, also known as text format and ASCII format (pronounced as-kee), is a universal format that almost all computer operating systems can interpret and use. ASCII stands for American Standard Code for

Information Interchange. You will use your plain-text resume whenever sending your resume as text within an email message to an employer, or when storing it at a commercial resume website.

Scannable: The scannable resume is the paper resume you send to employers who scan it into databases. The process removes almost all formatting features, making the resume less attractive. The point to keep in mind is that no one else's will look any more attractive than yours. Here, what's important is to create your resume so that when it is scanned, your words are interpreted correctly by the optical character recognition (OCR) software.

HELPFUL HINTS AND DEFINITIONS FOR ELECTRONIC RESUMES

The Internet and the Worldwide Web: The Internet is a worldwide network of computers that can pass information back and forth. Internet Service Providers (ISPs) and a network known as "the backbone," with servers and routers, keep track of information and can reach the intended server to pull information from it. The Worldwide Web (or "Web") is the graphical portion of the Internet that presents text, drawings, photographs, video, and audio using what is commonly known as a "browser." Depending on your operating system, you may be familiar with Internet Explorer, Firefox, Safari, or Opera. These are all browsers used to present information to you over the Internet. The Internet provides the ability to send and receive electronic mail, or email, allowing you to send messages from your computer, or receive messages from another computer.

Resume Database or Job Website: A resume job website or database will store resumes, and is capable of retrieving them by a search using key words. There are commercial resume database websites that allow you to post your resume so employers and recruiters can access the database and find people whose background fits what they are looking for. Most are free to the job seeker. Many large and medium sized companies also have their own online resume application that will enable you to post your resume directly to them.

URL: A URL (Uniform Resource Locator) is a web address. Each website has a unique URL, enabling you to find and view that site. URLs mainly use lowercase letters, and begin with "http://www." followed by the domain name, such as careerempowering. The URL ends with an extension, such as .com, .org, .edu and .gov. which indicates the type of organization it is. So the entire address for careerempowering would be "http://www.careerempowering.com."

Text Editors: A text editor, such as Notepad in MS Word, allows you to edit your plain-text (ASCII) resume or any other plain-text document. From a text editor you can copy and paste your resume or document into an email message you are sending to an employer.

Getting Connected: If you can access the Internet you are ready to begin your job search. If you need to get a computer and connect to the Internet there are several Internet connection choices available: cable, wireless, DSL, and dial-up. Dial-up Internet access needs a working phone line to connect to a modem that is either inside your computer or plugs into your computer. When you click the Connect icon on your computer screen your computer dials your Internet Service Provider (ISP) and sends your unique user ID to connect you to the Internet. Dial-up service is the least expensive (and slowest) access to the Internet. Cable access currently provides the fastest access to the Internet. Cable Internet access also uses an external modem (different from that used by a dial-up modem) that is always on. This means you have instant access to the Internet at any time. DSL and wireless Internet access fall somewhere between cable and dial-up in cost and speed. In general, whatever method of Internet access you choose, the rule of thumb is, the faster the access, the greater the cost.

Free Email Services: Having an email account is part of a successful online job search. It provides an easy means of sharing information with potential employers and job search contacts. See page 114 for a list of free email services. Hotmail, Yahoo, Gmail, and a host of other free email service providers offer free email accounts to anyone. Because you will be using email to communicate with potential employers it is important to create an email address that is businesslike. A good tip when sending email is to email yourself all the versions of your resume. You then can have access to your resume anywhere there is Internet access just by logging into your email account.

If You Don't Have a Computer: Most libraries now offer Internet access. You have to sign up for a session, usually no more than an hour at a time, but you can do a lot of job searching in an hour. Most email programs now provide access from any computer that is Internet connected. If you're unemployed you may have access to computers at your state Employment Security offices, often known as WorkSource Centers, One-Stop Centers, or Job Service Centers.

Attachments: Attachments are formatted files that can be added to an email message. During a job search, typical attachments would be a resume or cover letter. People often send MS Word attachments, and computers can open and read them. Once opened, you can save the resume as a Word document. People also attach plain-text resumes. Many companies have policies that prevent employees from opening email attachments from unknown people because of the potential for damage from rogue computer applications called computer viruses.

Storage: You can take your resume along with you in many ways. There is of course the old standard, the floppy disk. However many new computers no longer come with floppy disk drives, so it may be wise to store your resume and cover letter on a "thumb drive," "USB drive," or "flash drive." All of these terms refer to a small device that can store far more than your resume and cover letter; they are also much more durable than a floppy disk. You can attach them to your car keys, wear them as a necklace, or carry them in your pocket. All computers built in the last six years come with USB plug-ins. Prices on USB drives vary according to their storage capacity. Compact disks (CDs) and digital video discs (DVDs) represent two other ways to store your important information. Both need a device called a recorder to "burn" your data onto a blank disk. You then can take the disk with you and access your information from any computer that has a disk drive.

CREATE A KEY WORD RESUME

Creating a key word resume is the first step in producing a resume you can post to resume Internet websites. The first priority for a resume is that it must be searchable and retrievable. Key words make your resume searchable and retrievable.

Searchable and Retrievable

Once a resume makes it into a database, a recruiter can request all the resumes of people with a certain background. They do this by setting up a search for only those resumes that contain the key words they want. If the employer wants a highly skilled mechanical engineer the key words might be: mechanical engineer, BS, and PE (professional engineer). The resumes presented to the recruiter will all be from practicing mechanical engineers who have a BS in engineering, and they will have been doing it long enough to have gained the professional designation Professional Engineer. Your challenges are to learn the key words employers might use to find someone with your background, and then to make sure your resume includes them.

Put Key Words into Your Resume

The best time to start identifying your key words is when you're writing your job sketches. Of course, if you've already created your resume, now is the time to see which key words are already in your resume, and which key words you should add.

The most common way for recruiters to find a resume in a resume database is through key words. The term "key words" simply means that employers will determine the desired background of the ideal candidate, and then will decide which words and terms to look for.

To begin, list all the words and terms you think an employer might look for. Then look for ways to get those words into your resume. The best way is to place yourself in the position of an employer seeking someone with your background. In essence you are asking, "How would I find myself?" Key words can be single words or two-word terms and are usually nouns—such as marketing, Visual Basic, MS Windows, project management, graphic design, and behavior modification. Key words can also be gerunds, which are noun-like verbs—like "negotiating" and "analyzing."

There are several ways to identify key words:

1. Search the want ads in your field and notice which words they specify in the requirements and duties sections.
2. Talk to people in the field and ask what they believe the key words would be.
3. Read professional journals in your field to help identify the current hot terms.

Do all of these, but then come back to considering how you would find yourself if you were looking for someone like you. Produce as extensive a list as possible and then settle on the 20 most likely terms, and make sure they all appear somewhere in your resume. If some of these words were not already present, look for ways to include them in existing sentences, or create sentences that include them.

It's helpful to understand how databases are used to extract resumes. In experimenting with different searches, we tried several approaches. When we used five key words, we typically found too few resumes because only those with all five key words were selected. When we used only one or two words we sometimes got too many. After putting in the key words, the database would show how many matches had occurred. When there were too few we removed a term or tried other words to get the right number of matches.

Once a resume came on-screen it often took only 20 seconds to see whether that person displayed the needed experience. If they didn't, with a simple mouse click we were on to the next resume. This might happen, for example, if we were looking for a computer programmer with three or more years of Visual Basic experience. If Visual Basic was our only key word, then every resume that used that term would come up on-screen. Sometimes, however, the person had merely studied Visual Basic and had no professional experience. If three years of actual job experience with Visual Basic didn't turn up, that person was quickly removed from the search.

When doing a key-word search, resumes will appear on the screen one by one, with the key words in the resume highlighted. The reader will skim through each resume to decide which people are good candidates. When a qualified candidate pops up on the screen, the reviewer can print that resume. Those not so qualified will simply remain in the database awaiting future openings.

The right key words separate the wanted resumes from the others in the database. At that point the candidate's experience, and presentation of that experience, determined whether the resume was chosen.

If your resume is poorly written and doesn't contain the right key words you won't be getting called for an interview. So what can you do to improve your chances?

Buzzwords

To develop your list of key words, begin by including all the buzzwords in your field. This would include the jargon, technical terms, and nomenclature in your specialty. List the current hot terms, the standard terms that have been around for a long time, and the new terms that may soon be hot. Once you have your list, decide which ones are right for you.

Synonyms. When you list a term, also list its synonyms. For example, if you list personnel administration as a key word, also list human resources management. If you list attorney, list lawyer also. So, if you had the term "human resource (singular) management," and the key-word search by an organization was "human resources" (plural) but without the word "management," there would still be a match on most but not all search systems. Because a match would not occur on some systems, you will want to use as many variations of the same key words as possible.

Abbreviations. If "registered nurse" is one of your key words, make sure that it appears somewhere in the resume as RN. If you are going to use "certified financial planner," make sure that CFP appears as well.

With the synonyms and abbreviations you are trying to cover all of your bases. If the employer uses "human resources management" as a key phrase, while you used "personnel administration" throughout your resume, the computer may not see your resume as a match and the employer will never read it. If you only use the term certified financial planner but the employer searches only for CFP, you also risk not having your resume viewed.

When using these terms, realize that personnel clerks often perform the first screening of the resume, and will not be familiar with all buzzwords in all fields. In principle, the first time you use an abbreviation that you suspect not everyone will recognize, spell out the full term and then show the abbreviation in parentheses. This is how it might appear in the Qualifications section for a registered nurse's resume: "Over ten years' experience as a Registered Nurse (RN), including five years' experience in Emergency Room (ER) and Critical Care (CC)." From that point on you can use the abbreviation without having to spell it out. You will also have ensured that the computer will be able to find both the term and the abbreviation.

Don't insert keywords in a resume merely because you feel an employer might look for them. They must be somewhere in your background. For example, when computer people list programming languages, most list those they've used on the job, as well as those they've studied. That's perfectly acceptable. Once your resume shows up on the screen, however, it is up to the employer to decide if your experience and knowledge match the need. Later, in a telephone or face-to-face interview, you must present how extensive your experience is.

With so many companies using computerized resume databases, it is in your best interest to ensure that your resume achieves maximum exposure.

Once a request is made for resumes with certain key words, all the resumes in the database are searched. When your resume comes up, the computer will find all your key words and highlight them on the screen. Where your key words appear makes no difference to the computer, but it may to a reader. For that reason many people prefer to include a specific key word section for resumes that are likely to be scanned or sent electronically.

Some of the resume tracking systems used by companies will rank the resumes based on key words, education, years of experience and other relevant information. Some give more weight to resumes that have key words early in the content. So you may want to include your key word paragraph when you know or believe it is likely that your resume will go into a resume database.

Many jobs ask for a bachelor's degree. If you have tons of experience, but never finished that degree, this could cause problems for you. If you believe you're qualified for a position, you will want to prevent yourself from being screened out merely because you're ten credits short. Of course, if you come up on an employer's screen, you'll have to have the goods or with a quick mouse click they'll be on to another resume. Here are some ways that can work:

BA (equivalent)

This example would be used by a person who has significant college credits, attended many seminars, and who perhaps has a certificate or two from recognized institutions.

Currently enrolled in BA program

Or

BA (to be completed in June 2009) [this resume was created in the late 2008 in preparation for a June 2009 graduation]

Any of these could be used if they are accurate.

Using a Key Word Section

If you have created a Qualifications section, a key word section will fit right into that format. For a salesperson it might work like this:

OBJECTIVE: Sales Representative

QUALIFICATIONS

Strong sales background. Consistently exceed quota and always become a top producer. Effectively build long-term relationships with accounts. Excellent at cold calling and adding new accounts.

Areas of experience include: Calling on key accounts; territory management; sell to OEMs, retail chains, wholesalers, and distributors; experienced with co-op advertising; marketing; advertising agencies; market research; consultative selling; international sales; tradeshows.

In this example the first paragraph already exists and it contains some desirable key words. The second paragraph is the key word section. Some of the terms in the key word section appear elsewhere in the resume but most do not. This person has just increased the likelihood that her resume will show up on the employer's computer screen when beginning a key word search.

If you choose not to make one of your qualifications paragraphs a key word section, you can insert a key word section at the end of your resume. Simply label it: Key Words. Then under this new section, type in a paragraph of key words (nouns and buzzwords) with each key word or phrase separated by a comma or semicolon. The computer does not care where key words appear, as long as they do appear. Such a key word section would look almost identical to the example just above.

A key word section, while helpful, is not essential. Your job narratives probably include many of the essential key words. However, adding this key word section allows you to view all of your key words or phrases at once, ensuring that you have not missed any important ones. Since it can be difficult to make sure that all of your key words, and all of their variations, including synonyms and abbreviations, are in the resume, a dedicated section is often appropriate.

Some databases rank your resume based on the number of times a key word appears in your resume. This ranking assumes that the more times the word appears in a resume, the greater the likelihood that this person has extensive experience in this field. On the other hand, some databases rank your resume not only on its key words, but on how recently you posted your resume. That option assumes the more recently posted resumes are from job seekers who are actively seeking employment.

What all this means is that you should show the primary key words in your resume more than once (be careful, and don't overdo it). Then make sure that you update your resume for any particular job search website every couple of months.

That's how you create a key word resume. Having taken care of the key word portion of your resume, it will now be important to create your plain-text resume, which you can send to employers by email, and your scannable paper resume, which can be sent to those employers who will electronically scan your resume into their database.

CONVERT A WORD-PROCESSED
RESUME TO AN ELECTRONIC RESUME

To create a resume that will look consistently good when emailed, scanned, or viewed within a text editor, you must use the simplest formatting possible. This means sacrificing the advanced formatting features of your favorite word processor, such as italics, columns, bolding, and custom fonts.

Follow these steps to create a resume that will look good no matter where you send it. These directions will work for MS Word 6.0 and up. Ignore any "lost formatting" warnings that may occur as you work to convert your resume from a MS Word document to a "Plain Text" document.

IMPORTANT: Be sure to save a backup copy of your resume before converting it.

If you are using a word-processing package other than MS Word, the steps will be the same, but some of the special techniques and methods that we suggest are unique to MS Word.

1. Open your formatted resume in your word processor. Make sure your chosen key words are already in your resume. This should be your final version that says everything exactly the way you want it. You will notice that the file name for your resume ends with ".doc": this three-letter unit is called a file extension, and .doc is the file extension used by MS Word up to Word 2007. Word 2007 uses a ".docx" file extension.

2. Go to the File menu and select Save As (see Figure A). In Word 2007 first click the "Office Button" then select, "Save As" and then choose, "Other Formats"(see Figure B). Choose "Plain Text (.txt) in the "Save as type" drop-down menu at the bottom of the dialog box (see Figure C).

Figure A   **Figure B**

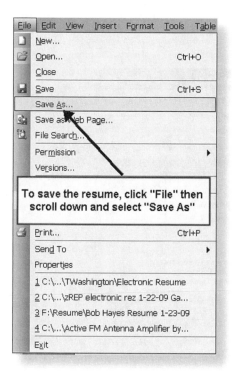

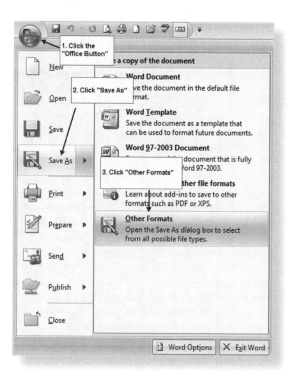

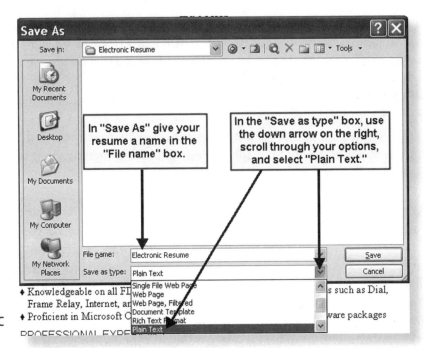

Figure C

In the "File name:" box, give your resume a name. Select a name you will be able to recognize, something like *resume electronic* or *electronic resume*, along with the date created. (This can also show you which version of the resume is being modified.) After naming the resume and selecting "Plain Text" as your format, press "Enter" on your keyboard. You will immediately see a warning box (see Figure D).

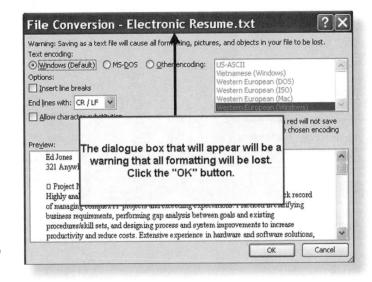

Figure D

Figure E

Go ahead and click "OK." Another warning will then appear informing you that all of your formatting will be lost (see Figure E). Ignore this warning as well, and click "Yes." Be sure to note which folder you have saved your resume in so you can find it later.

3. Close your resume but do not close your word processor. Then click "File" and within MS Word you should see a list of the most recent files opened, including your text resume. Notice it ends with the new file extension, "txt" indicating it is now "Plain Text (see Figure F).

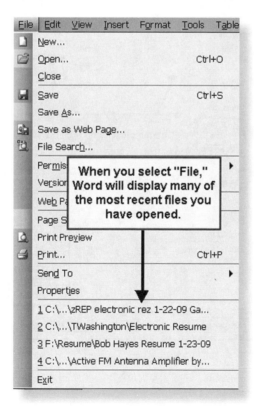

Figure F

The font for your text resume should be "Courier" or "Courier New." The Courier font family is a fixed-width printer font, meaning that all the characters have the same width. Most plain-text editing programs use Courier. Be sure to check that the font size is set to 10.

4. From the File menu click "Page Setup" for Word 2003 and change your left and right margins to 1.7" each (see Figure G).

If you are using MS Word 2007, click the "Page Layout" tab, then "Margins," and at the bottom select "Custom Margins." In the dialogue box that appears use the arrows to set the left and right margins to 1.7.

This process should ensure that none of the lines in your resume will exceed 65 characters. This is important because some computer monitors are limited to 65 characters on a screen. This 1.7" rule will work if your word processor has converted your type to 10-point. If it is 12-point you should set your margins at 1.4" left and right.

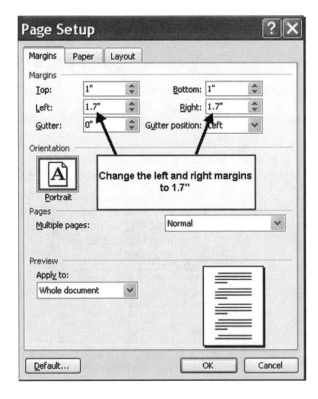

Figure G

Quick Tip: To confirm that none of your lines exceed 65 characters, highlight the longest line in your resume. Click on the left margin of the line until an arrow appears, then left click your mouse and the line is highlighted. Go to the Tools menu and select Word Count, look at "Characters (with spaces)." This will tell you how many characters (including the blank space between each word) are in your longest line. If the longest line is indented from the left margin, add the number of spaces to the number you just read, and make sure the combined total is fewer than 65.

In Word 2007 highlight the longest line of text in your text document and click on the word "Words" that has a number after it. A dialogue box will open with information about the number of characters in the line with and without spaces and even more information.

5. Check to see if you've used any tabs. If so, remove them. Without removing the tabs your plain-text resume will not look the way you want it to.

6. Save the resume by going to the File menu and selecting "Save As." Select "Close" and then immediately reopen the file. There should be line breaks at the end of each line. You'll know there are line breaks if you see a paragraph sign (¶) at the end of each line. If you see no paragraph signs and no dots between words, it means that function has been turned off. To show those signs, hold down the shift and control keys, and press the number 8 key. You'll immediately see the line breaks.

7. Now is your opportunity to edit your resume so you can get it looking the way you want within the limits of a plain-text resume. Now that all the tabs are gone, all text will probably be flush left.

    If you want to indent some portions such as job descriptions you can do that with the space bar. To indent a line, put the cursor in front of the first word in the line and press the space bar to create as many spaces as you need. If you want to create spaces between words, simply use the space bar to create as many spaces as you want.

    You can also do other editing functions. You can capitalize words you want to emphasize, such as your name, the section titles such as Education and Employment, or job titles. This helps add clarity because saving your resume as plain-text will remove bolding and italics. If you want to create a bulleted list you can use the asterisk (*), hyphen (-), or plus sign (+) in place of bullets. This change is needed because when you convert to plain-text, any existing bullets will automatically be turned to asterisks. If you want to double-space between categories or between paragraphs, this is the time to do it.

8. Once you have finished editing your plain-text resume, save it one more time.

Quick Tip: For those not familiar with copy and paste we'll walk you through the process. To copy the text in your resume, start by highlighting the entire resume. To do that click on Edit, then click on Select All (see Figure H).

Then, with the text highlighted, go back to the Edit menu and click on Copy. Next, open your email software to start a new email message. Put your cursor in the space where you want the text to appear for an email message. Go back to the Edit menu and click Paste. Your entire resume will now be pasted in the email.

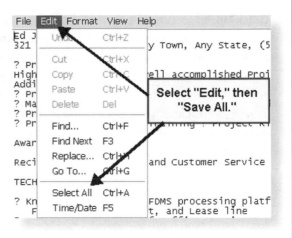

Figure H

Once you have completed the pasting process in the email, address the message to yourself and click Send. Then open your emailed resume and print it out. If you're satisfied with the appearance, you're ready to send it to employers.

Having completed all of these steps you are ready to advance to the process of sending your resume to employers or to commercial resume databases.

WARNING: Do not send your resume as a file attachment to an email message unless the employer specifically requests that you do. Pasting your resume directly into the email will ensure that you are not passing on a virus with the message.

To see your results, close your document and your word processor. Reopen the file in a plain-text editor such as Notepad. To open your resume in Notepad, click on the Start button at the lower left corner of your screen. Click on Documents and then click on your resume. It should now appear in Notepad. Checking your resume in Notepad ensures that it is in plain-text format. It also ensures that your resume will look exactly the same to employers when you email it to an employer database or send it to a commercial database.

If you haven't used your plain-text resume for a while, this method of opening your resume in Notepad may not work for you. In that case click on the Start button, then "Accessories," then click on Notepad (see Figure I).

Click on File, then click on Open. The dialog box will have a portion that says "Look in:" Click on the folder where you originally saved it. When

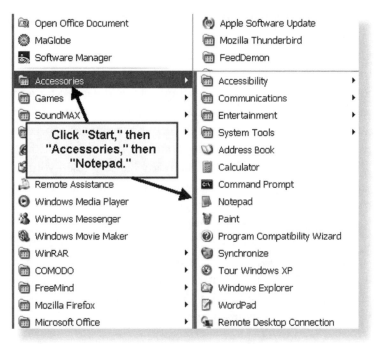

Figure I

you find your text file, click on it and it will come up in Notepad. If your resume doesn't look quite right, you can still add or delete spaces and you can double-space between categories or between paragraphs. When you're through, save the document by clicking on File and then clicking on Save.

Test your plain-text resume by emailing it to yourself. Highlight (select) all the text in your resume, copy it, and paste the text into an email message you are emailing to yourself. The reason you send your resume to yourself the first time is to test the formatting that you just finished working on. If your resume comes to you exactly the way that it was sent, you have a successful plain-text resume.

HOW MANY PAGES?

A computer does not care how long your resume is. It can store and retrieve a ten-page resume as easily as a one-page resume. The answer to the question about the best length of a resume remains relative: It should be long enough to sell you and not so long that a person hesitates to read it. Most resumes are one or two pages in length, with a three-page resume being appropriate for some people.

Electronic resumes are often a little longer because of the short 65 character lines for plain-text. So our advice is that one-, two-, and three-page resumes will work fine. Just make sure that everything in the resume is there because it helps sell you.

SOME SYSTEMS WILL ACCEPT ONLY ONE RESUME AT A TIME

The systems at some corporations, Boeing for example, will keep just one version of your resume in its database. In such a system, if you have previously sent a generic resume, but now you are sending a targeted version for a specific position, that new resume is the one that will stay on file. If you haven't been invited for an interview in four weeks, resubmit your generic resume so it becomes your resume on file. Your targeted version will have already done its work. HR or the department looking to fill the position will already have accessed your targeted resume. You may or may not get an interview, but from that point on you want HR or a hiring manager to view your generic version. As soon as you see a specific job to apply for, tailor your resume for that position and submit it.

In most database systems it is easy to update your resume. If you have moved, added a degree or certification, or completed a successful project, update your resume and resubmit it. Just remember to keep track of your user name and password for each site. A good routine to follow is to write down your user name and password immediately as you create it.

USING YOUR ELECTRONIC RESUME FOR YOUR JOB SEARCH

Sending your electronic resume to potential employers can be well worth the small amount of effort it takes. Resume websites are now used by a growing number of people in a wide range of occupations. If you have never used a resume website, take time to browse some. Most of them have a lot in common, including clear instructions and ease of use. Getting familiar with them can guide your choice of which to use.

POSTING YOUR RESUME TO DATABASES

Most resume websites store your resume text (but not its formatting or layout) and make it available to employers who search for people with specific skills and experience. These are easy to use and free for job seekers. Sites include Monster.com, Hotjobs.com, and CareerBuilder.com.

How It's Done

First, let's look at the database-style resume websites. Follow the site's links to register with the site. Each site will want to get some basic information about you. Rather than refer to it as registering, some will say they want you to "create a new account" or "store your resume." You'll generally have to select a user name and a password, although some sites assign these to you. Many people use their own name or a nickname for a password. Record this information precisely. Keep track of the user name and password you use at each site.

You could try to use the same user name and password with each site, but if neither is available, you'll have to select another.

The resume you're going to submit to the websites will be your plain-text version. The text isn't pretty, but it is functional.

Once you've created a text-only resume, the basic procedure for most websites is similar. Fill out the forms on your screen (with your name, address, and other vital pieces of information), and then paste your entire resume into a larger window provided for that purpose. That's about all there is to it.

Some sites also prompt you to supply a cover letter in another window. Create a short cover letter that hits your key skills and experience. In the world of electronic resumes, cover letters are often ignored, so if you want yours to have impact, keep it short and to the point.

PRIVACY

If you're concerned about your employer discovering you're job hunting, or concerned that your name and email address are available to marketers, follow the link to the site's privacy policy statement and read it. Some sites don't have one available. Those that do usually state that they will not disclose specific or personal information to outside parties without your permission. The organization behind the resume website may "offer third-party services and products to you based on the preferences that you identify in your registration and at any time thereafter" (in other words, send you spam), as in the case of Monster. com. If you're employed you may want to post your resume only at the safest sites. The safest sites require the organization interested in you to email you and tell you who they are. You can then reply if you are interested. With other sites, the resume database will contact you by email and ask you to reply if you're interested in the organization, which will then be revealed to you.

If your concern is that your present employer may see your resume on the Web and find out that you are looking for a new job, look for options in each site that allow you to make your resume nonsearchable. This means the website will contact you for permission to show your resume to interested employers instead of including it in the results of any search conducted by any employer. Not all resume websites offer this choice.

Another way to control the privacy of your posted resume is to remove the names of your last two employers, and instead of your name and address at the top, just list your email address. Also at the top would be a request that interested organizations email you and identify themselves and provide more information about the position. Such a technique could cause some employers to skip you, but those really interested would not be deterred. For maximum privacy, get a new email account that you will use just for the job search. Create an email address that does not contain your first or last name or your initials.

Like other websites, many career and resume sites use "cookies." Cookies are small files placed on your computer by websites you visit in order to recognize you when you return and also to target online ads to your demographic. You can adjust preferences within your computer to refuse to accept some or all cookies, but doing that will stop you from visiting some sites.

USEFUL FEATURES OFTEN INCLUDED IN RESUME WEBSITES:

- Clear instructions, including information on how many characters will fit on each line (so you can put in manual line breaks)
- A window where you can paste the entire resume
- An option for a confidential resume, which means the website will contact you for permission to show the resume to interested employers; this can prevent your current employer from stumbling across it
- A statement of the website's privacy policy
- A preview button that allows you to view the resume after pasting it into the window.

TIPS TO KEEP IN MIND WHEN BUILDING AND POSTING YOUR RESUME:

- Record your user name and password for each site. Sometimes you will select these; at other sites they will be assigned to you
- Start with a finished resume. Save it as a text (.txt) file. It will lose any special formatting such as centering, bold and italic type, and bullets. You can then copy and paste this version into the "paste your resume here" windows provided by the websites
- Check on how long the site will keep your resume.

A SCANNABLE RESUME

Although more and more companies prefer electronic resumes sent by email, many still scan resumes into their database. When a paper resume comes in, someone in HR will scan the resume and use the optical character recognition (OCR) software to post it to the resume database. At that time it becomes available to a manager who can then find it through a key word search.

Scanners, and the OCR software that translate the images into words, have limits. Many cannot properly interpret italics, and if the print is too small, the OCR software will not recognize the letters, creating typos throughout the resume. In the next five years scanners and OCR software may reach a level of sophistication where they can even read the handwriting of doctors. Until that time arrives, it is best to follow the rules that almost ensure a one hundred percent accurately scanned resume.

Take the time to insert all your key words so employers can find you. Personnel file drawers containing resumes are called black holes because usually once a paper resume gets in a file drawer it never sees the light of day again. At least now, if you understand the following rules for creating a scannable resume, your resume will pop up on many computer screens and you'll have the opportunity to sell yourself.

Paper resumes sent to employers, who then scan them into their database, must be formatted in such a way that all the words you've used to describe yourself are entered exactly as you composed them. If done incorrectly, your scanned resume might end up in the database riddled with typographical errors. Resumes with such errors rarely result in interviews.

TIPS ON USING YOUR RESUME

Whenever possible, send your resume to a specific person. If the organization is identified in the ad, call and ask for the best person to address your cover letter to. Make sure you ask how the name is spelled and the person's gender. Mr. Chris Smith is a lot different from Ms. Kris Smith. Although not every organization will give you a name, many will. Then address your cover letter to that person with the correct title. While you have a person from that organization on the phone, also ask if they scan resumes. If they don't, send only one version of your resume, the one that visually looks the best. If you simply don't know if your resume will be scanned, or if the organization has over one hundred employees, send both versions. Few companies under one hundred employees scan resumes.

CREATING A SCANNABLE RESUME

When a resume arrives at an organization that scans and stores resumes, it first passes through an electronic scanner, which takes a picture of the document. The OCR software will analyze the resume to change it from an image to a plain-text file and store it in a database. Problems can occur both in the scanning and analyzing stages. If the contrast between the paper and letters isn't good, the scanner may not take a good picture of the page. This could occur when a resume with black ink on dark paper is scanned. If the letters are too small or if an unusual font is used, the OCR software simply cannot recognize the letters and the resume will be unreadable.

Scanners and OCR software are constantly improving, so the newest high-end hardware and software may have little trouble with typical resumes. The problem is that many organizations are still using older equipment, and you have no way of knowing who is state-of-the-art and who is not. What this means is that to get through the OCR door, the great looking resumes that people create with their computers and laser printers need modification.

Although it seems like extra work to transform the original resume into a scannable version, it will require only a bit more time if you follow a few simple suggestions. Following these instructions should lead to a resume that can be scanned and stored with 100% accuracy.

Because many companies are still scanning paper resumes into their data-bases, it's important to send something that will scan properly. Much of the scanning software will have no trouble with many of the items mentioned. But it's better to be safe than sorry. Consider underlining, for example. Since some scanners have trouble with underlining, it is simply better to remove it. Under-lining and using too small a font can cause typographical errors. Words the OCR software had trouble with will use a tilde character, which looks like this: ~. The resume with lots of errors and tilde marks (~) will rarely earn a thorough read. The following sentence appeared in the resume of one of our clients:

> Placed over 100 people with disabilities into competitive jobs, a rate 30-40% above the norm.

After scanning the sentence became:

> Placed ove~ 100 people with disabilities into competitive jobs, a rate 3040~ above the nomm.

You can see why it is important to create a scan-friendly resume. The ~ symbol is substituted for the original characters by the OCR when it notices that a letter or symbol is there but that it cannot properly decipher it. In the 30–40% portion, the OCR did not detect the hyphen; it also could not deci-pher the percent sign. The word "norm" became "nomm". In this case the problem occurred because the resume used a small, 10-point serif font. We recommend 11-point sans-serif fonts for resumes that will likely be scanned.

THE KEYS TO CREATING A SCANNABLE RESUME

Below are 18 points which, if followed, will result in your resume being scanned with almost total accuracy.

Use an 11-point font

We have long recommended an 11-point font size because it is the most readable. It also happens to be what scanners and OCR software prefer. When we tested different font sizes and typefaces (such as Arial and Times Roman), they all did better with 11-point type than with 10-point. For your name at the top of the first page, 14- or 16-point font sizes are fine.

Use a sans-serif typeface

We like serif fonts like Times New Roman for resumes, but your scannable resume should use a sans-serif font like Helvetica or Arial. Letters with serifs have the little extra strokes in parts of each letter.

> This is Times Roman. It has serifs.
> This is Arial. It does not have serifs. It is a sans-serif (i.e. without serifs) type-face.

Resumes using a sans-serif typeface scan slightly better than those with serifs. In those typefaces that have serifs, the letters sometimes touch, and this can give fits to a scanner. Typefaces come in many names, and often there are only slight differences between them. Some sans-serif typefaces that will scan well include Arial, Helvetica, Univers, and Century Gothic. Most sans-serif typefaces will scan well. Sans-serif typefaces from Word 2000 that will scan well include:

This is Albertus Medium

This is Antique Olive

This is Arial, the most commonly sans-serif typeface used in resumes (It is almost identical to Helvetica, another popular font)

This is Century Gothic

This is Franklin Gothic Book

This is Lucida Sans

This is Tahoma

This is Univers

This is Verdana

Keep your lines to 75 characters or less

Some OCR applications allow no more than 75 characters per line on the screen. If a line in your resume has more than 75 characters, your resume on screen and on paper may look like this:

Eastside Employment Services, Renton, WA 1984–1993
EMPLOYMENT COORDINATOR – Met with clients with
    disabilities and assessed
their mental and physical skills. Matched clients with prospec-
    tive
employers and sold those employers on the benefits of hiring
    each client.
Successfully placed over 100 people with developmental dis-
    abilities in

Here, a line-wrap problem has occurred because not all the words could fit on the line. It doesn't look pretty, and most firms will simply not take the time to improve this awkward appearance.

A basic rule is that if you use an 11-point font and have margins of 1.6 inches on both sides you should be safe from line-wrap problems. To be sure, count the characters (don't forget to count the spaces between words as characters too) in your longest line. Remember that you can count the number of characters in one line automatically: Highlight your longest line, go to Tools, then click on "Word Count." Look at "Characters with Spaces." But note that if your line is indented, you need to add the number of characters in the indent, as shown below:

Data Systems, 1973-Present

SENIOR PROJECT MANAGER, Little Rock, Arkansas, 1989-Present.
Negotiate contracts, schedule deliveries, and troubleshoot all phases of
computer installations. Work closely with customers to determine their
needs, then gain contractual commitments from manufacturing and field
engineering.

In this example, you would first count the characters in the line starting with "needs." That line has 69 characters. But since that sentence was indented two spaces in from the company name, you would have to add them and count it as 71, still well within the 75-character rule. This job description would not create a word wrap problem.

Use white or light-colored 8.5 x 11" paper and print on only one side

Scanners need maximum contrast between the letters and the background. They also do best with standard 8.5 x 11" paper. When we scanned a resume with black letters on dark blue paper, the errors immediately went from zero to about 15. A few people print their resumes on 11 x 17" paper to create a presentation folder. The sheet is folded in half, with printing on all four pages, the first page acting as a cover. This style is not well accepted, and it causes major problems for scanners.

Avoid the use of underlining

Some OCR handle underlining just fine, but problems can occur when the underline touches the lower part of letters such as "j", "g", or "p".

Avoid the use of bolding

Although most applications handle bold letters without any problem, some do not. Avoid bold type.

Avoid fancy fonts

Some of the unusual fonts that are available are difficult for scanners to read. We fed one OCR application a resume using a script typeface

which looked like this.

To the scanner it was total gibberish. Such a resume will be tossed out by most employers. Other fancy fonts that would not work well include: **Bauhaus**, Papyrus, *Forte*, ALGERIAN, Footlight, Matura, Tempus, *Lucida Calligraphy*, and Bradley Hand.

Don't use bullets or hollow bullets

Bullets are removed from a resume during scanning so you might as well not even use them. Hollow bullets on a paper resume can be interpreted as zeroes or as the small letter "o" when scanned, so avoid using them.

Put your name on the top line and use one line for each telephone number listed and one for email

Many scanning applications assume that the first line of a resume contains your name. Therefore, for your scannable resume, have only your name on the top line. It will also increase accuracy if you give one line for your home phone and another line for a cell phone number. Your email address should also be on a separate line. If you have a web resume, put your web address (URL) on a separate line as well. Although it is considered best to have a single line for each item on a scannable resume, you could put both phone numbers on one line as long as you put at least six spaces between them. Typically you would write "Home" after your home number. Another common approach is to put (h) or (H) after your home number and (c) or (C) for cell phone. Put parentheses around your area code: (425) 879-0098. Or try 425-879-0098, or 425.879.0098.

Use caps to give emphasis to key areas

Since we've already advised you to remove some of the nice word-processing touches that make a resume attractive, about the only design choice you have left is to capitalize certain words for emphasis. Your job titles and your subject headings like Education and Employment could be capitalized. Your use of capitalization is retained in the plain-text version.

Send a resume unfolded, unstapled, and flat in a 9 x 12" manila envelope

Creases in letters can cause a scanner to misread words in those lines. Although there is an extra cost to sending your resume unfolded, it will scan better. Besides, even if the firm does not scan resumes, it will have a nicer appearance. The resume pages will be taken apart before scanning, so leave them unstapled. Use a paper clip instead.

Avoid the use of italics

Many scanners do just fine with italics, but italics can cause problems for others. In part this is because with italics the characters come so close to merging with one another the OCR software cannot make out what the letter should be, a problem similar to some of the more exotic fonts.

Avoid the use of shading

There's really no reason to use shading, but some people use it on resumes just because it's available. Scanners need clear contrast between the letters and background. Shading destroys that contrast. Shading like this will really make a scanner go bonkers.

Avoid the use of columns

Many scanners handle columns just fine, but some scanners assume each column is a separate page.

Avoid the use of boxes or vertical lines

Vertical lines can fool a scanner, which may read them as the letter "I." Vertical and horizontal lines and borders add nothing to a resume, so just leave them off.

Avoid compressing space between letters and between lines

Today's word-processing packages enable one to compress the space between letters and between lines. That allows you to fit more words onto a page, but it can also cause problems for scanners. Stick to using the standard spacing between letters, lines, and paragraphs.

Print only on one side of the page

Print on just one side of the page. Printing on both sides of a page can create shadows and gives scanners real problems.

Never send a resume by fax unless requested

The quality of a fax degrades the sharpness of the letters so much that errors are certain to appear. If you are asked to fax a resume for the sake of speed, send your scannable version by mail the same day so that they will have your high-quality resume as well. Or, consider sending only your scannable resume, but sending it by next-day air or second-day air. If you fax your resume, try to fax it directly from your computer since this will create a higher-quality document when they receive it.

Pulling It All Together

Although we have given you many points to follow, they are simple to apply. These rules do, however, eliminate some of the nice visual touches that are possible with today's word-processing programs and laser printers. But once a resume is scanned and goes into the database, all of those things are stripped off anyway. The bolding, italics, shading, or other special formatting you've used will not appear when your resume is printed after being stored. So if there is any chance the resume will be scanned, you might as well remove those elements at the beginning and make sure the scanner will read it with total accuracy. As scanning applications improve, some of the advice provided above will change. But for now this is what you must do to ensure that your resume is accurately scanned and stored.

If you decide to send two copies of your resume—one for scanning and one that visually looks the best—you could attach a note to the scanning resume that says, "Resume version intended for scanning purposes."

Although not all cover letters are scanned into databases, you should still take the time to create a strong cover letter, because many employers use cover letters to learn about you. It too should use a 11-point, sans-serif font.

The resume on the next page is an example of a resume that should scan perfectly with almost any scanning application. It uses 11-point Arial type and its longest line does not exceed 75 characters.

Make effective use of your electronic resume. As valuable as the hundreds of commercial employment websites can be, keep in mind that far more jobs are posted at company websites. Many organizations choose not to advertise their positions. Based on observation they've concluded they get higher caliber applicants by posting positions only on their own company website. Think about it. Using websites like Careerbuilder are fairly passive. Many people lack focus and use such sites to apply for jobs almost haphazardly. Those who target specific organizations tend to be more focused and seem to offer the work ethic and drive that many companies seek. See page 286 for information on Reference USA where you can create a list of organizations that fit your profile based on location, industry, and size.

ADRIAN MASTERS
2199 Roxanne Avenue
Long Beach, California 90815
(213) 645-0968

OBJECTIVE: Import Manager

QUALIFICATIONS

Strong import and transportation experience with knowledge
of customs regulations and procedures. Consistently establish
procedures that cut costs and provide timely delivery of product.

EDUCATION

B.A. - International Business, UCLA (1992)

EMPLOYMENT

Raha Sportswear, Long Beach, California 10/97-Present

ASSISTANT IMPORT MANAGER—Manage a staff of five who monitor
$95 million in wearing apparel imports and a $44 million letter of
credit line. Proposed, developed, and implemented an ocean freight
consolidation program which has reduced ocean freight costs by 30%
and provides better tracking control. Planned and developed a manual
tracking system which for the first time has enabled the company to
analyze the performance of vendors.

Breslin Inc., Los Angeles, California 5/93-8/97

IMPORT SPECIALIST—Coordinated the transportation of all retail
purchase orders through communication with brokers, agents, and
product managers. Recommended the establishment of a specific
footwear rate, saving an estimated $30,000 in ocean freight rates.

Appara, Los Angeles, California 4/90-5/93

IMPORT CLERK/ALLOCATION CLERK—As Allocation Clerk, adjusted
inventories and future shipments to meet store orders. As Import Clerk,
tracked all imported product to assure consistent flow of goods by
communicating with brokers, truckers, and foreign agents.

ELECTRONICALLY SUBMITTING YOUR RÉSUMÉ

ASCII

There are two primary ways to submit an ASCII (plain-text) resume—online and by email.

Most employment and employer websites have electronic application forms that include a spot in which to paste your resume. As with any application, make sure you follow the instructions.

When emailing, many professionals see benefits in pasting the resume into the body of the email itself, giving the reader immediate access. One click on the email and there it is! No muss . . . no fuss. At that point the reader can review it or cut and paste it into the organization's resume database for later scrutiny. A cover letter can also be pasted into the email so that the cover letter will be seen first. Keep it short so the reader will quickly move onto the resume.

Another option is to enclose the resume in the form of an attachment. Some companies, however, do not accept attachments for fear of viruses and other cyber intruders.

Word-Processed

The benefits of a visually attractive word-processed resume versus a text version have previously been covered. Submitting such a document requires the use of an attachment. Since, as we have seen, some organizations are attachment-averse, it is advisable to contact them in advance to check out their policies. Don't bother calling those organizations that specifically prohibit the use of attachments.

Using an attachment means having the reader take an additional step in accessing your resume than if you plugged it into the body of the email. Hoping the reader will take the additional step of opening a second attachment containing a cover letter might be overreaching a bit. If you want to include a cover letter, paste it into the resume file and send it as a single attachment. This is especially helpful for those resumes that get forwarded to several parties. The odds of each of them opening the cover letter as a separate file are probably low.

PART TWO

Sample Résumés
To Use As Guides

Sample Résumés To Help You

The following sample resumes demonstrate how the entire resume fits together to tell a story. Visit our website at (www.careerempowering.com) for additional entries. Just click on Books and Articles by Tom Washington and Gary Kanter. Then click on *Resume Empower!* and Sample Resumes.

The sample resumes in this book and on the website have been provided to give many ideas on how to create the best format for you and to highlight your strengths, skills, and results.

Various fonts (typefaces) have been used so you can determine which you like best. The name of the font appears at the top right of each resume.

Though this book presents the basic principles for writing the empowered resume, it cannot provide examples for all positions. If you don't see your job, don't panic: the ideas presented in *Resume Empower!* can be used universally.

As you read the resumes, notice that the people being described seem like real, living, highly capable people, a quality rarely found in resumes. Strive to make your resume as interesting as theirs. Do everything possible to bring results into your resume.

Essentially, all occupations and people fall into 19 categories. Those 19 categories include:

Recent college graduates	Administrative/Office people
Those returning to work after long gaps	Government employees
	Teachers
Those over 50	Engineers/Scientists
People who use portfolios	Accounting/Finance
Military people	Professionals
Computer and IT specialists	Nonprofit organizations
Salespeople	Manufacturing/Laboring
Career changers	Healthcare professionals
Managers/Supervisors	Retailers

RESUME SAMPLES*

*Note Before You Read The Sample Resumes: Many of the sample resumes you'll see were originally two pages. They were reduced in length to enable you to concentrate your attention on key elements of the resumes.

Graduating
College Students/Recent Grads

Although you may not have a lot of work experience, make the most of what you have, especially any experience related to what you want to do. Bookkeeping, for example, is valuable experience for an accounting major. It's not the same as accounting, but it is excellent, practical experience and is recognized as such by employers. A forestry major would emphasize any work with a timber company, even if it was only menial summer work.

As a recent or soon-to-be graduate, you have four things to sell: your education, your personality and character, related work experience, and general work experience. If you have little or no related work experience, most of your resume will be devoted to revealing your personality, character, and work ethic. Employers need to sense the type of employee you will be. College graduates typically remain with their first employers for just a few years, so it's fair for employers to seek those who will quickly contribute to the organization.

Internships and jobs where you've had a high level of responsibility, are particularly valuable. In John Etter's sample resume on page 176, only one job was actually described because its value was so much more relevant than the other summer jobs.

The myth of the one-page resume is never more prevalent than in the case of the new grad. Employers need reasons for their hiring decisions, and if you offer a record of excellence you have immediately separated yourself from the pack whether you use a one-page or two-page resume.

Describing some or all of your summer or part-time jobs can be valuable in demonstrating your work ethic, maturity, and results.

Look for ways to reveal your personal qualities. Offices held in high school and college reveal leadership and responsibility. Your achievements in office can be impressive, as can class projects that demonstrate value. Try a Special Projects section or include the projects as part of your Education section. Perhaps you were in a group with business students who developed a marketing plan for a small company or in a group of industrial engineering students who solved an actual manufacturing problem.

Below is a Special Projects section by a student who was very active on campus:

- Planned and organized the University of Puget Sound 2007 Spring Parents Weekend and set a new record for attendance. Arranged programs and activities, obtained speakers, made hotel arrangements, ordered food, and headed up a four-person committee. Increased attendance 20% over the previous year. Evaluations by parents indicated it was the best organized program since its inception in 1980.
- Published the first Parents Association Newsletter, which was sent to 3,500 parents of UPS students. The first two editions were well-received and the newsletter has become an official school publication, published three times each year.

Lettering in sports indicates learning the value of teamwork and coopera-tion. Excellent grades indicate discipline and intellectual capacity. Participation in debate and theater can reveal communication skills, analytical thinking, and willingness to take risks. Participating in school committees and organizations reveals responsibility and a sense of community.

The Qualifications section of a resume is an excellent place to describe and call attention to some of the qualities you want an employer to know about, as the example below demonstrates.

OBJECTIVE: Mathematics/Statistics
QUALIFICATIONS

- Excellent training in math and statistics.
- Maintain excellent relations with supervisors. Always a valued employee. Loyal, cooperative, and easy to work with.
- Work well under pressure, learn quickly, hard working.

You may have noticed that none of these statements was backed up with hard facts. The student who wrote this statement picked qualities she knew to be true about herself, which she can elaborate about at an interview.

When selecting these qualities make sure you can back them up when asked to. Don't offer them just because they sound good. You might get the interview, but you'll never get the job unless the "real you" matches the "you" on paper.

Value comes in a variety of forms. Demonstrating you paid a substantial part or all of your college expenses by working is a powerful statement of ded-ication and time management. Being willing to travel or relocate can be an immediate plus for companies where that kind of flexibility is valued.

Simple statements in a Personal section will suffice.

PERSONAL
Earned 60% of college expenses
Willing to relocate

College Graduate   **Century Schoolbook**

JOHN ETTER

426 Harris Hall
Burlington, Vermont 05401
(802) 795-2631
jetter@realcheap.net

OBJECTIVE: Entry-Level Training and Development Position

QUALIFICATIONS

Excellent program development skills. Established new intramural programs and increased participation by women 130%.

Strong research and writing ability. Published an article in the *Vermont Historical Society Quarterly*.

Speak well before the public. Won numerous debate tournaments and placed fifth in the 2007 national tournament.

Cooperate well with supervisors; reliable and responsible; work hard and complete projects on schedule.

EDUCATION

B.A. - History, University of Vermont, will graduate June 2008 (3.6 GPA)

Business Courses: History of 20th Century Business, Macroeconomics, Microeconomics, Communications

PUBLICATIONS

"Effects of the Abolition Movement in Burlington, Vermont 1826 to 1866"
Vermont Historical Society Quarterly, January 2008 issue

AWARDS

"Outstanding History Senior" selected by the History Faculty (2008)

Fifth place, national debate tournament, extemporaneous speaking (2007)

EMPLOYMENT

University of Vermont, Burlington, Vermont 9/07 to Present

Director of Intramural Sports - Planned, staffed, and organized the intramural sports program. Working with a tight budget, assessed equipment needs, received bids from sporting goods suppliers, and purchased sports equipment. Supervised two assistants and recruited and supervised dozens of volunteers. Developed a new concept in women's athletics and actively promoted the program. Participation by women grew from 24% in previous years to 55%. Participation by men increased from 54% to 64%. Developed successful refereeing clinics along with new sportsmanship rules that dramatically reduced fights and complaints regarding calls by referees.

Summer Employment:

Records Clerk, Stephenson Steel, Ascutney, Vermont 6/07 to 9/07
Mail Sorter, U.S. Postal Service, Ascutney, Vermont 6/06 to 9/06
Laborer, Isaacson Contracting, Ascutney, Vermont 6/05 to 9/05
Farm Worker, John Tyler, Ascutney, Vermont 6/04 to 9/04

College Graduate   Arial

POLLY GLADSON
275 S. Pine Blvd.
Henniker, New Hampshire
(603) 971-2653
pg@beartrap.com

OBJECTIVE: Entry level accounting position with a CPA firm

QUALIFICATIONS

Excellent college training and on-the-job experience. Have worked closely with a CPA firm and helped prepare taxes. Prepared documents for an IRS audit. Have practical business experience handling all bookkeeping functions at a busy restaurant.

EDUCATION

B.A. - Accounting, New England College, 3.21 GPA (June 2008)

EXPERIENCE

Gulliver's Restaurant, Henniker, New Hampshire (9/03 to Present, full-time)

Waitress (9/07 to Present). Provide outstanding service and consistently receive the highest tips among the restaurant staff. Highly professional.

Bookkeeper (4/05 to 9/07). Responsible for accounts receivable, reconciling charge slips, payroll, balancing five registers, recovering on bad checks, reconciling petty cash, and inventorying bar supplies monthly. Monitored costs by preparing monthly reports comparing gross sales to labor costs for each department.

Worked closely with accountant and prepared figures as requested. Each year helped auditor track and reconcile all financial transactions. A 2007 IRS audit stated the books were very complete and accurate. Highly respected and trusted - had full access to safe and every part of restaurant.

Podium Hostess (9/03 to 4/05). Redesigned the reservation system, which significantly improved service to customers. Developed excellent relations with customers and helped create a loyal clientele. Trained seating hostesses in all facets of the job.

Village Inn, Henniker, New Hampshire (6/02 to 9/03, full-time)

Hostess/Waitress - Greeted and seated customers, opened and closed the restaurant, and prepared the registers each day.

ACTIVITIES

Member, American Society of Women Accountants

Active in jazz dancing and dog obedience training

Those Returning To Work After Long Gaps

While the mother of the family remains the primary caregiver for the overwhelming majority of families, the *house husband* or *soccer dad* has become fairly familiar in this millennium. Regardless of gender, the issues facing the parent who returns to the workplace can be substantial.

One of the most common factors facing the returning parent is the uneasy feeling that the years at home were basically useless in terms of career skills.

The good news is, you are not alone! The interviewer across the desk from you probably knows a returning parent or has perhaps been one. It is a solid demographic and one that many employers either belong to or appreciate.

So, at the outset, don't consider the endless choruses of "The wheels on the bus go round and round . . ." at the preschool as time misspent. Volunteering in the classroom or on field trips, fundraising, coaching sports, or managing the concessions at events are just a few of the contributions you made in your "parenting career."

Parents with special expertise often teach classes or tutor students in special subjects ranging from computers to foreign languages and origami. These are definitely grist for the resume mill.

Some parents assist their spouses or partners in family businesses. This can include bookkeeping, reception, and assorted other administrative duties. As this is rarely accompanied by a paycheck it is often overlooked on the resume. Big mistake. Parenting, volunteering, and working are all exercises in time management. Appreciate them as such. So will the employer.

If you feel you need assistance getting started there is help at hand. Most community colleges have career assistance of some sort, usually at low or no cost. Local community organizations, YMCAs, and religious groups often have active job clubs and support groups. Recently divorced or widowed spouses might be eligible for "displaced homemaker" grants and programs. State employment services can provide valuable information about these programs. Also, many cities have regularly published employment magazines that provide calendars of events pertaining to employment, including times and locations where job groups meet.

When reviewing your previous work history, regardless of how dated it is, don't make the mistake of concluding that the quality of your experience has been diluted by time. If you were good . . . you were good. There is no statute of limitations on excellence. Write your job sketches as if the experience were current. As you take this refresher course in your background, you should begin valuing your achievements all over again. The employer will.

Regular volunteer activities and projects, if substantial, can be presented with the same authority as paid jobs, replete with duties, accomplishments, and results.

The decision whether or not to pursue additional education depends on your profession. Those in technical and scientific fields do need to be current. If you can achieve sufficient readiness through self-study and can sell that to the employer, terrific! Otherwise, a few classes at the local technical or community college might be sufficient. The final decision should be determined by research into the current state of your field. In many cases you will find you can hit the ground running, without the need for extensive and probably unnecessary preparation.

Below is the resume of a returning mom who had strong volunteer experience and was seeking a position managing a nonprofit organization.

Administrative Assistant   **Georgia**

SHARON COSGRAVE
526 South State Street
Wilmington, Delaware 19803
(302) 543-9161
sharron@chloethebeagle.com

OBJECTIVE: Administrative Assistant/Project Manager with a nonprofit organization

QUALIFICATIONS

Strong experience in developing effective new programs, motivating and coordinating large numbers of volunteers, and making office systems more efficient.

Excellent fund-raiser. Have written three successful grant proposals, one of which was funded for $20,000. Through PTA fund-raising activities, increased revenue 18% above the previous record.

EDUCATION

University of Delaware, Liberal Arts, 96 credits, 1985–1988

PROJECTS/ACTIVITIES

PTA President, Robert Frost Elementary, 2005–2008. Increased attendance at monthly meetings from 51 to an average of 92. Worked with principal and teachers to develop five new volunteer programs for parents. Participation in programs increased from 26% of parents to 58%. Because of active parent involvement, vandalism at the school decreased to almost zero.

Fund-raising Chairperson, Robert Frost PTA, 2005–2006. Coordinated the efforts of over 400 children and 95 adults in six fund-raising activities. Exceeded the previous record by 18%.

Board Member, Wilmington Crisis Clinic, 2000–Present. Analyze and approve annual budgets, interview and select new directors, and study proposed program changes. President of the board 2003–2005. Wrote grant proposal, which obtained $45,000 in federal funds.

President, Wilmington Chapter, MADD (Mothers Against Drunk Drivers), 1996–2000. Organized the local chapter and tripled dues-paying membership each year. Testified as an expert witness before the Delaware Legislature. Coordinated statewide lobbying efforts and helped pass legislation that significantly strengthened laws against drunk driving.

EMPLOYMENT

McClinton, Brandeis & Nelson, Wilmington, Delaware 1988 to 1991

Office Manager - Handled bookkeeping, payroll, bank statements, accounts payable, and accounts receivable. Purchased office equipment and supplies. Greeted clients, answered phones, scheduled court reporters for depositions, and developed an improved appointment and court scheduling system for eight attorneys.

Those Over 50

The greatest concern of people over 50 is age discrimination. While federal law prohibits discrimination on the basis of age, we know that it persists in both overt and subtle ways. Ageism is like every other form of discrimination: whoever you are, there is going to be somebody out there who is going to object to you. It is outside of your control. So treat it as an obstacle and get on with the job search.

In most cases, you will not be competing with substantially younger people. By virtue of your age you have achieved a certain level of experience, which, by definition, will rule out the young 'uns. You are presenting this level of knowledge, ability, judgment, and ability.

Back in the '80s, every corporation worth its stock options was recruiting twenty-something MBAs like the NFL drafts quarterbacks—complete with signing bonuses. This youth movement was exacerbated in the '90s, culminating with the legendary dot-com fiasco.

You don't need an MBA to figure out that even the best business school education cannot replace solid experience.

So, create the presentation that demonstrates those assets that set you apart from not just your more youthful competitors but from your peers as well.

Trenton is a 59-year-old insurance executive. His impressive experience speaks volumes about his track record. Feeling a bit nervous about his age, he chose to omit his earliest positions. His employment record is so strong that his minimal education has also been omitted. The Prior Employment section keeps us focused on the details of the more recent positions.

Sales and Marketing Management   Tahoma

TRENTON McGRATH

2215 Broadway North
Houston, TX 77012
(713) 785-2761
tmcgrath@menarefrommars.com

OBJECTIVE: Sales/Marketing Management

QUALIFICATIONS

Complete knowledge of Mortgage Lending/Mortgage Finance/Secondary Markets.

Recognized as an outstanding trainer and motivator of sales staffs. Substantially increased market share in each position held.

Broad marketing experience. Developed and marketed new products and services that have consistently been accepted in the financial community.

EMPLOYMENT

Diversified Mortgage Insurance Company, Minneapolis, MN 1/87 to Present

Regional Vice President 2/02 to Present, Houston. Moved into a troubled 16-state zone and have increased market share 61%, from 3.2% to 5.2%. Have aggressively marketed new services and became active with the Bond Business, Pension Funds, Swaps, and assisting lenders with Portfolio Sales. Travel extensively and work closely with four district sales managers and 20 salespeople.

Senior Vice President, Sales and Marketing 12/94 to 2/02, Minneapolis. Developed and implemented a reorganization of the national sales force, moving from 12 divisions to four zones. Reorganization has been credited with strengthening DMI's national market share. Took part in the development of the Mortgage Finance Unit which has successfully moved DMI into new markets. Developed strategies for participation in Mortgage Revenue Bonds, Pass Through Certificates, Pension Funds Issues, Builder Buy-downs, and Pay-through Bonds.

Vice President, Northwest Division Manager 9/92 to 12/94, Portland. Covering nine western states, trained and supervised a staff of nine account executives, three underwriters, and two secondary market managers. Increased market share in the territory by 88%. Traveled extensively throughout the territory and made calls on CEOs.

Product Manager 1/87 to 9/92, Minneapolis. Developed and implemented marketing plans for specialized insurance products for mortgage lending financial institutions: Error/Omission Coverage, Special Hazard Coverage, and Officers/Employees Liability Coverage. Responsible for national marketing of the products. Sales volume for these products increased an average of 22% per year.

American Insurance Company, Atlanta, GA 6/83 to 1/87

Director of Field Operations 6/85 to 1/87, Atlanta. Had total responsibility for sales production of six regional and 21 state managers. Introduced new mortgage life and disability insurance programs and created a highly effective sales training program.

Regional Manager 6/83 to 6/85, St. Louis. Supervised operations of four state managers and personally generated new business in metropolitan St. Louis.

Niagara Home Life Assurance Company, Palo Alto, CA 8/77 to 6/83

Assistant Vice President - Negotiated exclusive contracts with S&Ls for the sale of Niagara Home Life's Mortgage Life Plan and Disability Plan. Designed and implemented a specialized Insured Savings Plan for Savings and Loan depositors which had an excellent effect on insurance sales. Recruited and trained sales agents.

Prior Employment

Sales Agent/Trainer, Home Owners Security, Inc. 2/73 to 8/77

Sales Agent, Home Security Associates 2/71 to 2/73

People Who Use Portfolios

Architects, drafters, artists, designers, photographers, models, and writers use portfolios to help sell themselves. They often make the mistake of placing too little emphasis on a top-quality resume, assuming the portfolio alone will sell them.

As important as your portfolio is, don't shortchange yourself. There are lots of talented people out there with outstanding portfolios. Taking the time to develop an equally compelling resume will make an important difference to your job-hunting success. Your resume can reveal qualities and background that may not be apparent from the portfolio alone. A portfolio can express your technical or creative ability, but a resume reveals where you've been and how you developed your ability. In fact, without an effective resume you might not get the opportunity to show that fantastic portfolio you so painstakingly assembled.

Consider reproducing two or three samples of your work on 8½ x 11" paper to enclose with your resume or hand to employers when you meet them. The benefit of this is to leave a visual reminder of your work for when the employer reviews applicants' materials in the future. Writers can do the same with clippings.

While we normally recommend minimal use of graphics in resumes, here's a case for an exception. Those in the visual arts can use the resume as a sample of their creativity and proficiency. Of course, the danger, as usual, is in obscuring the message in the medium.

Bobbie's resume adds a personal touch the portfolio itself could not provide. We see she is organized and responsible, with a wide range of communication and customer service skills. She comes across as a real person, not just a mix of artistic abilities.

BOBBIE BLANE
1127 Mariposa Drive
Santa Barbara, California 93110
(805) 651-2720
bblane@eclipse.net

OBJECTIVE: Graphics/Illustration Artist

QUALIFICATIONS

Develop excellent relations with clients and have satisfied even the most demanding. Specialty is personality portraiture used in advertising.

Excellent graphics and illustration training and experience. Skilled in design, layout, paste-up, lettering, story boards, and the use of darkrooms and stat cameras. Knowledge of printing procedures and experienced in preparing work for printing. Have operated printing presses and other printing-related equipment. Prepared work for black-and-white and full-color reproduction, as well as two- and three-color.

EDUCATION

Bachelor of Fine Arts, Illustration, Seymour Art Center (2003)

EMPLOYMENT

Freelance Work 2003 to Present

ARTIST – Have painted and sold 65 portraits and scenes using watercolor, graphite, pen and ink, egg tempera, and oil.

Have provided graphics and illustration for numerous projects: notebook cover, Advancetec (2007); brochure cover, Barr & Associates (2006); map and tour guide, Santa Barbara Museum of Natural History (2005); catalog and advertising design, Briton Engineering (2005); work order design, Armor Advertising (2005); logo and menu design, Silk Oyster Restaurant (2005); logo, business card design, Donner Electronics, Inc. (2004); magazine illustration, *Interpersonal Psychology* (2004); catalog design, Sunstra Inc. (2004); scratchboard portrait of deVinci for ad appearing in *Smithsonian* (2003); layout, design, illustration, *Infoworld* (2003).

Jonathan Edwards Galleries, Santa Barbara, California 2001 to Present

ART DEALER – Assist customers in purchasing art works for both personal viewing and as investments. Help customers in understanding the artist and the art piece. Have developed an excellent reputation with customers for knowledge, helpfulness, and tact.

Redecorate the gallery as new works are shown and touch up damaged pieces. Commissioned through the gallery to do portraits. Currently showing several personal works of children and scenes including *Cool Mist, High Noon, Children in the Sun*. Help design the monthly newsletter and provide calligraphy and design expertise for gallery signs.

Military Personnel

To write an empowering resume, the person transitioning from the military, like all other career changers, needs to demonstrate value and transferability of skills.

Aside from some highly specialized functions, most military positions have counterparts in the civilian world. Whatever your job, if you did it well you can demonstrate skills that are valuable on the outside.

USE YOUR STRENGTHS

Analyze your background carefully and emphasize those skills and experiences that will sell you into a civilian job. Even the most specialized military jobs are composed of generic processes and procedures. Present those activities in straightforward step-by-step terms.

For the overwhelming majority of military transitioners, your job narratives will be nearly indistinguishable from your civilian competitors. Managers will write about managing. Officers and NCOs supervise people, manage projects, coordinate events, and so on. Cooks write about cooking, IT professionals can talk computers and networking. And, of course, there are doctors, nurses, lawyers, mechanics, pilots, technicians, clerks . . . all of whom have stories to share.

Things to Avoid

As you write your resume, scrupulously avoid military jargon, also known as militarese. Let a civilian read your resume to determine if your descriptions are understandable.

USING EVALUATIONS AND LETTERS OF COMMENDATION

Quoting or paraphrasing your fitness reports, evaluations, and letters of commendation can boost the power of your resume. Praise from superiors is always beneficial. Two such entries are usually sufficient, so choose wisely.

If you wish to include additional excerpts from your fitness reports, create an Addendum. For a specific example of an addendum on a military resume, see page 190. Captain Paul Handle is a retired military person who used extensive quotes from evaluations as an addendum to his resume. After giving his name as "Captain Paul Handle" at the top of the addendum, and referring to himself as Captain Handle on the first line, he was thereafter simply able to refer to himself as Handle, even though in the fitness reports he was always identified by rank. These quotes were heavily edited, with only small portions of each evaluation included. When skipping portions of the evaluations there was no attempt to use ellipses (. . .) to signify a gap. Instead, it was all woven together to make a strong statement about Handle that allowed commanding officers to say things he couldn't say about himself. Feel free to take a copy of your addendum to interviews and present it to the employer if it seems appropriate.

If a chronological resume does not seem to be working for you, take a good look at the clustered, hybrid, or functional resumes. See page 121 for a functional resume which worked well for Jason Ryerson.

In the first sample military resume, Sanders does an excellent job convincing the reader that he is totally dedicated to safety. It is clear that the record he set for the most consecutive months without a major accident was driven by his dedication and development of a comprehensive safety program. In the second and third sample resumes, Tolson and Handle clearly sell their technical abilities.

Safety Management   **Century Schoolbook**

PETE SANDERS
237 Durham Way
Durham, California 95938
(213) 628-9714
petesanders@realfast.org

OBJECTIVE: Safety Administrator

QUALIFICATIONS

Developed a comprehensive safety program which resulted in six years without a serious accident to any of the 800 personnel.

Proven ability to set up effective, low-cost, industrial safety programs which rely heavily on instilling a safety consciousness in all employees.

Totally familiar with OSHA regulations and compliance procedures and have worked closely with OSHA inspectors.

WORK EXPERIENCE

U. S. Army 1978 to 2008

Safety Officer - 1984 to 2008

While Safety Officer at Ft. Bradley for ten years, was responsible for the safety of 800 air field personnel ranging from mechanics, machine operators, and vehicle operators to supervisors and management staff. Developed a comprehensive safety program which set a Ft. Bradley record for safety. Awarded a six-year safety award for 72 consecutive months without a major accident (over $25,000 property damage or loss of life).

Directly supervised three safety technicians and coordinated the efforts of 20 officers responsible for safety in their immediate areas. Held monthly safety seminars to promote and enhance safety awareness within each specialized group.

Made daily and weekly inspections of offices, maintenance facilities, and mechanical, paint, electrical, and machine shops, to ensure compliance with safety regulations, and performed on-the-spot corrections for minor infractions. Identified potentially hazardous practices and recommended changes.

Formulated and administered safety policies and procedures to ensure compliance with federal and state safety acts. Worked closely with OSHA inspectors and developed excellent knowledge of OSHA regulations.

Airfield Safety Officer/Pilot, Ft. Bradley, California 1994 to 2008

Airfield Safety Officer/Pilot, Munsun-ni, Korea 1988 to 1994

Airfield Safety Officer/Pilot, Ft. Lewis, Washington 1984 to 1988

Pilot, Ft. Benning, Georgia 1978 to 1984

EDUCATION

Business - California State University, 85 credits (1994-1997)

SAFETY EDUCATION

Accident Prevention, U. S. Army Agency for Aviation Safety, 640 class hours (1985).

U. S. Air Force Crash Investigators School, 320 class hours (1985).

Aviation Safety Officers Course, University of Southern California Safety Center, 960 class hours (1981). Course covered reconstructing accidents, investigative procedures, evidence acquisition, analysis of causation factors, methods of accident prevention, and gaining employee cooperation.

Electronics Technician   **Arial**

RICK TOLSON
PreComUnit USS Antrim
1102 S W Massachusetts Avenue
Seattle, Washington 98134
(206) 641-2737
rickt@baldeagle.com

QUALIFICATIONS

During ten years in Naval Communications gained broad experience in troubleshooting electronic systems. Specialty is recognizing system or circuit deterioration, isolating the fault, and restoring the system or circuit to normal operation through corrective procedures or by an alternate route. Personally construct, operate, and maintain all types of communication systems.

AREAS OF EXPERTISE

Constructing Communications Systems

Satellite Systems, High Speed Data Systems, Voice Systems, Teletype Systems, Continuous Wave.

Maintaining Communications Systems

Perform quality control and performance monitoring on audio and DC circuits.

Electronic Communications Equipment

Transmitters, transceivers, receivers, modems, multiplexers, demultiplexers, cryptogear, microwave, couplers, antennas, high level black patch panels, high and low level red patch panels, and numerous types of test equipment.

EDUCATION

Graduated Pisgah High School, Pisgah, Iowa (1998)

Navy Schools – Technical Control, Satellite Communications, Communications Supervision, Maintenance and Material Management, High Frequency Transmitters, Antenna Maintenance

WORK HISTORY

U.S. Navy August 1998 to Present

Tech Controller, 1st Class Radioman Assignments have included Naval Communications Stations, Naval Telecommunications Centers, and three Navy ships. Since 2001 have supervised numerous groups of technicians and trained them to use sophisticated communications equipment. While involved with the construction of an Arleigh Burke class guided missile destroyer, developed an extensive set of lesson plans to explain the construction of the circuits and also diagrammed all of the wiring and block schematics for this new class of ship. These two projects will save hundreds of training hours. Top Secret Security Clearance.

Electronics Maintenance   **Times New Roman**

PAUL HANDLE
3715 Pearl Ave. N.
Everett, Washington 98206
(425) 954-3721
phandle24@webstermebster.com

OBJECTIVE: Electrical, Electronic, Mechanical Maintenance

QUALIFICATIONS

Consistently rated superior in both technical expertise and supervisory ability. Constantly finding more effective methods of making repairs and reducing downtime of equipment.

EMPLOYMENT

US Navy, (Retired with rank of Captain), 10/74 to 12/08

Electronics Instructor 2/98 to 12/08. Provided comprehensive instruction to maintenance technicians and pilots covering aircraft electrical and electronic systems. Courses ranged from basic electricity and electronics to advanced solid-state theory and repair. Taught 13 separate courses averaging 80 classroom hours each. Course Manager for 5 of the 13 courses. Took difficult courses and made them more practical and easier to understand. Wrote numerous manuals and lesson guides which simplified previous courses. Students consistently outscored the students of other instructors.

Senior Supervisor 7/84 to 2/98. Supervised two shift supervisors and up to 35 technicians. Developed work schedules for personnel, scheduled maintenance, and provided overall management of a large maintenance shop. Trained new technicians and personally performed many repairs on state-of-the-art aircraft electrical systems, automatic flight control systems, and navigational systems.

Took over one command position where outdated maintenance and record keeping procedures had created serious maintenance problems. Reorganized the reporting and maintenance procedures and streamlined the operation. In 36 months the unit moved from "poor" to "excellent" in readiness reports.

Electronic Maintenance Supervisor 6/78 to 7/84. Supervised up to 20 technicians in the repair of electrical and electronic aircraft systems.

Aviation Electrician 10/74 to 6/78. Maintenance and service technician on aircraft electrical and navigational systems.

SPECIALIZED TRAINING - Navy Schools (75 courses, total of 2,400 class hours)

Advanced Electronics Courses (1977 - 2006)

Polyphase power and control systems (200 hours)

Advanced magnetic devices (240 hours)

Digital, analog, solid-state, and T.T.L. devices (400 hours)

Advanced syncro/analog/solid-state control and indicating systems (400 hours)

Hybrid solid-state inertial navigation systems (200 hours)

High resolution hydraulic/electronic T.T.L. control systems (160 hours)

Component/miniature component repair, including P.C.B. (160 hours)

Aviation Electrician Course, 1974 (320 hours)

Verdana

Captain Paul Handle

PORTIONS OF SEMIANNUAL EVALUATIONS

Captain Handle's broad qualifications and maintenance know how on F-22 A Raptor electrical systems have enabled him to become a particularly valuable instructor. He is always striving to make difficult courses easier for the students to comprehend by ensuring that proper maintenance procedures are included in his lessons. His willingness to work at any task, no matter how large or small, has contributed materially to the mission of NAMTD. His conduct sets an example worthy of emulation by other officers. He has amply demonstrated a fair and unbiased attitude, readily accepting each and every person as an individual. Handle is industrious, thorough, and accurate in this work and extremely conscientious in all duties and endeavors. He is alert and stable, displaying a creative mind. He shows great ability to develop effective procedural methods and to prepare excellently written and easily understood lesson guides. He secures the attention and respect of his students whom he guides and directs with understanding and tact. He is frequently called upon by other rate groups of this detachment to help solve technical problems in the writing of lesson guides. He attacks these problems with a cheerful and aggressive nature, seeing any problems through to a successful conclusion. Success in his work is shown by the students' final grades and their comment sheets. January 2007

Handle is intelligent, exceptionally quick to learn, with the ability to grasp pertinent details rapidly. Given broad guidelines, he accomplishes assigned tasks in an enthusiastic and exemplary manner. Handle is a conscientious and concerned instructor who demonstrates a sincere feeling of responsibility toward his students and works very hard to ensure they receive maximum benefit from his instruction. He is equally at ease before a group of juniors or seniors. He is very effective in conveying his thoughts clearly and fluently, both in casual conversation or when presenting a formal lesson. During this reporting period, he has been assigned the task of writing the avionics portion of AZF under the individualized instruction format. He willingly assisted other instructors with this new format and readily assumed the responsibility of insuring that uniformity was met by all rate groups. He spent many hours researching instructions. Acting as liaison between rate groups, he arranged and conducted meetings to achieve this goal. January 2005

Handle has been extremely instrumental in the training of the less experienced men assigned to the branch. He can be counted on to do any assigned task correctly, efficiently, and safely. January 2003

Handle is a dedicated, knowledgeable First Class Electrician who strives to ensure work is completed safely and that the proper maintenance procedures are utilized. He keeps his superiors informed of all potential trouble areas and draws on his vast experience to propose viable solutions. He leads with an easygoing, unobtrusive manner, never interfering with the personal initiative of those he supervises. He plans the work load efficiently and utilizes a smooth rapport with the men to carry out the work. January 2001

*Computer
And IT Specialists*

The computer world is a unique field that requires a special type of resume. This is especially true for programmers. Since the typical programmer stays only 24–36 months with an organization, managers usually look for someone who can step right in and do the job, based on past experience with the same hardware, language, and operating system. This is a source of great frustration for new and veteran programmers who can quickly master any new technology and only require an opportunity to prove it.

For programmers, IT specialists, and technical project managers, it is generally best to list all languages you know, as well as all hardware, operating systems, and applications you've been exposed to. Listing outdated or obsolete languages, systems, or tools can be valuable, since there are still legacy systems around and few who know how to troubleshoot them. On the resume, it is sufficient to only enter the skill . . . not the skill level. That assessment will take place at the interview. Some technical job announcements will request you rate yourself on each skill. This practice is often problematic, as the "expert" in one company might not be qualified to carry the flash drive of a "knowledgeable" user in another. Of course, prior to applying, it is a good policy to completely review the position to determine if your skill level and knowledge are in the ballpark to begin with.

Another reason to include all of your knowledge and skills is that, of them all, technical resumes are probably most frequently scanned electronically. Even though the job announcement or ad mentions a handful of key skills, showing a wider breadth of experience provides numerous value-added benefits.

The technical resume can be fairly simple to write because it consists of several distinct sections that practically write themselves. Start with Areas of Experience. Typically, it will consist of Languages, Systems, Special Programs, Computers, Conversions, and Applications. Applications can be further divided into New Applications and Maintenance. It should be easy, almost like filling in the blanks.

Because programming and other computer jobs are so project-oriented, it is often better to place more emphasis on projects than on job narratives. A

Special Projects section will work great (see Special Projects at page 76). If you will be using projects to define your skills, write a brief job narrative that presents the generic tasks and activities you perform in each. Then introduce the projects.

Since employers usually use resumes as a basis for interviews, be sure to choose projects that are most representative of your skill range and that can be expanded at the interview. Create job sketches for each project. Edit as you go, cleaning out unnecessary words and descriptions. When you are done, what should remain is a description of the mission, your role, any obstacles you overcame, and the results.

Software Engineer   **Century Schoolbook**

PERRY T. ELLISTON

23444 NE 35rd Street #A-7 Kirkland, WA 98033 (425) 555-3344 perryt@elliston.net

OBJECTIVE: Software Engineer

QUALIFICATIONS

- Strong experience in software design and development at Microsoft and a national software company.
- Proven ability to manage multiple tasks, projects, and assignments simultaneously.
- Award-winning professional with a reputation for service, satisfaction, and quality results.
- Creative troubleshooter able to quickly identify and resolve problems at all levels.
- Effective communicator able to clearly present complex information to diverse audiences.
- Demonstrated ability to quickly learn and utilize new methods, systems, and technologies.
- Track record of successfully completing tasks, projects, and assignments on time and within budget.
- Regularly commended by clients, managers, and associates for vision, follow-up, and excellence.

EDUCATION

AS – Computer Programming, Spokane Community College (2001); *Phi Theta Kappa Honor Society*

Specialized Coursework: C/C++, Java, VB, SQL

AA – General Studies, Spokane Community College (2001)

ADDITIONAL TRAINING

- Introduction to Developing with Windows Workflow Foundation & Visual Studio 2005, Microsoft (2007)
- Introduction to Developing with Windows Presentation Foundation & Visual Studio 2005, Microsoft (2006)
- Micro/Macro Economics, Financial Accounting, Norton Community College (2005–06)
- What's Wrong with this Database Management Picture?, Fabian Pascal, 352 Media Group (2003)

PROFESSIONAL HISTORY

Microsoft, Redmond, Washington 2006 to Present

SOFTWARE DESIGN ENGINEER – Global Support Automation. Perform a wide range of design and development functions on a variety of search, display, authoring, reviewing, publishing, and support tools for the Knowledge Management Team. Work both independently and in cross-functional groups.

Key Projects and Assignments

- **Visual KB:** Designed components for three versions of this document search and display tool. Created administration screen for creating and managing product specific portals (3.0); added new content types and implemented new integration features with other systems (3.1, 3.2). Planned and created technical specifications for these new features. The platform used was ASP.NET 2.0, C#, web services, XML, XPath, XSLT, XSD, and SQL Server 2005.

- **Term Compare:** Initially assigned to debug and update automated Word content style-checker tool. Conceived of and designed special functionality and several efficiency upgrades that were integrated prior to launch and commended by client for improving efficiency and productivity. Technologies used were Word API using a COM add-in, C#.

- **KAM:** Designed and implemented key components of a hierarchal product selector and worked closely with UX team to improve user friendliness of authoring experience. Improved code quality and reduced code-base by over 1,000 lines of code by refactoring and rewriting parts of the application. The platform used was ASP.NET 2.0, C#, web services, XML, XPath, XSLT, XSD, and SQL Server 2005.

- **Prescriptive Content:** Designed and developed HTML and CSS templates on new iteration for guided content on the Microsoft support site. Additionally, authored new OS/browser detection script to guide users through appropriate content. Content Managers commended templates for ease of use.

- **CX Author:** Created an original Word-based proof-of-concept authoring tool which can open and save a custom XML format. Placed a demo video and the source code on Microsoft's internal toolbox website. The platform is VSTO (Visual Studio Tools for Office), C#, .NET and Word.

- **Regex Process:** Created a text processing tool that allows user to quickly transform a document by performing multiple search and replace actions. Tool was published on Microsoft's internal toolbox website. It is built on C# and regular expressions.

Escalade Technologies, Boston, Massachusetts 1999 to 2006

TECHNICAL ARCHITECT/POST DEVELOPMENT SENIOR PROGRAMMER – 2003 to 2006. Implemented and managed two new service areas for this prominent national commercial web development company. Worked closely with clients to design functional and technical specifications for applications. Worked with customer support teams to provide add-on features and functionalities for existing websites. Consistently commended by clients and managers for exceptional knowledge, skill, vision, and leadership skills.

Prior Company Assignments

TEAM TECHNICAL DIRECTOR (2002-2003)

PROGRAMMER (1999-2002)

Company Awards

- "Block Award" for launch/technical assistance on Earthlink (2005)
- "Block Award" for work deploying new CRM system, Creative Manager (2005)
- "Block Award" for technical assistance on MS Visual Studio Express CD project (2005)
- "Elevate" Award for "going above and beyond the call of duty" (2004, 2005)
- "Create" Award for "producing an exceptionally high quality work product" (2004)

COMPUTER SKILLS

- C#; Javascript/Jscript; Regular Expression syntax; XML / XSL, XPATH, XSD; VB and VBScript
- Database design and development; SQL (Microsoft / Transact, Access, Oracle)
- FreeBSD, Redhat, and Debian Linux – installation, configuration; mail, web and database server configuration and administration. Knowledge of BASH, shell scripts, Apache, MySQL
- Systems Administration – Active Directory, networking, IIS, file servers

Computer Science   Arial

RHONDA V. COOPER

22133 148th Avenue SE #D333 Burien, Washington 98146 206-555-1335 cooper@msn.com

QUALIFICATIONS

- Successful experience in project management, business analysis, and supervision for major regional, national, and international corporations.
- Creative troubleshooter able to quickly identify and resolve problems at all levels.
- Effective communicator able to clearly present complex information to diverse audiences.
- Solid leader able to build and mentor highly motivated and productive teams.
- Track record of completing projects on time and within budget.
- Demonstrated ability to turn around underperforming and troubled projects.
- Respected by customers, managers, and other stakeholders for integrity, follow-up, and commitment to teamwork.

EDUCATION

BS – Computer Information Systems, University of Phoenix (1995)

SDLC METHODOLOGIES

Anderson's Method I, Fujitsu's Macroscope, Price Waterhouse, Microsoft Solutions Framework, Wireless Unified Process, Rational Unified Process

REPRESENTATIVE PROJECT & LEADERSHIP HISTORY

Verizon, Redmond, Washington 2004 – Present

SQA SENIOR ANALYST – 2007–Present. Verify, validate, and assess artifacts for traceability and completeness, as well as policies and procedures to ensure projects meet SDLC SOX compliance controls and release readiness. Work closely with Project Managers to assure all stakeholders have sufficient resources, budgets, schedules, and information. Gather project measurements and create scorecard through automated tool. Assist project teams with artifact reviews for approvals. Assess and report quality of control key artifacts, such as project plans, requirements, test plans, and deployment plans. Report project progress weekly and escalate non-compliance issues.

Provide coaching on Systems/Software Development Life Cycle (SDLC), Software Quality Assurance (SQA), appropriate tailoring use of the SDLC Process, effective and measured defect detection, and rigorous stakeholder involvement and approvals.

Recognized for substantially improving quality, efficiency, and IT development efforts while reducing operating costs through collaborative process improvement, measurements, analysis, process coaching, and quality planning.

TEST ANALYST – 2004–2007. Performed localization testing for two World View intranet CRM applications in multiple languages. Set daily goals with Project Manager for execution. Reviewed business requirements, updated test cases, validated data integrity, and documented product defects.

Managed Clear Quest/Issue Tracker defect triages with development and production support teams. Verified fixes through regression and User Acceptance testing to identify efficiencies/deficiencies in testing process.

Issued resolution and analysis of defect or environment problems. Instructed and mentored testers. Worked with Deployment Leads and Test Design to determine which tests needed to be run during deployment. Recognized as SME on projects and applications as well as for possessing proactive attitude toward problem solving and issue resolution.

Boeing, Seattle, Washington 2001-2004

PROCESS ARCHITECT AND MPD TEST FOCAL – 2002–2004, Everett, WA. Received *Exceptional Performance* recognition from Boeing, Everett, for supporting, redirecting, and improving statement of work management as a Process/Systems Analyst and as Testing Focal for Development and Deployment. Led integration of cross-functional processes across a multitude of stakeholder groups. Managed deliverables and communicated results with stakeholders. Advanced as MPD Test Focal for the 787 Manufacturing Process Definition Team as SOX auditing readiness champion through the SDLC processes.

FUNCTIONAL ANALYST/LEAD COORDINATOR – 2001–2002. Planned, coordinated, and executed unit, functional, integration, and user acceptance test efforts for two COTS teams (Khalix and Cognos) within the Finance Department. Collaborated with team members, internal staff, vendors, managers, business customers, and developers to define and create functional specifications through participation in initiating CMM and ISO standardizations for SOX compliance. Managed and led the QA efforts between developers, test teams, and Business Users through initiating collaborative efforts and teamwork.

Premera, Seattle, Washington 1996-2001

TEST MANAGER – 1999–2001. Promoted into this position following brief tenure as an Analyst and Test Lead. Simultaneously led two multi-state projects, supervising autonomous teams of testers, developers, and four customer support teams from throughout the Northwest. The first project included the integration and implementation of a secure four-state customer/physician communication network. The second was the relocation of the physical mainframe from Seattle to the Midwest. Both projects were successfully completed with no interruption in customer service.

Prior Experience with Premera: Software Test Analyst 1998–1999 Tester, Business Liaison Analyst 1997–1998, QA Tester & Analyst 1996–1997

COMPUTER SKILLS

Hardware: Mainframe, Client Server, Standalone PC

Software Development: Automotive, Banking, Credit Card and Bank Accounts, Healthcare, Manufacturing, Government, Retail, Telecommunications, Travel

Development Models: Object Oriented, Agile, Iterative, Waterfall, RAD, JAD, RUP

Testing: BVT – Build Verification Test, UAT – User Acceptance Testing, Benchmark, Functional, Integration, Performance, Ad Hoc, Regression, Stress, Web Internet / Intranet, Rational TestManager, Rational Test Suite, Mercury TestDirector, WebSphere

Technical: C++, C #, Java, HTML/DHTML, JavaScript/VBScript, XML, Perl/PHP, COBOL, DB2 CICS, JCL, Oracle, SQL, Unix, CORBA, AMDOCS, RDBMS, Linux, Novell, Netware, Windows NT, Sybase, IBM RS/6000

Salespeople

Salespeople typically hate to write. That fact is generally quite evident in their resumes, most of which are poorly written, poorly designed, and reveal very little of substance. Taking just four to five hours of your time to write a quality resume could net you an extra $250,000 in your lifetime earnings.

The sales resume is usually one of the easiest to write because it is so results oriented. Sales resumes rarely require extensive details about duties because sales managers already know what you do. What they care about is the bottom line. Don't tell a sales manager how hard you worked or how many phone calls you made or how many sales calls you went on. Did you sell? That's all that counts.

There are a number of ways to show results:

- Earning sales awards
- Ranking within your sales organization
- Improving the position of territory compared with other territories in the company
- Increasing sales
- Increasing profits on sales
- Increasing market share
- Setting sales records
- Introducing new products
- Restoring inactive accounts
- Pioneering a new territory
- Increasing penetration
- Maintaining a high customer retention rate
- Maintaining a high referral rate
- Building customer loyalty
- Designing effective programs

Use whatever is most appropriate. If you know your market share or can estimate it pretty closely, use that figure. Market share is effective because it provides an excellent means of comparison. During an economic boom with high inflation, the gross sales of even a mediocre salesperson will increase 5–8%

annually. To increase market share, however, means you have taken business away from competitors and increased your share of the pie. It means you're doing something right.

Showing increases in market share is great, but companies rarely provide that territory-by-territory information. So use whatever you do have.

Feel free to use a combination of numbers if you have them. Increases in revenue, dollars, margin, market share, etc. Provide a context that includes your ranking in the district, region, and nationally, whichever is most impressive. If your gains were modest due to an industry slowdown or economic slump, did you exceed others in production? What about the industry average during that time? What about severe economic times? Did you maintain your customer base while others were losing theirs?

The example below contains most of the ways to show success in sales. Each job narrative speaks to one of those achievements, including improving the territorial ranking, increasing market share, receiving numerous monthly sales awards, and percentage increases.

B & N Machinery, Tempe, Arizona 6/05 to Present

Marketing Representative - Developed and implemented marketing strategies that increased heavy equipment sales to the construction industry in Arizona. Took the territory from 7th (out of 8) in the company to 2nd during the first 36 months.

John Deere, Phoenix, Arizona 10/01 to 6/05

District Representative - Assisted 26 dealers in Arizona and New Mexico in marketing John Deere products. Set up five new dealers and developed their sales, parts, and service departments. Moved seven dealers from near bankruptcy to very strong financial positions. Increased market share 33%.

Gerald BMW, Phoenix, Arizona 1/99 to 10/01

Salesman - Each year won the Professional Sales Counselor award for sales excellence. Out of a sales force of 12, was salesperson of the month 8 times in 34 months.

PointSystems, Trenton, New Jersey 1/97 to 1/99

Sales Representative - Sold a full line of point-of-sale equipment to local and regional chains. In two years increased territorial sales 44%.

Olivetti Corporation, Trenton, New Jersey 1/93 to 12/96

Sales Representative - Sold cash registers, self-service terminals, and printers throughout metropolitan Trenton. Worked closely with store managers and sales staffs and provided excellent training in selling Olivetti products. Ranked 2nd in sales in 1996 out of a regional sales force of 18.

Always save your sales reports. Whenever you start a new position, get data on the condition of the territory prior to your arrival. If you don't have the actual numbers, provide good-faith estimates, that you are prepared to explain.

Medical Sales   **Georgia**

ERIN B. ANDERSON

2199 West Drive

Las Vegas Nevada 89115

(702) 555-8115

ebanderson@columbia.com

OBJECTIVE: Medical Device Sales

QUALIFICATIONS

- Successful blend of training and experience in marketing, sales, and the medical field.
- Proven ability to develop new business and expand existing accounts.
- Demonstrated ability to identify, contact, and deliver presentations to key decision makers.
- Regularly selected for special assignments to assist underperforming sales teams.
- Track record of quickly learning new methods, systems, technologies, and products.
- Respected by customers, employers, and associates for dedication, follow-up, and excellence.

EDUCATION

B.S. – Business & Communication, Arizona State University (2005)

A.A. – Licensed Practical Nurse, Western Nevada Community College (2002)

SALES TRAINING

Three-week Comprehensive Sales Training Program, Yellow Ads USA
> Key Modules: Prospecting, Cold Calling, Creating Effective Ads, Developing Sales Proposals, Mock Sales Appointments, Needs Analysis, Sales Presentations, Negotiating, Closing, Follow-up (2005)

SALES EXPERIENCE

Yellow Ads USA, Las Vegas, Nevada 2005 to Present

SALES REP-MEDIA CONSULTANT – Introduced Yellow Ads to the Greater Las Vegas Area. Yellow Book had recently purchased the existing Transwestern World Pages, which had demonstrated dramatic failures in customer service and fulfillment, leaving a hostile customer base.

Visited existing customers throughout the metropolitan area to reclaim existing business and prospected for new accounts. As Yellow Ads was not yet in the market, primarily sold a concept, utilizing existing editions from other markets. Was additionally tasked with managing artwork on existing accounts but still was in the top one-third in production the first year. Was a major contributor in the team winning *Most Dollars Sold* for the premier edition.

Successful Las Vegas experience led to selection to assist the underperforming Reno sales team to achieve its goals. Successfully focused on reclaiming canceled accounts.

Expanded skills and responsibilities in order to market new offerings such as pay-per-click advertising for all major search engines including Google, Yahoo, and MSN, as well as for yellowbook.com. Currently the fourth top producer among 35 representatives.

MEDICAL EXPERIENCE

Methodist Hospital, Las Vegas, Nevada 2002 to 2004

LPN – Worked ICU and Surgical and gained experience with many types of medical equipment.

Sales Representative   Tahoma

DANIELLE R. BIDEN
1850 Elm Drive
Santa Rosa California 95405
(707) 555-9889
drb@homenet.com

OBJECTIVE: Sales Representative

QUALIFICATIONS

- Successful experience in creating, implementing, and managing domestic and international marketing and sales programs.
- Customer-oriented professional with a reputation for service and satisfaction.
- Track record of substantially increasing sales, revenues, and market share.
- Effective leader able to build highly motivated, productive, and diverse sales teams.
- Proven ability to develop strong relationships with customers, distributors, and marketing representatives.

EDUCATION & TRAINING

Business Studies, University of San Francisco (1998–2002)

PROFESSIONAL HISTORY

NATIONAL COMPONENT TECHNOLOGY, INC., SANTA CRUZ, CALIFORNIA 2005 TO PRESENT

NATIONAL SALES MANAGER – Developed the domestic and international outside sales programs of this international hi-tech product manufacturer. Created a network of 14 regional representatives and numerous worldwide distributors. Recruited, trained, and coached new representatives. Designed and created collateral, marketing, and sales materials which effectively professionalized the company's image.

Developed and implemented sales and marketing strategies, policies, and procedures. Worked closely with management and sales team to develop realistic goals and forecasts. Implemented company's first comprehensive quality control checklist and immediate customer service program, which dramatically improved customer satisfaction by reducing operating problems and returns. In three years took sales from $1.2 million to $8.1 million.

DALMAN CORPORATION, SANTA ROSA 2002 TO 2005

PRINCIPAL/SALES MANAGER – Directed all sales and marketing activities of this property acquisition and management company. Performed extensive research to identify both prospective properties and buyers throughout the West Coast. Key buyers included ARCO, Albertson's, and Value Village. Developed marketing and sales campaigns for various properties in cooperation with owners. Coordinated sales effort with local business and governmental agencies to successfully lease the Lacey Corporate Center.

Managed six downtown office buildings tenanted by public and private businesses. Maintained less than 3% vacancy while consistently achieving market value rents.

ADDITIONAL EXPERIENCE

CORPORATE PROPERTY MARKETING MANAGER, Prudential Properties, San Jose, CA (1999–2002)
ASSISTANT PROPERTY MANAGER, Prudential Properties, San Jose, CA (1997–1999)

Sales Representative   Cambria

PAUL KIRSTEN

525 Bates S.W.
Beaverton, Oregon 97006
(503) 962-0013
paulakirsten@kellyrocks.com

OBJECTIVE: Sales Representative

EMPLOYMENT

Prescal & Hemsted Wire Rope Company, Beaverton, Oregon 3/01–Present

Sales Representative (2/04–Present). Sell wire rope through 18 distributors and through direct sales to OEM accounts, covering Oregon, Washington, and Alaska.

Key Accomplishments

- Between 2004 and 2008, built sales from $652,000 to $1,404,000.
- Have trained all inside sales staff in effective sales techniques.

Inside Sales Manager/Office Manager (3/01–2/04). Handled all inside sales, purchasing, inventory control, and traffic. Supervised the warehouse and shipping/receiving operations.

Key Accomplishments

- Reorganized the office and warehousing procedures which increased on-time deliveries and customer satisfaction.
- Coordinated a switch from a manual to a computerized inventory control and billing system. Increased productivity 32% and decreased errors 21%.
- Regional sales manager attributed most of the 43% sales increase between 2001 and 2004 to the new level of professionalism at the order desk.

Peterson Manufacturing Company, Coos Bay, Oregon 2/92–3/01

Sales Representative (3/96–3/01). Sold replacement parts for the barkers and chippers manufactured by Peterson, covering Oregon, Washington, Idaho, and Montana.

Key Accomplishment

- Increased sales of replacement parts 16%.

Inside Sales (2/94–3/96). Called on customers of Peterson products and sold replacement parts. Worked closely with purchasers of new machines to ensure an adequate inventory of the parts most likely to need replacing.

Key Accomplishment

- Increased sales of replacement parts to existing customers by 18%.

Expediter (2/92–2/94). Responsible for expediting, scheduling, and inventory control in the manufacturing of custom-made wood barkers and chippers.

Key Accomplishment

- Significantly increased total production and on-time deliveries.

EDUCATION

B.S. - History, University of Oregon (1992)

Sales Manager   **Century Gothic**

WARREN DRISCOL
927 Honeycut Drive
Atlanta, Georgia 30032
(404) 527-6819
warrend@kirklandusa.net

OBJECTIVE: Sales/Marketing Management

QUALIFICATIONS

Strong Sales and Marketing background. Significantly increased territorial market share in each position held, with increases ranging from 45–330%.

EDUCATION

B.S. - Forest Engineering, University of Georgia (1982)

EMPLOYMENT

Ubasco Machinery Company, Atlanta, Georgia 8/99 to Present

FOREST PRODUCTS SALES MANAGER - As Ubasco's first Forest Products Sales Manager, responsible for selling to key accounts and for training the sales staff in methods of increasing sales of earth-moving equipment to forestry related companies. Perform extensive market research to target sales and identify sales potential. Gross profit has been increased from 14% to 18% and unit sales have increased an average of 16% per year.

John Deere Tractor Company 7/82 to 8/99

FOREST PRODUCTS SALES REPRESENTATIVE, Atlanta, Georgia 8/94 to 8/99. Developed and implemented marketing strategies to increase sales to the forest industry through 24 Southeastern John Deere dealers. Worked closely with the dealers and trained their salespeople to sell earth-moving equipment to the forest industry. Created a special training program which covered sales techniques and forestry applications of John Deere equipment. Increased net sales 148% and market share from 6% to 20% between 1994 and 1999.

DISTRICT REPRESENTATIVE, Bangkok, Thailand 11/91 to 8/94. Responsible for increasing sales and service levels among all dealers in India, Sri Lanka, Bangladesh, Thailand, Taiwan, South Korea, and the Philippines. Identified new market areas, developed marketing strategies for dealers, and trained sales forces in effective sales techniques. Increased John Deere's market share from 14% to 21%.

PRODUCT/MARKET REP, Hong Kong 2/85 to 11/91. Conducted market studies and consulted with dealers on applications and modifications of John Deere equipment. Developed an extensive market study on the uses of wheel loaders in Asia and concluded a huge untapped market existed for wheel loaders to replace track-driven loaders. Made sales calls with dealers throughout Asia as they visited customers. Businesses immediately switched to wheel loaders. Increased sales of wheel loaders an average of 76% each year between 1985 and 1991 and captured over 60% of that market.

MARKET REP, Spokane, Washington 7/82 to 2/85. Acted as machinery application consultant to dealers. Studied mill and mining operations and made recommendations for the most appropriate John Deere equipment.

Career Changers

*And the day came when the risk to remain tight in a bud was
more painful than the risk it took to blossom.* —Unknown

Career changers come in two flavors: those who move by design and
others who are moved by circumstance. The former are often seeking
greater job satisfaction and a lifestyle more in tune with their values.
The latter are those who have been displaced by a shifting economy, technologi-
cal environment, and outsourcing. Others find they can no longer physically or
emotionally handle the rigors of their current jobs.

Whatever the reason, career changers face major challenges in preparing
their resumes.

The first order of business when preparing your resume for the new career is
to identify every experience related to that line of work, and then get it into the
resume. The Qualifications section is often an excellent place to do this.

When you start describing your employment, you have two main goals:
(1) to show you were successful at what you did; and (2) to emphasize any
parts of your jobs that are related to your current objective. Your successes are
important. Employers are dubious enough about hiring a career changer; they
certainly want a person with a proven record of success. Essentially you'll be
saying through your resume, "I've been successful in the past, and I'll be successful for you, too."

Emphasizing related experience is important. There is no law of propor-
tionality in resume writing. That is, even if the bulk of your responsibilities was
in administration but you actively participated in sales, and you want to move
into sales, you do not have to stress the administrative side. Quickly describe
that side of the job and move into sales as convincingly as you can without
embellishment.

Career changers tend to have longer Qualifications sections than those who
have years of experience in the same field. Career changers sometimes do better
with a hybrid, functional, or clustered resume. Read pages 117 to 139 for a
full explanation and several examples. Rosalyn (on page 205) used a lengthy

203

qualifications section very effectively. The points made in Qualifications could not have been adequately made in the Employment section. Notice how she emphasized related training and development experience.

Paula does everything possible to show she is sales oriented and that her efforts have consistently increased revenue. Although she has never held a job labeled "Sales Representative," it is very easy to picture her being successful in sales.

Training and Development   **Times New Roman**

ROSALYN RODRIQUEZ

2315 Dixie Avenue Charleston, South Carolina 29406
(803) 976-4204   roz@bahston.com

OBJECTIVE: Position in Training and Development

QUALIFICATIONS

Broad background in planning and developing programs. Skilled in determining program needs through task analysis. Have planned and organized numerous programs, including the Council for Exceptional Children 2006 State Conference.

Extensive knowledge and experience in determining needs, setting behavioral and learning objectives, and developing assessment tools. M.A. in Curriculum and Program Development.

Expertise in selecting appropriate teaching techniques to match the audience. Quickly establish rapport with groups.

Outstanding record in education. Received ratings of excellent to outstanding in all evaluations.

Evaluated and selected speakers and consultants for educational topics and conventions.

Extensive budgetary and purchasing experience with instructional materials.

Excellent writer. Wrote three successful grant proposals and published two articles on curriculum development for the *Journal of Education*.

Extensive knowledge of statistics and research methodologies for determining effectiveness of programs.

Strong abilities in performing and graphics arts. Directed, stage-managed, and designed sets and costumes for numerous theatrical productions.

Designed and produced newsletters, manuals, and brochures using desktop publishing.

Extensive experience writing, producing, and editing video programs.

EDUCATION

M.A. - Curriculum and Instruction, University of South Carolina (1991)

B.A. - Art, Arkansas State Teachers College (1985)

EMPLOYMENT

Teacher, Charleston Public Schools, Charleston, South Carolina 9/92 to Present

Teacher, Greenville Public Schools, Greenville, South Carolina 9/85 to 9/92

ASSOCIATIONS

Member - American Society for Training and Development 2002–Present

Member - Council for Exceptional Children 1995–Present; State Bylaws Chairperson 2005 to Present; Chapter President 2003; Chapter Vice President 2002

Entry-level Sales   Verdana

PAULA PROJASKA

1247 Morton Drive
Ottawa, Ontario K1Z 1A6
(613) 743-1726
paulap@polkadot.com

JOB OBJECTIVE: Sales

QUALIFICATIONS

Proven ability to sell products and services. Quickly develop product knowledge and relate very well to people at all levels.

EDUCATION

B.A. - Public Relations, Trent University (1994)

EMPLOYMENT

Four Winds Hotel, Ottawa, Ontario 1995–Present

Executive Assistant (2002–Present). Implemented numerous training and staff development programs which have raised guest service to the highest level found in Ottawa. Increased communication and cooperation between departments and implemented an effective cross-training program. Since 2004 hotel revenue has increased an average of 14% per year. Work closely with the Chamber of Commerce and perform PR functions with other local businesses and organizations.

Food Services Coordinator (1997–2002). Introduced new food and room services which increased room revenue 11% per year and food/beverage revenue 12% per year. Supervised a staff of 60.

Assistant Food Services Coordinator (1995–1997). Coordinated all food services, including room service, coffee shop, dining room, lounge, and meeting rooms. Supervised a staff of 20. Designed a new training program which instilled more professionalism in the staff. Annual turnover was cut from 20% to 5%. As service improved, room revenue and food and beverage revenue each increased 40% in two years.

Managers/Supervisors

Managers are hired to get fired. — BASEBALL MAXIM

Providing results in a resume is important for everyone, but is especially critical for managers. Being a manager is unique in that most of your accomplishments come through the efforts of others.

If you have not done so already, start quantifying your results when they occur.

Be aware of your mission, your starting point, and results. If you decreased rejects, what was the existing level and where did you bring it to? If you improved customer satisfaction, where was it when you took over?

It often helps to indicate the size of your department, the number of direct reports, and the dollar value of your department's budget, but include this information only if you feel it will help sell you.

See pages 40 to 52 for more on results.

Do not get caught in the trap of thinking that your results must be super impressive. If rejects are reduced from 2.1% to 1.9%, that is still a 10% decrease and is very significant. Use your results to show that wherever you are, you constantly look for ways to improve your operations.

Retail Manager   **Times New Roman**

LINDA V. MAILER

2700 Boulevard Road Apt D-16, Wilmington, Delaware 19805   (406) 256-8691
mailerlv@msn.com

QUALIFICATIONS

- Successful experience building and managing large teams and sales organizations.
- Customer-oriented professional with a reputation for service, satisfaction, and results.
- Proven ability to manage multiple tasks, projects, and assignments simultaneously.
- Creative troubleshooter able to quickly identify and resolve problems at all levels.
- Solid leader able to build, mentor, and develop highly motivated, productive, and loyal teams.
- Regularly selected as a member of the opening management team for new stores.
- Recognized as a major contributor in leading one store from $12 million to $60 million in annual revenue with the second highest volume in a four-state region.

PROFESSIONAL HISTORY

Kmart Corporation 1984 to 2007

EXECUTIVE/ASSISTANT STORE MANAGER – Wilmington, DE, 1995 to 2007. Selected as a member of the management team that opened what became the second highest volume Kmart store in a four-state region. Recruited, trained, and supervised a 20 department managers and 200-member sales and service team. Directed the installation of fixtures and merchandising plans. Implemented policies and procedures. Delivered presentations throughout the community introducing Kmart to the community. Directly managed guest services, cashiering, apparel, and food services. Grand Opening exceeded all corporate expectations and goals.

Developed and administered budgets for each department. Monitored performances to assure maximum expense control while not sacrificing service and quality. Trained each department head in effective management techniques, payroll, and cost control.

As Assistant Manager, directed storewide operations on a regular and as-needed basis. These included safety, security, financial management, operations, human resources, delivery schedules, and community relations. Regarded by Store Manager as "Right Hand Person."

Success of all-around performance led to increased responsibilities and the leadership of all operations for 55,000 non-apparel items ranging from electronics, entertainment, and toys to perishables, automotive products, pharmacy, household goods, and seasonal product lines.

Credited as a major contributor in the store growing from $12 million to $60 million in annual revenue.

Prior Target Assignments

EXECUTIVE, Trenton, NJ (1991–95)
OPERATIONS MANAGER, Trenton, NJ (1989–90)
OPENING EXECUTIVE/ASSISTANT MANAGER, Harrisburg, PA (1988–89)
CUSTOMER SERVICE MANAGER, Albany, NY (1986–87)
ASSISTANT RECEIVING MANAGER, Erie, PA (1985–86)
RECEIVING ASSISTANT, Erie, PA (1984-85)

EDUCATION

Liberal Arts Studies – Pennsylvania State University (1982–84)

Chief Financial Officer

Arial

ALISHA T. GREER, CPA

1012 N Boulevard #1403 Tampa Florida 33607   (813) 555-7805   aliashg@comcast.net

OBJECTIVE: Chief Financial Officer

QUALIFICATIONS

- Successful experience building and managing financial reporting systems in the public and nonprofit sectors.
- Proven ability to manage multiple tasks, projects, and assignments simultaneously.
- Creative troubleshooter able to quickly identify and resolve problems at all levels.
- Solid leader able to build, mentor, and develop highly motivated, productive, and loyal teams.
- History of improving efficiency and productivity to respond to rapid growth without corresponding administrative expense.

PROFESSIONAL HISTORY

Southeastern Credit Union, Tampa, Florida 2004 to Present

CONTROLLER – 2006 to Present. Manage a 14-member accounting team in assuring accurate and timely financial reporting for one of the region's largest credit unions. Report directly to CFO. Oversee all external financial and regulatory reporting for the Credit Union and CUSO affiliations. Drive development of organization's financial plan for presentation to senior management. Ensure accounting and reporting systems are in place, designed, and functioning to support the operations of the Credit Union. Coordinate key elements of CPA and regulatory audit processes. Respected by management and peers for vision, integrity, and follow through.

Special Achievements

- Created a system to enable various departments to better control monthly expense reports and facilitate annual budgeting and forecasting processes.
- Improved department productivity to accommodate 52% organizational staff growth without expanding personnel count.
- Increased department's Leadership Index from 94 to 97 (2007).
- Increased department's Workgroup Index from 85 to 91 (2007).

Special Committees and Assignments

- Asset Liability Management Committee
- 401(k) and Pension Investment Review Committees

ACCOUNTING MANAGER – 2004 to 2006. Managed the team that led the $500,000 conversion project from a legacy DOS-based financial system to PeopleSoft. Project was completed on time, within budget, and with zero interruption in service.

ADDITIONAL EXPERIENCE

AUDITOR, Floridian Equity Corporation Tampa, FL (2002-2004)
SENIOR FINANCIAL ACCOUNTANT, NY Life Capital Corporation, Miami, FL (1999-2002)
AUDITOR/SENIOR AUDITOR, Arthur Anderson & Associates, Miami, FL (1995-1999)

EDUCATION

BS – Accounting, Florida State University (1995)

Administrative Personnel

As an office worker your primary responsibility is to demonstrate that you possess strong office skills, that you are hard working and efficient, that you are easy to work with, that you are reliable and resourceful, that you can take on greater responsibility, and that you look for ways to improve office operations.

Either in the Qualifications section of the resume or in a section called Office Skills, you can list the types of computers you have used, knowledge of operating systems such as Windows, and experience with various applications software such as Word, Excel, SAP, and others.

Demonstrating that you are a hard worker, efficient, and easy to work with is usually best covered in the Qualifications section and in the cover letter. If you really feel you have these qualities, simply tell the reader through the resume and cover letter. Another excellent way to sell these qualities is to show that you are a results-oriented person. By selling your results you will sell the fact that you are efficient and easy to work with.

Do not feel that you must list every single duty that you had on each job. We've seen clerical resumes that were unreadable because they simply consisted of a long, boring list of duties. You may have had a duty that you performed in each of your last six jobs, but in the resume you may choose to include that duty only in your earliest jobs or only in your most recent, in order to show you have experience in that area. Of course, with a key skill you would list it in any job where you used it.

As with any resume, the key is to demonstrate quality and results. Since office performance isn't usually measured in quantifiable figures, applicants often tell us that they have no results to speak to.

Au contraire!

Everyone has results. If you cannot quantify, qualify! What is your attendance record? Do you consistently produce quality work on time? Are you the one selected for special projects and the most complex assignments? Do you get commendations from other staff, departments, and customers for going the extra mile? Have you heard the words "couldn't have done it without you" from others? How about your evaluations? Quote and paraphrase the good stuff.

Of course, if you have improved a procedure that increased productivity, go with it! Perhaps you designed a form that streamlined the invoicing process and reduced receivables. Or you found a new vendor and saved the company money on office supplies. The amount may not be all that impressive but the example of your initiative is.

Results don't have to be huge to make an impact on an employer. The mere fact that you made contributions is the compelling factor. Dedication, competence, initiative, creativity, and integrity are all traits you can present as your contributions to the organization.

Administrative   **Lucida Bright**

SANDRA L. DENIS
139 Line Road SW
Atlanta, Georgia 30331
(404) 555-6543
sdenis@aol.com

QUALIFICATIONS

- Strong education in medical records technology combined with excellent administrative experience.
- Quality-oriented professional with a reputation for dependability, flexibility, and accuracy.
- Proven ability to coordinate multiple tasks simultaneously.
- Work effectively both independently and as part of a team.
- Accurately maintain and process detailed files and records.
- Consistently recognized as a valuable and contributing team member in all situations.

EDUCATION

AS – Health Information Technology, Atlanta Technical College (2004)
<u>Specialized Coursework</u>: Business Computer Applications, Medical Terminology, Quality Improvement, Transcription, Legal Aspects of Healthcare, ICD9 Coding, CPT Coding

ADDITIONAL TRAINING

Ambulatory Records, SHIMA (2006)
Arthroscopic Procedures/Plastic Repair Procedures, SHIMA, 7 hours (2005)
HIPAA, GDOL (2004)

PROFESSIONAL HISTORY

Atlanta Medical Center, Records Division, Atlanta, Georgia 2004 to Present

<u>RECORDS TECHNICIAN</u> – Process patient release of information requests and perform a variety of other activities for this busy medical records section. Review requests for accuracy, completeness, and adherence to legal requirements. Assist other staff as necessary in all areas including chart retrieval and distribution, data entry, and general administrative duties. Recognized for dependability, flexibility, and attention to detail.

Key Manufacturing, Valdosta, Georgia 1990 to 2004

<u>ACCOUNTING COORDINATOR</u> – Managed all financial activities of this specialty manufacturing company. Maintained detailed accounting, inventory, and customer records. Provided timely and accurate customer service. Assured all records were complete and within contract specifications. Processed all receivables and payables. Prepared quarterly tax reports and detailed government compliance statements. Increased administrative capacity to match rapid company growth without the need for additional staff.

COMPUTER SKILLS

Word, Excel, Access, Health Data Management

AFFILIATIONS

- Georgia Health Information Management Association
- American Health Information Management Association

Government Employees

As with any resume, demonstrating results will help you get more interviews and more job offers. Your goal should be to demonstrate that you design and implement successful, cost-effective programs, or that you are highly skilled at your work. Quantify your results whenever possible. Do your best to show the before and after. If you were head of a program to improve air quality in a metropolitan region you should be able to provide accurate figures. If you worked with a summer youth program you might be able to indicate that you obtained more private sector jobs for youths than in previous years.

In addition to specific results, you should look for ways to demonstrate that you work well with the public. Show that you have a real feel for public relations, that you can sense in advance when there will be a public outcry over a new policy, and that you can defuse tense situations.

If your job will involve you with elected officials or citizen boards, demonstrate that you know how to deal with them. Show that you make persuasive recommendations and that your recommendations are usually approved. Show that you work well with community groups to gain their support for your programs, but that you are not afraid to stand up to them when necessary.

If your work is more in the planning area, describe your overall responsibilities and then mention key projects by name that you were involved with. Also, provide key information so the reader will understand the size and scope of the project/program, as well as the complexity.

Government Administrator   Verdana

TONYA P. LINDEN

725 Charles Street Boston, Massachusetts 02114 (617) 752-7337 tpl17@msn.com

QUALIFICATIONS

- Successful experience in management of public agencies, coordinating statewide programs, and administering multi-million dollar budgets.
- Proven ability to manage multiple tasks, projects, and assignments simultaneously.
- Skilled administrator able to develop and effectively manage large budgets while maintaining cost controls.
- Effective leader able to build and mentor highly motivated, productive, and loyal teams.
- History of developing community, industry, and government consensus on policy proposals and implementation issues.
- Recognized for upgrading financial procedures resulting in greater accountability and substantially improved audits.

EDUCATION

JD – Boston University School of Law (1990)

MA – Business/Health Care Administration, University of Illinois (1987)

BBA – Management/Marketing, University of Illinois (1985)

PROFESSIONAL HISTORY

Department of Health & Human Services, Boston, Massachusetts 1995 to Present

CHIEF ADMINISTRATOR – Family Health Division, 2000 to present. Direct all operations of this major division with over 350 employees and a $550 million annual budget. Report directly to Assistant Secretary of Family Health. Oversee such vital state programs as immunization; maternal health; child, adolescent and infant health; genetics, breast and cervical cancer, family planning, tobacco prevention/control; HIV and AIDS prevention. Mentor programs on policy, legislative and budget development.

Represent division to other departments and agencies as well as to the public. Manage budget development and implementation process. Recognized for upgrading accountability in financial reporting of all programs resulting in dramatically improved audit results.

Special Assignments & Projects:

- Serve on agency management team, digital government steering committee, and represent management on union negotiating team.
- Served as facilitator of statewide HIV Prevention Study Committee, which brought together public agencies, community-based organizations, academia, and legislators with divergent interests. Many of the committee's final recommendations have been implemented (2001).

TONYA P. LINDEN – Page Two

EXECUTIVE DIRECTOR – Health Systems Quality Assurance Division, 1998 to 2000. Supervised 16-member staff that provided licensure and discipline services to medical and mental health practitioners. Supervised an additional eight legal staff members who provide legal services to over 30 health care professions. Developed and managed a budget of $2.7 million.

Served on management team that developed policies on such diverse topics as prescribing for chronic pain, nurse delegation, physician-assisted suicide, self-directed care, medical marijuana, and criminal background checks for health care practitioners.

Conducted community forums across the state to develop policies for the implementation of newly adopted laws regulating Chemical Dependency Professionals. Established substantial community support, resulting in the rules being adopted with no opposing testimony at the final hearing.

LEAD STAFF ATTORNEY – Health Systems Compliance Division, 1995 to 1998. Supervised work of six legal staff members. Reviewed investigative reports, prepared legal analyses of cases, and recommended appropriate case disposition/action. Drafted proposed formal disciplinary orders for presentation to numerous boards and commissions.

As the first staff attorney to Dental Compliance Commission cleaned up a backlog of 165 cases and demonstrated the value of in-house counsel. Reduced the number of costly contested hearings from 70% to 15%, eliminating costly utilization of Attorney General's personnel and resources.

ADDITIONAL EXPERIENCE

ASSISTANT ATTORNEY GENERAL, Office of the Attorney General, Boston, MA (1992–1995)

ASSISTANT GOVERNMENTAL AFFAIRS LIAISON, Cambridge Public School District (1990–1992)

LICENSE

- Massachusetts Bar Association; Legislative, Equality in Practice, and Civil Rights Committees

SPECIAL AWARDS/RECOGNITION/COMMUNITY SERVICE

- Bunker Hill Community College Board of Trustees (1998–present)
- Suffolk County American Leadership Forum, Board of Directors (2003–present)
- Boston University School of Law Board of Governors (2002–present)
- American Civil Liberties Union, Civil Libertarian Award (2003)
- City of Boston Urban Policy Committee (1996–1998)

Government   Century Schoolbook

——————— LAURA DONOHUE ———————

401 Eastman   West Arlington Heights, Illinois 60015   (312) 871-2652
laurad@starwave.com

QUALIFICATIONS

Excellent organizational ability. Develop new systems that increase productivity and
quality of work.

Broad speaking experience. Frequently speak to groups of 100–500 people. Received a
standing ovation at an annual convention for making a difficult subject easily understood.

Strong public relations experience. Work effectively with organizations and individuals
while solving problems and explaining policies. Quickly gain the respect of all parties.

EDUCATION

Graduated - Colville High School, Colville, Washington (1990)

EMPLOYMENT

United States Railroad Retirement Board, Chicago, Illinois 11/96–Present

Contract Representative - 11/04–Present. Explain and interpret complex laws and
regulations related to retirement, disability, and unemployment benefits. Interview
claimants and obtain necessary documents. Substantiate evidence and determine
eligibility and amount of benefits.

Provide training sessions for union and management groups to explain changes
in regulations. Successfully introduced a group interview procedure for explaining
unemployment compensation when claims rose from 250 to 2,100 per month. Developed
numerous systems which decreased backlog and increased staff morale.

Unemployment Claims Examiner - 11/96–11/04. Interviewed claimants and
former employers to determine eligibility for benefits. Monitored job finding efforts of
claimants and assisted in their obtaining new positions. Developed a new system for
coding claims and won the Region Accuracy Award in 2002.

Social Security Administration, Chicago, Illinois 6/90–11/96

Service Representative - 4/94–11/96 Provided assistance and technical information
about Social Security, Medicare, and Supplemental Security Income to beneficiaries
and the general public. Resolved problems, untangled red tape, and helped make the
system work. Received a cash bonus award for suggesting improvements in Social
Security forms.

Secretary - 6/90–4/94. Ran the office efficiently, answered correspondence, and
compiled statistical reports.

Personnel Administrator   **Century Gothic**

CHARLES PARSONS

1226 3rd Avenue N.W.   Minnetonka, Minnesota 55343
(612) 378-5162   cparsons@byte.com

QUALIFICATIONS

Over twenty years of progressively responsible experience in all areas of Human Resources Management. Highly successful in planning, organizing, and coordinating a wide variety of Human Resources Development programs.

EDUCATION

M.P.A. - Public Administration, Tufts University (1988)

B.A. - History, Western Kentucky University (1985)

EMPLOYMENT HISTORY

Personnel Management Advisor

U.S. Office of Personnel Management, Minneapolis, Minnesota   7/05 to Present

Responsible for promoting Human Resources Management practices with state and local governmental organizations in Minnesota, Iowa, and Wisconsin. Plan, design, and implement Human Resources systems including policies, procedures, job evaluation, compensation, benefits, recruitment, selection, employee relations, employee development, management information systems, organizational development, and safety.

As project manager, develop and adhere to budgets, supervise and train staff, and coordinate activities with client agencies. Most recommendations have been adopted, with agencies experiencing improved quality of service, increased morale, and greater productivity.

Classification and Pay Manager

Hennepin County, Minneapolis, Minnesota   9/98 to 7/05

Developed, implemented, and directed the classification and pay function for a totally new, comprehensive personnel management system. Unit became a highly respected part of the County Office of Personnel. Designed and developed the County's first uniform pay system. Promoted, planned, and coordinated a Personnel Management Information System which significantly increased the amount of personnel data available for management decisions. Improved service delivery 35% by instituting a personnel generalist approach.

Supervisor of Classification and Pay

State of Minnesota Merit Employment, St. Paul, Minnesota   7/95 to 9/98

Selected, trained, and supervised the professional staff that maintained and improved the State classification and pay systems. Developed improved classification and pay policies.

Administrative Consultant

Public Administration Service, Chicago, Illinois   8/88 to 7/95

Provided administrative, organizational, and personnel management consultative services to state and local governments nationwide for this highly respected, nonprofit consulting organization established in 1933.

Contract Administrator   **Times New Roman**

Doreen Caffey
13206 127th N.E.
Kirkland, Washington 98034
(425) 821-4454   dcaffey@lucyinthesky.com

OBJECTIVE: Contract Administrator

QUALIFICATIONS

Broad contract administration experience, covering solicitation preparation and advertisement, contract awards, claim settlements, negotiation of changes, and terminations.

Strong ability to recognize potential problems, research the problem, and propose solutions or alternatives.

EDUCATION

B.S. - Sociology, Oral Roberts University (1998)

EMPLOYMENT

U.S. Forest Service, Seattle, Washington, 7/98 to Present

Contract Administrator - 6/05 to Present

Responsible for preparation of solicitations for bid, advertising solicitation, and opening and awarding contracts. Handle complete contract administration including negotiation of changes, settlement of claims, suspension of contracts, ensuring timely contract completion, and termination of contracts for default and convenience of the Government.

- Developed procedures which have reduced the time necessary to let a contract from 90 to 72 days.
- Work with corporate sureties in takeover agreements and claims against bid, performance, and payment bonds.
- Research previous contract law interpretations and work closely with the Office of General Counsel when contract appears or bid protests have been docketed.

Voucher Examiner - 7/98 to 6/05

Made payment to vendors for supplies and services. Prepared monthly report of obligations (accounts payable).

- As Property Accounting Clerk for the forest, converted a massive manual property accounting system to a computer system thereby increasing accuracy and substantially reducing maintenance costs.
- Worked with accountant and budget analyst in preparation of the General Administration budget for the forest.

Teachers

As with many professions, teachers can all look alike in their resumes. After all, don't teachers stand in front of a classroom and . . . teach? Or is there more? What are you teaching? Who are you teaching it to? What are the demographics of your school or region? Are there special issues of poverty or a transient student population? Have you developed unique tools and materials to better educate these students? Have you been able to gear your lessons to the different learning styles of the pupils? Have you been successful? How do you know? Are your students better prepared for the next grade when they leave your class? Do you encourage family involvement through regular conferences and status reports?

Many teachers impact their schools through various committees such as curriculum development and textbook selection. Others serve on advisory committees in such areas as student discipline, after-school activities, and facilities management. Teachers often participate in district committees and task forces. Some become active with non-educational organizations. All are valid for the resume.

Education programs vary from university to university and department to department. There are a plethora of specialized programs for both undergrads and post-grad students. Everything from Computers in the Classroom to the updated focus on the three R's. A Specialized Coursework Section can be extremely demonstrative of these disciplines.

It is critical that the reader realizes that you are an energetic, enthusiastic, proficient teacher. The combination of your resume and cover letter can accomplish that. Your cover letter provides an excellent place to state a concise version of your teaching philosophy and exactly what it is that makes you an effective educator.

Teacher   Verdana

JOANNE N. MAXWELL

3345 Seerey Street Las Vegas, NV 89131 (702) 555-6555 maxwelljn@nev.net

QUALIFICATIONS

- Successful experience as an educator and administrator in diverse settings.
- Solid leader able to build, mentor, and develop highly motivated and productive teams.
- Recognized for designing and implementing innovative and effective curriculum for training staff and students.
- Regularly selected for special projects and assignments due to exceptional organizational, communication, and public relations skills.

EDUCATION

MA – Administration/Educational Specialist, University of Nevada-Las Vegas (2007)
MA – Curriculum & Instruction, University of Nevada-Las Vegas (2003)
BA – Elementary Education/Psychology, Oklahoma State University (1993)

PROFESSIONAL TEACHING/ADMINISTRATOR HISTORY

Petersen Elementary School, Las Vegas, Nevada 2000 to Present

TEACHER/ASSISTANT VICE PRINCIPAL – Perform a wide range of educational and administrative functions for this ethnically diverse elementary school. Developed and teach curriculum to third grade students, and provide ESL and literacy assessments for academic placement. Provide mentor training for third grade teachers, manage student assessments and academic progress on statewide database, and interpret assessment data for remediation and academic placement purposes.

Provide student monitoring and discipline. Maintain positive ongoing contacts with parents, handle conflict resolution of students and parents, and implement IEPs for students.

Designed and implemented staff development/in-service trainings and workshops on ESL, literacy, math, and technology. Co-authored school improvement plan and quarterly updates. Published bi-monthly school newsletter and created content for school website. Prepared press releases and district reports.

Chaired 25-member accreditation committee, authored accreditation annual report, and archived data and anecdotal records. Wrote two state grants and received $200,000 to purchase books, training, and software programs for school. Managed and archived data for grants evaluation, including narrative reports and field interviews.

Additional assignments included Site Council Leader, Student Teacher Mentor, Grade Level Chairperson, Learning Improvement Team, ESL District Liaison.

Bayberry Elementary School, Solstes, Nevada 1995 to 2000

PRIMARY MULTIAGE TEACHER/TRAINER – Managed 24 first, second, and third grade students in a single classroom. Served as trainer and supervisor for multiage teachers, artist-in-residence student sponsor, PTA teacher representative, Community Program teacher, Safety Patrol advisor, accreditation team member, student teacher mentor, and grade level representative. Wrote third grade curriculum for entire district as well as assessments for placement benchmarks.

Reservation Primary School, Kirk, Oklahoma 1993 to 1995

TEACHER – Significantly improved the reading and math scores for third graders.

PROFESSIONAL CREDENTIAL

Nevada K-8 Teaching Certificate

Educator   Bookman Old Style

BRENDA BERKELEY

5693 Smugglers Cove Road
Portland, ME 04017
(207) 876-3562   brendab@outofthebox.com

OBJECTIVE: Educator

QUALIFICATIONS

Strong teaching background. During nine years of teaching have obtained excellent results with children and have instilled a desire to learn. Thoroughly enjoy working with kids and seeing their personal growth.

EDUCATION

MA - Curriculum Development, Boston College (2002)

BA - Education/Speech Therapy, University of Maine, Farmington (1999)

PROFESSIONAL EXPERIENCE

Portland School District, Portland, ME 1999–Present

Educator - 2006–Present. Teach first through third grade to high risk students. As chairperson of the Staff Training and Development Committee, completed a needs assessment and identified numerous training needs among teachers and teacher's aides. Sold the teaching staff on the need for training and developed a training program which has met all of its objectives.

Program Coordinator/Educator - 2004–2006. Coordinated all aspects of the Early Childhood Special Education Program, including hiring and training of staff and support professionals, and the design and implementation of curriculum. Marketed the program throughout the community and in six months tripled the size of the program to 190. Persuaded parents to participate in special events with their children, resulting in a 70% increase in parent involvement. Spoke to business, community, and physician groups, gaining community support for the program and enabled professionals to make appropriate referrals.

Communication Disorders Specialist - 1999–2004. Provided therapy to students with communication disorders. Participated in all aspects of Project Redi, a screening program for kindergartners, including the selection of assessment procedures, training staff, and analyzing statistical reports. Presented information on the process to other schools which resulted in their adopting similar procedures.

Engineers/Scientists

By all means keep your resume interesting. Listing key buzzwords will certainly help because human resources people and hiring managers will be looking for evidence of experience in specialized areas. Be careful, however, not to exclude the human achievements that set you apart from a well-programmed automaton.

There are a lot of good *techies* out there with credentials comparable to or even more impressive than yours. For each program you have mastered your competition has mastered three. As in every occupation, though, it is not always the most "qualified" candidate who gets the job.

It is critical to demonstrate that you are good at what you do, solving the most complex problems, and completing projects on schedule and within budgets. If you designed a product that became a hot seller or a feature that made an existing product soar, mention it. Did you take over a troubled project and turn it around? Did you identify critical bugs that were delaying a release? Did you work cooperatively with internal and external customers? Don't underestimate the "people stuff."

Combine general and specialized knowledge. Some employers are looking for people versed in highly specialized areas. Others prefer those who have demonstrated they can specialize but also have sufficient all-around skill and knowledge to handle multiple projects and problems.

A way to pitch both is with a statement in Qualifications that might read "Over 10 years experience in _____, with specialties in ____, _____, _____, and _____." In the job narrative you can expand on the overall functions and work your way into the specialized pieces of it.

In the job narrative, you might say "Responsible for all areas of _____, including _____, and _____."

Quantify results whenever you can. In your job sketches list the objectives or specifications of the product or research project. Then determine if you met the specifications or goals. Once you've determined that you met the specifications, try to quantify some aspect. If you've got hard figures, by all means use them, but don't hesitate to use numbers even if you have to do some estimating.

Engineering and scientific fields are typically project oriented. Therefore, in the first paragraph of your job narrative provide an overall description of the generic duties you perform across all projects. This is also a good place to demonstrate your overall accomplishments and recognition, such as consistently completing projects on time, group and individual citations, merit raises, and bonuses. Then, select three or four of your most *representative* projects. (See Special Projects, page 76). Present sufficient information to describe the scope of the project, your role, budget, obstacles you overcame, and results.

Scientist   **Arial**

Luan Xieng
1745 Maple Lane
Ann Arbor, Michigan 48105
lxieng@atoms.com

QUALIFICATIONS

More than ten years experience in the research and development of polymer materials, including mechanical, electronic, photonic, and biological applications. Strong computer skills including theoretical calculations.

EDUCATION

Ph.D. – Nanotechnology, MIT (2005)
M.S. – Organic Chemistry, Stanford (2002)
B.S. – Polymer Engineering, Beijing University (1995)

AREAS OF SPECIALIZATION

Chemistry: Broad experience in the multistep synthesis of organic compounds. Create polymer syntheses in the areas of polycondensation, free-radical polymerization, photopolymerization, organometal-catalyzed polymerization, and living polymerization.

Materials Sciences: Strong knowledge of the structure/property relationships of organic and polymeric materials, with a solid background in material physics, including mechanical, thermal, optoelectronic, and photonic properties.

Characterization Techniques: Proficient with characterization techniques on material structure, morphology, and thin films. Hands-on experience on NMR, IR, UV-vis, Fluorometer, GC-MS, Mass spectroscopy, DSC, TGA, GPC, Instron, AFM, and SEM.

Laser Spectroscopy and Optoelectronic Devices: Extensive experience with femtosecond Ti:Sapphire laser system and optical characterization techniques. Excellent knowledge of optoelectronic devices such as light-emitting diode, photovoltaic, and field-effect transistors.

Biotechnology: Able to provide materials design for optical sensors and sensor processes.

RESEARCH EXPERIENCE

Postdoctoral Research, University of Michigan 2005–Present

Synthesis of polyelectrolytes: Developed a facile synthetic approach for conjugated polyelectrolytes which led to a series of new materials for applications in biosensors and multi-layer polymer light-emitting diodes.

Mathematic model for binding constant: Developed a new and simple model for studying the interaction between polyelectrolytes and biological species (determination of their binding constant and fluorescence quantum yield of the complex).

Doctoral Research, MIT 2003–2005

Design and Synthesis of Nonlinear Optical (NLO) Materials: Designed and synthesized two-photon absorbing chromophores and polymers, provided a new understanding of the structure/property relationships of a series of novel two-photon absorbing chromophores, and achieved the highest two-photon absorption efficiency to date of a polymer.

Optical Characterization: Developed a two-photon-induced fluorescence technique for two-photon cross-section measurement, using a femtosecond laser system.

Masters Research, Stanford 2001–2003

Semiconductive Polymers for Optoelectronic Devices: Developed a new approach to design blue-light-emitting conjugated polymers. Investigated optoelectronic properties of conjugated polymers.

Research Scientist, Beijing University 1995–2001

Structural Polymers: Chemical modifications of polymers, e.g., polyimide (PI), polyaryletherketone (PEK) and polyethersulfones (PES), for use as structural and membrane materials.

Functional Materials: Designed and synthesized organic and polymeric nonlinear optical materials. Studied nonlinear optical properties. Synthesized chiral polymers and investigated chirooptical and nonlinear chirooptical properties.

Electronics Engineer   **Lucida Bright**

JOHN MYERSBY
9023 York Street
New Westminster, BC V3L 453
(604) 271-3157   jmyersby@orca.com

OBJECTIVE: Electronics Engineer

QUALIFICATIONS

Excellent engineering background including experience with microprocessing design. Work effectively with teams of engineers and project managers.

EDUCATION

B.S. - Electrical and Computer Engineering, Simon Fraser University (2000)

EMPLOYMENT

Ransey Systems, Vancouver, BC 6/05 to Present

Senior Engineer - As part of a team of Software Quality Assurance Engineers, evaluate CAD/CAM software and make recommendations for improvements before software is made available to users within the company. Review functional specifications to ensure all portions are testable and fully meet user needs. Analyze test results, identify problem areas, and make final recommendations.

Performed a cost improvement study which documented savings through the Software Quality Assurance Program of $400,000 annually. Program has eliminated duplication of testing, produced a more organized software development process, and resolved problems at earlier stages.

Mutual Signals, Vancouver, BC 7/99 to 6/05

Manager of Engineering Services - 4/01 to 6/05. For this firm which designs, sells, and installs industrial and municipal signaling and alarm systems, designed systems and oversaw installations. Analyzed job specifications to determine necessary equipment, did takeoffs from blueprints for bids, modified or designed/built equipment, and provided technical support on sales calls. Oversaw installations and tested large systems upon completion. Played a key role in enabling the firm to grow an average of 18% per year.

Electronics Technician - 7/99 to 4/01. Installed and tested systems and did takeoffs from blueprints, as well as supervised technicians at installation sites.

Accounting/Finance

There are four ways you can excite an employer: demonstrate you can make money for the organization, save money, solve problems, and reduce the stress and pressure the boss is under. Those in accounting and finance are typically able to demonstrate all four when they succeed in quantifying their results. In your job sketches, concentrate on recalling past projects you worked on and determine what the results of those projects were.

With so much financial and accounting information computerized these days, it should be relatively easy to review past reports and demonstrate what your successes have been.

Although you will certainly want to let employers know what your duties were, devote the greatest amount of time to determining what your results have been.

Although many accountants have experience in converting from one computerized accounting system to another, make the most of your experience. If a firm anticipates a conversion in the next few years, your conversion experience could make you very valuable. Don't just indicate that you were involved in conversions, but also indicate the level of success. If the conversion was smooth, if the consultant indicated you had done a good job of preparing for the conversion, or if it was completed on schedule, say so. No conversion takes place without a hitch, so to say that it was a smooth conversion merely means that bugs were quickly fixed and that it was completed on schedule or close to schedule.

Look for various types of results. Did you produce new management reports or modify existing reports to make them more useful and timely? Many reports are extremely time sensitive, so if you reduced the time needed to produce a report from 14 days after quarter-end to 10 days after, that would make a strong statement.

Did you computerize an operation that had been done manually? Calculate the number of man-hours saved. If it eliminated the need for a position, indicate that as well.

Perhaps you improved the accounting operation so well that your audits were much improved. Perhaps you could say that exceptions were reduced by a certain percentage or from ten the previous year to only one, or perhaps none.

If you were involved in accounts receivable perhaps you could state that 90-day and over receivables were reduced by a certain percentage or that days outstanding were reduced from 40 to 30.

Other accounting people have found ways to reduce the transaction time on billings or reduce invoicing errors. Others have developed systems to avoid double-paying invoices on their accounts payable.

Finance people have found ways to reduce interest expense on loans, have taken companies public and raised new monies, negotiated larger lines of credit, and found ways to reduce taxes.

Accountant/Controller   Tahoma

PAUL HUSTED
406 Ash
Boise, Idaho 83702
(208) 361-2918

OBJECTIVE: Senior Accountant/Controller

QUALIFICATIONS

Strong accounting experience with a broad background in auditing, business and individual taxes, and cost control programs. Effectively implement computerized accounting systems.

Excellent manager. Consistently obtain high productivity from employees.

LICENSES

CPA, Idaho State Certification (1988)

EDUCATION

B.A. - Accounting, University of Idaho (1984)

EMPLOYMENT

Brandon Refrigerated Service Inc., Boise, Idaho 3/00 to Present

CONTROLLER

- For this refrigerated freight hauler, prepare financial statements and supervise 12 payroll, rate, billing, and AP/AR personnel.
- Extensively involved in customer relations, establishing credit ratings, approving credit, reviewing and approving customer claims, and making collections.
- Manage the cash flow of the company. Developed a major cost-control program which has cut overhead 15%.
- Maintain the smooth functioning of a sophisticated computerized accounting system.

Bestway Freight Lines, Boise, Idaho 8/93 to 3/00

CONTROLLER

- Responsible for financial statements and tax preparation.
- Supervised ten employees handling rates, billing, payroll, claims, and AP/AR.
- Oversaw the payroll system covering six separate union agreements.
- Developed the company's first cost studies and identified areas for substantial savings.
- Cut the shop force from 21 to 14 with no reduction in work completed.
- Worked closely with vendor and contract programmer while converting to a new computerized accounting and payroll system.
- Implemented a computerized system to track commodity transactions which reduced required staff time each month from 180 to 6 hours.

Robert Perkins, CPA, Boise, Idaho 6/84 to 8/93

STAFF ACCOUNTANT

- Performed audits and developed financial statements for a wide variety of clients.
- Handled state and federal taxes for individuals, trusts, estates, partnerships, and corporations.
- Provided management services and designed cost-control programs.

Professionals

The term "professions" usually includes such occupations as medical doctor, attorney, professor, accountant, psychologist, and counselor that usually require specific degrees, certifications, and licensure.

Professionals often find resumes hard to write because it can be difficult to quantify results. Despite the difficulty, almost everyone can come up with results and find ways to sell those results in the resume.

Remember that your goal is to cause people to want to meet you.

Although you may have done many things in your career, emphasize those things that you would like to do more of in the future. Devote more space and detail to those things.

Use your occupational jargon and buzzwords as appropriate but don't overdo it.

Professionals often do well by including special projects in their job descriptions, or even having a separate "projects" section if many of the projects have occurred off the job or as part of a professional society.

As in every occupation, each position has built-in success criteria. Attorneys try cases, win judgments, negotiate settlements. How is your track record in those areas? Have you developed business? Created or expanded a legal specialty?

Accountants interpret numbers. Are you a CPA with corporate clients? How have you helped them improve the financial health of their businesses? What kinds of audits have you performed? Have you identified deficiencies? Embezzlement? Mitigated IRS judgments?

Whatever your profession, determine how successful you are by the feedback from your clients, students, and patients. What kinds of outcomes have you achieved in terms of your specific mission? What kind of reputation have you established among your peers?

Professional committees and task forces as well as awards and recognition are of value. Publications and conference presentations speak volumes.

Attorney   **Cambria**

VINCENT D. COLE
303 Maple Drive Sacramento, California 95823
(916) 555-7609
vcole@calnet.com

OBJECTIVE: Attorney at Law

QUALIFICATIONS

- Successful career as an attorney in both public and private practice.
- Client-oriented professional with a reputation for solid legal knowledge and thoroughness.
- Effective communicator and litigator.
- Demonstrated ability to build caseload and revenues due to strong community network and track record of success in trying complex civil and criminal cases.
- Built private firm from start-up to one receiving national referrals.

EDUCATION

JD/MPA – Policy Analysis, University of California-Davis (1985); High Honors

BA – Political Science, California State University-Northridge (1981)

ADDITIONAL TRAINING

Mediation Training, University of California-Berkeley (48 hours)

Advanced Trial Lawyer Training, Stanford University/American Trial Lawyers Association (65 hours)

PROFESSIONAL HISTORY
Maron Keating Carver & Cole, Sacramento, California 1992 to Present

FOUNDER/PARTNER – Established this full-service firm from start-up. Specialize in criminal, personal injury, and employment law. Quickly developed a reputation for quality representation resulting in substantial referrals. Expanded to include additional specialties including business, tax, and corporate services. Firm has represented a diverse client base including individuals, municipalities, small businesses, and churches. Perform key managing partner roles in such areas as recruitment and firm strategy development. Have successfully expanded practice to include clients from throughout the country.

Loomis & Jones, Sacramento, California 1991 to 1992

ASSOCIATE – Recruited by the partners of this firm specializing in insurance defense. Built criminal, personal injury, employment, and plaintiff practice, generating revenues that accounted for one-third of all receipts in 1992.

PRIOR LEGAL EXPERIENCE

ASSOCIATE, Powers Clawson & Taft, Sacramento, CA (1990–1991)

ASSISTANT CITY ATTORNEY, Sacramento City Attorney's Office, Sacramento, CA (1988–1990)

PROFESSIONAL CREDENTIALS

- State of California Certified Mediator
- Member of The California Bar Association
- Ninth Circuit Court of Appeals

AFFILIATIONS

- National Bar Association
- California Trial Lawyers Association
- American Trial Lawyers Association

Training and Development Specialist **Century Gothic**

DEBRA SLAWSON
1503 Adrian
Minneapolis, Minnesota 55102
(612) 281-6964   dslawson@sesame.com

QUALIFICATIONS

Broad experience in designing, teaching, and supervising training programs in a large training department.

Develop effective teams and establish a strong sense of commitment.

EDUCATION

M.S. - Curriculum Design Administration, University of Minnesota (1986)
B.S. - Education, Moorhead State University, Minneapolis, Minnesota (1983)

EMPLOYMENT HISTORY

Prodigital, Inc., Minneapolis, Minnesota 10/99 to Present

Medical Training Administrator 10/05 to Present. Design and implement workshops nationwide which train medical professionals in the uses and benefits of digital radiography. Consult with Prodigital subsidiaries to assess training needs and help them establish training departments.

Developed a comprehensive program to train the 15-member technical training staff in effective teaching techniques. Ratings from customers have improved 40% since the program was implemented.

Clinical Application Training Supervisor 6/02 to 10/05. Administered and monitored week-long training workshops for domestic and international customers. These workshops have firmly established Prodigital's reputation for providing excellent service and training after the sale. Developed programs for introducing new product lines to the national sales force. Hired, trained, and supervised a staff of three medical trainers.

Training Specialist 10/99 to 6/02. Designed and created one-week product orientation courses for customers. Due to the success of the courses, the format and procedures were adopted for all training courses.

Thompson Manufacturing Co., St. Paul, Minnesota 9/93 to 10/99

Training Support Manager 8/97 to 10/99. Developed sales training courses and materials for new and experienced salespeople. Took highly technical data and constructed practical, understandable courses.

Technical Training Specialist 5/95 to 8/97. Identified needs and designed a five-week technical training program for domestic and international specialists. The program became the model for other workshops within Thompson.

Administrative Assistant to Product Planning Manager 9/93 to 5/95. Researched market trends and studied products and marketing plans of competitors.

Prior Employment: Teacher 9/83 to 6/93

Nonprofit Organizations

To most people, the terms nonprofit and not-for-profit connote social services and limited compensation. Nonprofits, however, exist for a variety of reasons. Today every racial, ethnic, gender, socioeconomic, and religious demographic has nonprofit organizations incorporated for their benefit. AARP and NAACP are examples of national nonprofits that exist to serve definable populations.

Cities, counties, and even countries have nonprofit organizations created to enhance their economic well-being. These range from local merchants associations and chambers of commerce to international trade organizations. Similarly, most industries have nonprofit adjuncts that include trade associations and lobbying organizations.

Credit unions are nonprofits in the financial world. National charities include the Multiple Sclerosis Society, United Cerebral Palsy, and the Make-a-Wish Foundation.

There are nonprofits that provide international philanthropy, such as the Bill & Melinda Gates Foundation and the Ford Foundation.

The major consideration in joining a nonprofit lies in understanding the organization's mission and demographics. If you have a problem with its demographics, politics, religion, or other major activity, better look elsewhere for a job. Aside from that focus, the overwhelming majority of positions reflect those in all other sectors. These include all levels of management, such as CEO/Executive Director, CFO, IT, HR, and Operations. Of course, no organization can succeed without administrative support. Depending on their mission, nonprofits can employ case managers, counselors, therapists, social workers, field representatives, bookkeepers, accountants, receptionists, technicians, drivers, fleet managers, and more. In other words, every type of employee found in the for-profit world can be found in its nonprofit counterpart. So, as with any position, present yourself in the best possible light.

Don't feel that you will be disqualified if you have no specific nonprofit experience. On the contrary, more and more nonprofits are valuing those with experience in the private sector.

When seeking those nonprofits that are more social services oriented, emphasize and make sure to include any relevant community service you have performed or supported. If you have some long-term or substantial history, feel free to present it as a series of projects or even job narratives (See Special Projects, pages 76).

For those whose service is dated, use the section heading Community Service History or Volunteer History instead of providing dates. Then, just list your experience *sans* dates. You can fill in the dates at the interview.

Social Service Agency Management   **Times New Roman**

MARIAN OSTEGAARD
4006 Walton Avenue
Ypsilanti, MI 48197
(313) 264-2372

OBJECTIVE: Director of a Social Service Agency

QUALIFICATIONS

Strong social service administration background gained during 24 years with one of the most respected agencies in Michigan. Build accountability into programs, consistently hire the best, and create programs for staff that reduce turnover and increase skills. Establish and deliver services that the public needs and appreciates.

EDUCATION

M.A. - Social Work, University of Michigan (1986)

B.A. - Sociology, Psychology, University of Michigan (1983)

PROFESSIONAL EXPERIENCE

Counseling Services of Detroit, Detroit, MI 7/83 to Present

Assistant Executive Director 6/05 to Present

Direct the agency's counseling program, including six branch offices and 36 employees. Manage the salary budget, which represents 85% of the total budget. Created and implemented a new middle-management structure which has increased accountability of branch operations. Counseling productivity has been increased 24% through improved training and time management.

Unit Administrator 9/99 to 6/05

Managed three branch offices, and supervised 15 professional employees and eight volunteers. Taught Family Life Education classes, and acted as Field Instruction Supervisor for counseling interns. Provided consultation and training to other organizations, and spoke before numerous business and public groups. Organized a Citizen's Advisory Committee that led to increased local support.

Senior Counselor/Branch Manager 7/91 to 9/99

Opened and managed several branch offices. Responsible for counseling services, Family Life Education, Field Instruction, volunteer supervision, and public speaking.

Counselor 7/83 to 7/91

Provided counseling services to a wide variety of clients on individual, family, and marital issues.

Manufacturing/Labor

This category includes machine operators, assemblers, machinists, tool and die makers, technicians, laborers, warehouse workers, and carpenters, as well as any people who work in what are usually referred to as "the trades."

The main goals for your resume should be to show the breadth of your experience, the tools and equipment you can use, and the fact that you are very good at what you do.

It may be appropriate for you to use a section called "Tools," "Equipment," or "Processes" to showcase special knowledge or experience.

As with all resumes, identifying results will help set you apart from the competition. Try to recall any improvements you have brought about. Perhaps you discovered ways to produce a product with fewer steps. For example, you found a way to produce a part using only three different machines instead of four. Perhaps you discovered that a hole was specified at plus or minus .001, but you determined that for the product's purpose, .005 was actually quite acceptable, and as a result fewer parts were rejected. Perhaps you discovered a faster way to assemble a component and thus increased productivity by 15%. Or you found a way to maintain equipment more effectively and reduced downtime. The possibilities are endless.

Use your cover letter and resume to demonstrate that you learn new equipment and technology easily and that you are always looking for a better way to do things.

Of course, the most important attributes you want to share involve your work ethic. Are you dependable? Responsible? Are you regularly selected for special projects? Are you the go-to-guy/gal when a project needs a boost? Are you the one who trains and mentors new employees?

Machine Operator   Verdana

PAUL YOKIHANA

13097 Mona N.E.
Honolulu, Hawaii 96821
(808) 292-3724
pyokihana@mahimahi.com

OBJECTIVE: Machine Operator

QUALIFICATIONS

- Strong mechanical, tool, and woodworking ability.
- Excellent knowledge of the working characteristics of a variety of hardwoods.
- Easy to get along with. Cooperative. Flexible.

EDUCATION

Woodworking, Kauai Community College, 60 credits (2000)

EMPLOYMENT

Exotic Woods Inc., Honolulu, Hawaii 6/01 - Present

Machine Operator

- Responsible for production of domestic and exotic hardwood molding for this small picture frame manufacturer.
- Handle all operations including selecting wood, ripping, rabbeting, shaping, rough sanding, finish sanding, staining and oiling.
- Set up and operate joiner, table saws, wide belt sander, molder-planer, radial arm saw, and wood shaper.
- Duties include operation of hand sanders and chopsaws.
- Occasionally finish and assemble frames.
- Train new employees and ensure smooth operations in the shop.
- Produce a very high quality product which has helped the firm to almost triple its business since 2001.

Previous Employment

Maintenance, CST Inc., Honolulu, Hawaii 5/96-6/01

Waiter, Spring Winds Resort Hotel, Kapaa, Hawaii 4/94-5/96

Quality Control Inspector   **Century Schoolbook**

RITA SAWYER

1202 Guthrie Avenue South
Tulsa, Oklahoma 74119
(918) 693-4217
rita@sooner.com

OBJECTIVE: Quality Control Inspection

QUALIFICATIONS

Excellent training and experience in all phases of quality control inspection. Work
hard and produce excellent results. Work well with engineers, production supervisors,
production workers, and vendors.

Broad experience with many measuring devices, including Vernier calipers and
scales, micrometers, sineplates, air gauging equipment, durometer and Rockwell
hardness testing, XYZ coordinate measuring machines, optical comparators, roughness
measurement equipment, and height gauges. Experienced in surface plate inspection.

EDUCATION

Graduated - Keota High School, Keota, Oklahoma (1993)

TRAINING

Advancetech, Certificates in: D.C. Electronics, A.C. Electronics, Semiconductor Devices,
Digital Technology, Geometric Tolerancing

EMPLOYMENT

Advancetech, Inc., Tulsa, Oklahoma 10/01–Present

Quality Control Inspector - Responsible for all first article inspections and final
inspections for this sheet metal fabricator. Using blueprints, calculate dimensions
and bend factors to check and approve flat pattern layouts. Verify proper sequencing
of production plans. Receive and log incoming sheet metal and other products. When
parts do not meet customer's specifications, work closely with engineers to discover
if the fault was in the original design or in the fabrication process. With discovery of
fault, work with engineers to correct it. Through improved processes reduced rejects by
customers over 20%.

Electrotech Laboratories, Oklahoma City, Oklahoma 3/97–10/01

Quality Control Inspector - Inspected incoming vendor-supplied sheet metal
and small precision parts. Used hand measuring devices as well as XYZ measuring
machines and optical comparators. Inspected for conformance to geometric tolerances.
Inspected and tested electrical components and electrical subassemblies.

K & I Industries, Muskogee, Oklahoma 8/93–3/97

Machine Operator - Set up, operated, and maintained six Brown & Sharpe and two
Traub single spindle screw machines. Inspected manufactured parts. Recorded setup
procedures for ease of manufacturing the part in the future, saving approximately 100
hours per year among five machine operators.

Healthcare Professionals

In your resume you will want to make the most out of your experience. Demonstrate that you seek opportunities to further your knowledge, show that you are good at what you do, and prove that you are a dedicated professional.

Health professionals often have a hard time because it can be difficult to quantify results. You should, however, look for every opportunity to identify your results and, if possible, quantify them.

Results will most often be found in a special project you worked on. Perhaps you were part of a committee that examined a process and recommended improvements.

List any awards you may have received, such as employee-of-the-month or year. Awards demonstrate that people think highly of you. Indicate on the resume the reasons for receiving the award rather than merely listing it.

Seminars, workshops, and special training are always valuable to list. Extensive lists can be presented as a third page or addendum. See page 110.

Showcase your areas of experience. This can easily be done by using a paragraph under Qualifications, which might read, "Broad experience in _____, _____, _____, _____, and _____." If you have numerous items you want to mention you could have a separate category below the Qualifications section which would be called "Areas of Experience."

If you know yourself to be a highly qualified health professional, please do not be satisfied with merely listing your duties and showing your years of experience. Demonstrate your successes and effectiveness.

Nursing Administrator

Arial

ELEANOR SIEVERS
3116 Indale Avenue
Athens, Georgia 30606
(404) 643-8014

OBJECTIVE: Director of Nursing/Administrator for Nursing Services

EDUCATION

M.A. - Hospital Administration, University of Houston (1986)

B.S. - Nursing, University of Texas (1981)

PROFESSIONAL EXPERIENCE

University Hospital, Athens, Georgia 4/94 to Present

Associate Administrator for Nursing Services 4/02 to Present.

Direct the activities of a 520 FTE nursing staff with a $60 million budget in a 380 bed medical center. Responsible for all inpatient units including medical, surgical, and cardiac intensive care units, an eight room operating suite, and a level one trauma/emergency department.

- Work directly with four Division Directors and twelve Nursing Supervisors.
- Developed new standards for care, and set up daily mechanisms which ensure compliance.
- Established more effective budgetary and staffing monitoring systems which save over $400,000 per year.
- Opened six critical care beds and added a head nurse.

Division Director, Acute Care 1/98 to 4/02.

Responsible for this eight unit division with a 205 FTE nursing staff—190 beds, $26 million budget. Established workable and effective budgetary controls.

- Installed and coordinated a capital equipment purchasing system which saved $85,000.
- Implemented two medical services.
- Established, trained, and supported a service for ventilator-dependent quadriplegics in the rehabilitation unit.
- Trained staff in troubleshooting ventilators and working with patients.

Nursing Administrative Supervisor, Medical/Surgical 4/94 to 1/98.

Had responsibility for two 24-bed units with a 69 FTE staff.

- Established a six bed telemetry unit and a cardiac patient teaching program.
- Developed a primary nursing care model and upgraded the staff from mostly aides to mostly RNs.
- Increased the role of head nurses by giving them greater budgetary and administrative responsibilities.
- Established preoperative standards.

The Methodist Hospital, Houston, Texas 5/81 to 4/94

Nursing Administrative Supervisor, Acute Medicine 3/91 to 4/94.

Administered two medical units with 62 beds and a 65 FTE staff.

- Trained new staff as the units moved from mostly aides to a staff of RNs.
- Worked with head nurses as they were given more managerial responsibility.

Inservice Instructor 3/88 to 3/91
Head Nurse, Cardiac Unit 4/85 to 3/88
Staff Nurse, Intensive Care, Intensive Care Unit, Cardiac Unit 5/81 to 4/85

Registered Nurse   **Georgia**

PETER SIMMONS

1527 Broadway #217
Irvine, CA 92713
(714) 523-7615
psimmons@comcast.net

OBJECTIVE: Emergency Room Nursing

QUALIFICATIONS

Highly trained and experienced. Considered by supervisors to be an excellent emergency room nurse. Strongly motivated, provide quick, accurate assessments, and work effectively with doctors and other ER staff. Develop excellent rapport with patients.

EDUCATION

Diploma, School of Nursing, St. Luke's Methodist Hospital, Cedar Rapids, Iowa (1994)

Certificate - Emergency Medical Technician (1993)

EMPLOYMENT

University of California, Irvine Medical Center, Orange, CA 10/01-Present

Staff R.N. - Emergency Room - In this busy, twenty-two bed emergency room, work with up to sixty patients per shift. As the triage nurse on the seven-nurse staff, stabilize patients, make critical decisions, and handle the flow of patients. Receive a high number of trauma patients.

Scripps Memorial Hospital, San Diego, CA 6/98-10/01

Staff R.N. - Emergency Room - Night shift charge nurse for this eight-bed emergency room. Worked with many cardiac, respiratory, and psychiatric emergencies. Independently assessed patients and initiated diagnostic procedures. Ordered x-rays and lab tests. Consulted with patients by telephone and determined appropriate actions.

Las Cruces Memorial Hospital, Las Cruces, NM 5/96-4/98

Staff R.N. - Emergency Room - Performed all emergency room functions at this sixteen-bed emergency facility. Trained nursing students and supervised the outpatient methadone treatment program. Also assisted in the minor surgery department and the bronchoscopy department.

Mercy Medical Center, Roseburg, OR 6/94-4/96

Staff R.N. - Emergency Room - Treated many motor vehicle and sawmill accident trauma patients at this twelve-bed emergency room. Charge nurse last ten months. Also functioned as mobile intensive care nurse working by ambulance with an EMT and respiratory therapist. Taught IV therapy, CPR, and assessment skills to EMTs as part of an extensive training program.

Pharmacist   Tahoma

BARRY KOCH

1706 5th N.E.
Ryersly, Pennsylvania 18512
(412) 562-3216

OBJECTIVE: Director of Pharmacy

QUALIFICATIONS

Strong pharmacy management experience. Proven ability to introduce cost saving measures while increasing quality and productivity standards. Work effectively with all levels of hospital administration and have significantly improved relations with other departments.

EDUCATION

B.S. - Pharmaceutical Science, Northwestern University (1988)

PROFESSIONAL EXPERIENCE

Ryersly General Hospital, Ryersly, Pennsylvania 6/88 to Present

Assistant Director of Pharmacy & IV Therapy 3/98 to Present. Maintain overall responsibility for ordering medications and supervising and scheduling 15 staff pharmacists and technicians. Implemented a mobile cart system with pharmacists making rounds and dispensing medications at nursing stations. System increased quality control and improved relations between Nursing and Pharmacy staff.

Developed a centralized piggyback program, which relieved nurses of the duty of mixing solutions and turned it over to pharmacy technicians. Program has given techs greater responsibility and has significantly reduced errors and increased quality standards.

Responsible for keeping Pharmacy, Medical, and Nursing staffs current on effects and uses of new medications and developing policies regarding their use. Consult extensively with doctors on difficult cases. Currently developing a clinical program to provide more in-service training for doctors and nurses and completing development of a kinetic counseling program to better serve doctors. Represent the Pharmacy Department on the Pharmacy and Therapeutic Committee. Actively involved in helping the committee produce a complete formulary.

Staff Pharmacist 6/88 to 3/98. As staff pharmacist monitored and recorded patients' medications and IV therapy. Provided consultations with doctors, nurses, and patients to ensure proper therapy. Ordered all medications and kept the department well supplied. Designed a diabetic program which reaches 100 diabetics annually and helps them maintain more effective therapy.

Retailers

In your resume do everything possible to demonstrate that you are good at what you do. Just by your job title most employers will know your basic duties, so combine these with your results. Retailing is one of the most statistics-filled industries, so make use of the data available to you.

Add any duties not typically associated with your standard job title that demonstrate flexibility and willingness to take on added responsibility.

If your job entailed special projects, provide descriptions of the projects and emphasize the results achieved.

If you are primarily in sales, emphasize your sales success, including increases in volume and margins as well as how you stack up against the records of your peers in your department, store, or region.

If you are a buyer, do everything you can to show that you have a good sense of trends and that you can sense what will become the next hot item or style.

If you are a department or store manager, you would emphasize increases in sales, your department's or store's ranking within the chain, increases in profits, or increases in market share. You might also mention such things as inventory turns, sales per square foot, or sales per employee work hours.

Make mention of any involvement in planning or coordinating an opening of a store or of a major remodel. Show that you make effective use of co-op advertising and that you work well with manufacturers for special promotions. If you introduced a special new line of products or opened a new department, you could mention the increase in sales.

As a manager you can mention such things as your ability to train staff and your ability to decrease turnover and increase productivity.

Retail

Cambria

WILLIAM E. CONSTANT
55 Everett Avenue #B26
South Portland, Maine 04106
(207) 555-3466
constantbill@hotmail.com

QUALIFICATIONS

- Successful experience in purchasing, inventory control, sales, and personnel management for regional retail companies.
- Appreciated by customers for providing excellent and customized service.
- Proven ability to manage multiple tasks, projects, and assignments simultaneously.
- Demonstrated ability to build and mentor highly productive and loyal teams.
- History of upgrading and improving processes resulting in greater efficiency, productivity, and profitability.

EDUCATION

Business Studies – Andover College (2000-2001)

PROFESSIONAL HISTORY

NECC Natural Markets, Portland, Maine 1999 to Present

GROCERY COORDINATOR – 2002 to present. Manage a wide range of purchasing, sales, personnel, and logistical operations in support of $8 million in annual sales for this major regional natural foods supermarket. Report directly to Store Manager. Monitor all grocery and dairy items to assure adequate inventory. Perform regular and special purchasing. Inspect incoming orders for quality, spoilage, and accuracy of shipments prior to acceptance. Reduced *mispicks* from largest vendor 40% through careful documentation and reporting.

Implement special sales and promotions to assure proper and timely turn of time-dated items. Create sales strategies based upon seasons, previous product performances, and sales records of similar products. Coordinate co-op sales with vendors. Have consistently exceeded all vendor and store goals in both revenue and margin.

Train and supervise a team of up to 30 checkers, clerks, and courtesy staff for both day and night shifts. Immediately resolve personnel and customer issues. Developed innovative system for measuring productivity of night crew. Recognized for fair and effective leadership.

Developed and implemented coding system for bulk bakery items that was so successful it was expanded to all stores.

Fill in for Store Manager and Assistant Manager as needed. Schedule all staff and manage security. Oversee vendors and contractors. Open and close store, reconcile all accounts. Consistently commended for quality in all areas.

Additional Experience: Assistant Manager, 2001–2002, Second Assistant, 2000–2001, Checker 1999–2000

CARLY MARSTAN
515 Hillside Circle
Mansfield, OH 44907
(419) 555-9899
carly221@gmail.com

OBJECTIVE: Sales

PROFESSIONAL SUMMARY

· Successful background and experience in retail sales and management.
· Consistently at the top or near the top in sales production.
· Recognized by customers and employers for providing top service and follow-up.
· Multiple award winner for excellence in sales and customer service.
· Noted as an excellent leader, trainer, and supervisor.
· Proven ability to quickly identify and solve customer problems.

EDUCATION

B.S. – Business Management, Ohio State University (1994)

ADDITIONAL TRAINING

"Improving Sales and Customer Service" – The Lamp Store
"Nordstrom Quality Selling and Customer Service" – Breskoff Department Store

SALES EXPERIENCE

The Lamp Store, Mansfield, Ohio 1999 to Present

SALES CONSULTANT - Provide sales and customer service for this retail chain store specializing in high-end lighting. Customers include developers, general contractors, and large property owners. Educate customers in products, styles, and costs. Provide product and system demonstrations. Arrange for installation as needed. Visit home and business sites when necessary. Consistently follow up with customers to determine satisfaction. Recognized by customers and management for providing exceptional service resulting in repeat business.

Train new consultants in product knowledge and sales techniques. Assist others in solving technical and customer service problems. Consistently exceed sales goals and have earned a manufacturer's and a designer's sales award.

Selected as "Most Pleasant Employee of the Year" by corporate management. Recognized for playing a major role in building store from number three to number one in chain with monthly revenues going from $450,000 to $660,000.

Breskoff Department Store, Cleveland, Ohio 1992 to 1999

SALES ASSOCIATE/CASHIER - Savvy Department. Provided extensive customer service in the sale of designer clothing to customers of this service-oriented specialty store. Assisted customers in the selection of appropriate fashions, garments, and accessories. Provided extensive product, material, and style information. Developed extensive personal customer book. Contacted personal customers regarding sales and special events/promotions. Consistently was among the top three department producers, finishing number one several times.

Retail Management   **Century Gothic**

Megan Hathaway
2401 Belle Haven Road N.W.
Roanoke, Virginia 24019
(703) 829-7913

OBJECTIVE: Retail Management

QUALIFICATIONS

- Experienced in all aspects of retail marketing, merchandising, and sales.
- Quickly promoted from sales to department manager.
- Receive frequent compliments for creative displays and effective layout of merchandise.
- Supervise employees very effectively. Obtain excellent results from a young sales staff.

EDUCATION

AA - Merchandising, Fashion and Design Institute of Los Angeles (1998)

EMPLOYMENT

Brodericks, Roanoke, Virginia 7/98–Present

Department Manager - 3/05–Present. Manage the luggage and young men's departments with a staff of twelve. Responsible for displays, merchandising, scheduling, price changes, merchandise transfers, and twice-yearly inventories. Interview, hire, and train new employees and write performance reviews.

Work closely with store buyers and manufacturers' representatives to maintain high-quality merchandise. Took the luggage department from #6 in the chain to #2 in sales in the first three years. Significantly improved the look of the young men's department through creative displays and new merchandising techniques. Have increased sales in young men's an average of 15% per year.

Assistant Department Manager - 6/02–3/05. Sold handbags, accessories, and designer ready-to-wear clothing. Supervised and trained a staff of ten salespeople.

Salesperson - 7/98–6/02. Sold handbags, accessories, and young ladies' clothing. Received Salesperson of the Month six times with a store sales staff of 60. Over a twelve-month period, took over the duties of assistant department manager.

PART THREE

References,
Recommendations,
Cover Letters, and
Marketing Letters

References

The resume is not the proper format in which to present references.

References rarely come into play prior to the interview phase of the hiring process. References are usually not requested until the employer has determined you to be the top choice or at the very least a top finalist. Jumping the gun can violate the privacy of your references by providing contact information to any number of people who may happen to have access to the resume.

It is never too early, however, to have your references lined up and ready to go. Make a list of the ones you believe will provide the most positive accounts of your strengths across your *entire* skill range. This is especially important for those applying for a variety of positions requiring multiple and diverse skills. Having several references enables you to select the ones most appropriate to specific positions.

It is a good practice to ask these individuals if they are willing to serve as references. You will rarely be turned down, but it is proper to ask. These people, in effect, are doing you a favor and should be treated accordingly. No one is ever obligated to be your reference.

It is also a good idea to discuss with them the nature of their testimonials. Some folks have been surprised by the lukewarm responses from people from whom they were expecting powerful statements. Also, make sure they understand the types of positions for which you are applying so they can tailor their statements. It often pays to suggest the specific skills, achievements, and results you would like them to cover. This is a good strategy to use with both recent and previous employers. It gives them a script to work from when the reference check actually comes. Don't focus only on your favorite past employers. Most bosses, even those you might not have had great relationships with, will be glad to help when asked. If not, they will usually be up front about it so you can move along to more fertile ground.

Notify your references any time you suspect they are going to be called. You can use the brief conversation to tell the person about the position, why you would be perfect, and any points you would particularly like covered.

Some job seekers include the statement "Personal and Professional References Available Upon Request" on the resume. This is unnecessary because every employer knows you will supply references.

Although not every employer checks references, assume that each will. Don't skimp in amassing your reference A-team. Strong statements on your behalf can be a powerful force in the hiring decision. Glowing recommendations from a solid group of references can also mitigate some negative employment experiences.

References come in two flavors: personal and professional. Personal references include friends, business associates, and former coworkers as well as people you know through professional associations and volunteer organizations. Although it is generally assumed by employers that personal references will say only nice things about you, they are often still contacted. As you are judged by the company you keep, choose carefully. Friends who have poor communication skills or tendencies toward tasteless humor at the wrong times should be avoided.

Personal references should be those who know you fairly well and can say something reasonably specific about your character or skill level. It doesn't help your cause when someone says, "I don't know her well, but . . ." This is especially true of any influential or well-known people you choose. Such name-dropping will only be of value if the individual knows you personally, not just your parents or some other family member. Their level of help can also be questionable if they were only acquainted with you as a child.

Professional references include current and former bosses, peers in other departments, and customers. Your most important references are usually former bosses. Many companies, however, are increasingly refusing to provide more than the barest of information—such as job titles and dates of employment—due to a rash of defamation of character suits in recent decades.

In reality, when pressed, a former supervisor who liked you might surreptitiously defy company policy and provide some positive information. Conversely, a boss who did not care for you may be only too happy, just as surreptitiously, to offer negative feedback.

If your most recent employers are enjoined by policy from providing recommendations, there are strategies you can use to compensate. Try locating supervisors or colleagues who have left those organizations. Peers and associates still working for your previous employer are often available for contact, being somewhat removed from the actual chain of command.

Vendors and customers can be enormously valuable. Bosses and supervisors, when permitted, often feel obligated, for one reason or another, to say positive things about former employees; vendors and customers are under no such obligation. The only reason they are serving as references is because they *want to*. To get the biggest bang for the buck, get their permission and discuss the nature of their statements in advance.

A reference page should provide basic information about each person: Full name, title, company name, business address, phone number, and email. Never provide personal (e.g., home) contact information unless the reference specifically directs you to do so. The person's relationship to you and knowledge of specific skill areas may also be included: supervisor, vendor, customer, associate.

Finding former bosses who can act as references is important because it frustrates employers when they can't obtain this information. Hiring you becomes more of a gamble and an absence of references can serve as a reason to go with someone who is perhaps less appealing, but safer.

As with all references, get permission from these former employers. Fill them in on what you've been up to since you worked together. Let them know the gist of what you would like them to say about you. A few reminders might be in order, so have an outline in front of you.

If you had a mixed relationship with the person, steer the conversation into those positive areas you want to cover. If you were terminated or left for less-than-positive reasons, assure the person how you have grown, matured, and succeeded since your days together. Don't be afraid to acknowledge the weight of the favor you are asking. You will be surprised as to the response.

If you are currently unemployed and were fired from your last job, you face an especially difficult situation. But there are strategies to mitigate the problem. First, ask your boss and HR what they will say about you. Feel free to indicate what you would like them to say. Often this can be negotiated if you don't like what they indicate they will say. The only way to be absolutely sure about what will be said is to have a friend call, or to use a reference checking firm.

There are reference checking services that will make these calls for you. Do an online search for "reference checking." Depending on the amount you wish to spend, you will get reports ranging from direct transcripts of the conversation to annotated versions. The latter include some interpretation of the speaker's tone and attitude toward you. For instance, "She was a real gem," can be presented both as a compliment or a slur, depending on the tone of voice.

In determining what your ex-boss or HR department will disclose about you, carefully select someone to call them. Ideally this would be a highly professional businessperson who could call from work. This is important, because the person you are wanting to reach may ask for your friend's phone number and promise to call back later. Your friend must be prepared to describe the position you're being considered for.

Make sure your friend has a checklist of things to ask. This would include:

- ☐ Strengths
- ☐ Weaknesses
- ☐ Initiative
- ☐ Dependability
- ☐ Professionalism
- ☐ Eligibility for Rehire
- ☐ Additional Comments _____

These days, many organizations, owing to fear of litigation, will provide only basic information such as title and dates of employment. If this is the case, your problem might not be as serious as you feared.

Regardless of the response, it is always helpful to contact the ex-boss, if possible, to negotiate what we call a *non-aggression treaty*. Most ex-employers do not wish to permanently damage your career prospects. With that in mind, see if you can come up with a reason for leaving that you both can live with. This might include something as simple as "left to pursue other challenges" or "mutually determined the position was not the right fit," and so on. It never hurts to ask.

Basic Reference Page

References for Sheila R. Page

Richard Morrisey
Sales Manager
ElectraVista, Inc.
10044 NE 8th Street, Suite A-102
Bellevue, WA 98004
(425) 555-1000 Ext. 313
rmorrisey@electravista.com
Relationship: Past supervisor

Sandra Gonzales
Regional Vice President of Sales
COMEX Corp.
816 65th Avenue NE
Redmond, WA 98052
(425) 555-1732
s.gonzales@comex.corp.com
Relationship: Past supervisor

Nancy Reeves
Purchasing Director
Northwest Electronic Manufacturing Group
33198 Third Avenue
Seattle, WA 98102
(206) 555-2002
npreeves@nemgroup.com
Relationship: Current customer

The following example provides a more detailed and directed reference page. Here, the candidate not only provides the basic contact information but the skill sets each reference will address. This strategy provides the employer seeking one or more of these specific strengths a road map to the specific destination.

References for Kenneth Wong

Past Supervisor
Able to comment on my ability to organize and plan projects that achieve predetermined goals and get completed on schedule and within budget. Also able to comment on my commitment to the organization and my team members.

Rob Jensen
Senior Project Manager
Qwest
2312 Fourth Avenue
Seattle, WA 98213
(206) 281-2309 (work)

Past Supervisor
Able to comment on my ability to take on complex projects with tight deadlines and motivate a team to achieve goals. Also able to comment on my supervisory ability and the ability to develop staff that is highly regarded and gets promoted.

Cynthia Gonzalez
Acquisitions Manager
Qwest
1981 Fifth Avenue
Denver, CO 80228
(303) 760-2398 (work)

Past Supervisor
Able to comment on my ability to negotiate with government entities and private organizations to acquire properties and rights of way that helped Mountain Wireless grow at a rate of 42% per year for six years.

Revokh Traczewski
Senior Vice President
Mountain Wireless
345 Mountain Drive
Boulder, CO 80303
(720) 764-0987 (work)

Letters of Recommendation

Letters of recommendation have the same purpose as your references. More often than not, the letters will come from the same people who are your references.

A letter of recommendation is an insurance policy, which assures that you will be covered if the person who wrote it has left the company, disappears, or is enjoined from providing recommendations by a new company policy.

The letter of recommendation also provides backup for those nice things you write about yourself in your resume and cover letters and articulate at the interviews. It provides an affirmation by a qualified authority (boss, customer, vendor) that your positive presentation of your skills, achievements, and results is more than just smoke and hyperbole.

Most employers have no objection providing letters of recommendation. The usual problem is in getting around to writing them. Some are too busy. Others would like to but don't know what to say or where to begin. Therefore it is often convenient to provide a list of suggestions and valuable points, including major projects worked on and key successes. Remind them of projects you worked on and some of your more notable accomplishments.

Letters can be critical for those who leave their positions under less-than-positive circumstances. The contents are usually negotiated with the employer and not intended as unqualified praise. Instead, the letter is a careful delineation of the strengths and achievements the employee did demonstrate that both parties feel confident in presenting. Feel free to remind your now ex-boss what some of your successes were. The employer who completes this type of letter will rarely turn around and offer a highly negative account during a reference check.

It is rarely appropriate to enclose letters of recommendation with resumes. Some research suggests that it might be helpful for people in entry-level jobs and for those seeking certain office/administrative positions. With that said, save letters to support your presentation at the interview.

The value of lukewarm or one-size-fits-all letters is also debatable. Such missives include "Rosalyn worked for me for six years in such and such a capacity and she is an excellent employee. I can recommend her without reservation. Should you have any questions feel free to call me." It comes across sounding like an afterthought . . . and so does the employee. It does, however, provide an opening for the interviewer to contact the past employer who, hopefully, will have something more definitive and positive to say about the candidate. Still, this is not the type of letter of recommendation that you would go out of your way to give to a prospective employer.

Cover Letters

Imagine you are sitting in a movie theater watching previews or trailers for coming attractions. Most of what you are seeing is silly, violent, bland, or just plain incomprehensible. Then, out of the blue, comes a trailer that, in one manner or another, captures your attention in a positive manner. It is entertaining, compelling, even funny. It piques your interest and makes you want to go see the movie. It has done its job.

Consider the cover letter the trailer for your resume. It exists to motivate the reader to "see the movie."

There is more.

It is a week later and you are in the theater, watching the movie. Every time one of the clips from the trailer comes on there is a connection. *That* was the piece of business you have been waiting to see again since first viewing it in the trailer. There is an actual feeling of emotional gratification. You have also been provided a glimpse into the universe in which it exists. You have context! It wasn't just some gratuitous event the director threw in but an important component of the story.

In the same way, the claims you made in the cover letter need to exist and have a context in the resume. If not, imagine what kind of emotional letdown you can expect from the reader, and then the subsequent result.

Unless prohibited by the prospective employer, resumes should be accompanied by a cover letter tailored to the specific job to which you are applying. This is true for electronic submissions, providing there's enough space. For these, we recommend placing the cover letter in with the resume document. There it will be the first thing the reader will see on opening the file. This strategy is especially valid for those resumes forwarded to the different recruiters and managers within your targeted employers groups. It assures the cover letter will be included for all parties to see and consider.

The value of the cover letter is that you can tailor it to hit specific hot buttons for a particular position. With careful planning and execution, your cover letter will assure an employer that you understand the requirements of, are qualified for, and can succeed at a given job.

Don't throw away your chance to make an inviting first impression by sending a general letter merely stating your availability and interest. Orient your letter toward obtaining a specific job, *just that job and nothing but that job*!

Think It Through

Writing a customized cover letter takes thought and preparation. For example, before you can assure an employer that you are a perfect fit for a position, you must assure yourself. This requires determining how well your experience and skill set meet the job's requirements.

Start by gathering as much information as possible about the company and available position. Try to obtain a job description or other specifications. If a job description is not available, talk with networking contacts and hiring authorities, review company documents, or visit the Internet or library to research the profession and industry. We'll discuss a method for tailoring your cover letter on page 269 (Tailoring Your Cover Letter to Increase Your Interviews).

Most job descriptions are written with the mythical "ideal candidate" in mind. This is similar to fantasizing about the similarly mythical "ideal mate," and nearly as impossible to find. Few candidates, if any, have the sum total of all the skills, experience, and attributes employers are looking for.

In many cases, they aren't even looking for the person with the full-meal skill deal. Job titles and classifications exist primarily for the benefit of the payroll office, providing a systematic method for paying people. Similarly, the job description is often an amalgamation of everything everyone in the company with that particular designation does. Yet, when the hiring manager needs a new employee, HR will invariably run the standard boilerplate classified ad.

So, don't be intimidated if you are not a perfect match. You might have the perfect skill set the company needs at this time. That is why internal research can be so important; it lets you get to know *exactly* which of your cards to play.

If you cannot develop that information, the best strategy is to select those pieces of the job in which you feel most qualified and make your case.

Next, write down the job's duties and responsibilities. For each item, frame a brief explanation of why you're qualified. Include as many examples from your background as possible. From these, select the one or two examples that are most relevant to the job and company. Don't worry if you discard dramatic accomplishments in favor of more routine examples that better fit the job's requirements. What matters is that the employer sees your background as a good match with the opening.

Your mission in the cover letter (and later in the interview) is to express your strengths. Make your best pitch by emphasizing relevant experience. If you've included this information in your resume, direct attention to it through the cover letter, then elaborate. If you haven't included it in your resume, mention it in your cover letter. While it is usually an advantage to tailor both your resume and cover letter, when time is tight, create a special cover letter for the position and make some quick tweaks to your resume.

Here's where the cover letter earns its pay. For example, one of our clients determined that personnel supervision was a primary requirement for a job to which he was applying. His strongest supervisory experience, however, was earlier in his career and not fully delineated in the resume. Here is how he addressed the issue in his cover letter:

> During my nearly four years as engineering supervisor with Hi-Tech, I planned, assigned and directed the work of four engineers and three technicians. I maintained all hiring and firing authority, and provided regular performance reviews. I was noted by my staff and superiors as a firm yet fair manager who was always available to his staff. The unit consistently met its deadlines and budget constraints, earning two performance commendations from senior management.

A paragraph like this would describe your pertinent experience without diluting or adding undue length to your resume.

Target Hiring Authorities

The mantra of the job search is identifying and directly contacting the *hiring authorities*. Cover letters sent to HR departments can get lost or not forwarded to these hiring authorities with the resumes. Because your cover letter is designed to enhance your resume, try to increase the odds that a hiring manager receives them together. When possible, direct your letter and attached resume directly to the hiring manager. When snail mailing, use paper clips to attach the two documents and mention in your letter that your resume is enclosed. One good idea is to use the same header from the resume on the letter. It is an impressive way to brand your submissions, similar to using a personal letterhead. It's perfectly acceptable, however, to prepare cover letters on standard white paper.

Beware of the cover letter that presents you in pale generalities or empty superlatives. These one-size-fits-all cover letters are insulting, self-defeating, and destined for the trash can. Make sure you provide context for those nice things you say about yourself.

The Time Machine

Another way to look at the cover letter is as a time machine, linking your past (resume) with your future (new job). Your resume states what you've done; the cover letter states what you can do. It shows your potential, the major consideration in any hiring decision. Match your cover letter to the job you are pursuing, and, instead of rehashing your resume, expand on it. Take the reader from the past to the future and clearly show your potential for success in the new job.

Know Your Audience

It is critical to inform the reader that you understand the organization to which you are applying. One or two well-placed sentences can usually do the job. What do you know about the company? Have you used its products or services?

"As an avid golfer, I have used your line of clubs for over ten years. Long before I ever dreamed of representing you, I have been extolling the virtues of your products to anyone and everyone who would listen."

"In this era of increasingly impersonal service, I have been overwhelmed by the personalized service I have received, and continue to receive, at 1st Coastal Bank. This is the kind of philosophy that builds loyal customers such as myself."

Do you know people who are employed there? If so, what do they say about it?

> Joanne Gibson, your eastside branch manager, who I have known for years through our professional organization, assures me that there is no better place to work than XYZ.

> Roger Gray, your Regional Purchasing Manager, has been my customer for eight years. He is a quality individual and can't say enough about ABC.

> John McNamara at IBM believes you are one of the top management consulting firms in the country.

Has it been featured in the media for one or more achievements?

> *The Puget Sound Business Journal* described your company as "the small company with the big heart."

> The recent feature on your company in the *New York Times* business section convinced me that you are now the gold standard in the industry.

To get the clearest picture of how an organization views itself, visit its website and check out its mission statement. Next, check out the company history to get an idea as to its track record. Adapt these items into your cover letter.

> Like the ABC Company, I have a reputation for uncompromising customer service.

> The XYZ Agency was founded to provide free or low-cost housing services to previously unserved populations. My background in developing and implementing similar programs is perfectly aligned with that mission.

TO WHOM IT MAY CONCERN

As repeatedly mentioned throughout, always try to get your material directly to the hiring authority. This strategy, however, is becoming more and more difficult as managers are now well hidden behind layers of impersonal gatekeepers, email, and voicemail. Their identities are often protected with the same levels of security as the Manhattan Project.

But you have to send the stuff to somebody!

Most job announcements will provide some direction as to whom to address your materials. Usually, it is the ubiquitous "Human Resources Department." A phone call to HR requesting the name of the specific individual handling this position can be valuable. It can also yield nothing.

In these cases, the appropriate heading might read "Dear Human Resources." A little awkward but it's better than nothing.

Additional acceptable salutations might include:

Dear Sales Manager
Dear Service Manager
Dear Engineering Manager

Here are some headings to avoid:

To Whom It May Concern
Dear Sirs
Dear Sir or Ma'am

When in doubt use the term "Search Director." It is gender neutral and unlikely to offend anybody.

THE JOB'S THE THING

Use the *exact* job title as it is being advertised, not what you think the position should be called. Job titles vary from company to company and even within certain large companies. Titles such as program manager, project manager, and product manager are often used interchangeably in general conversation but within certain organizations can have major differences in status, responsibility, and compensation. In one company a sales manager's job is to supervise a workforce; in another it describes an individual contributor assigned to a specific region.

Most jobs have an associated reference number, which can be easily inserted in the cover letter to avoid any confusion.

I am applying for the position of Machinist (Ref #M-206) with the Coleman Company.

The cover letter is a piece of correspondence that introduces you to an employer. All resumes sent through the mail should be accompanied by a cover letter. The cover letter personalizes your resume and gives it greater flexibility. If your resume does not contain an objective, the cover letter is the place to express it. A cover letter provides an opportunity to share points that are not easily covered in a resume. So a resume and a cover letter represent the ideal vehicle to get across all of the key ideas you want an employer to know about you.

A resume that arrives without a cover letter is an incomplete presentation. There is no indication that you have any idea as to what you are applying for or where you're applying for it. It smacks of shotgunning, or shooting your resume to any and all targets out there. This is not a recommended or effective practice.

When answering a want ad, specify the exact job title in the cover letter. It is not necessary to specify the source of the ad or its date. The exact title will provide all the information HR needs. When an ad explicitly requests certain types of experience that you have, but that are not adequately covered in the resume, use your cover letter to fill in the details. The alternative would be to rewrite your resume slightly to include the necessary details. A highly targeted cover letter with a resume modified specifically for that job will usually provide better results.

View your cover letter and resume as a team. Each performs a different function, but they must work well together. Cover letters generally consist of two to four short paragraphs and seldom total more than twenty lines. The first paragraph should open with a strong statement about you that arouses interest and curiosity. Devote a middle paragraph to an accomplishment that will further arouse interest. Refer to the parts of the resume that make your strongest case. Don't be afraid to select specific entries from the resume and either present them exactly or paraphrase them.

Appeal to the employer's self-interest by supplying those specific examples or universal strengths that demonstrate your value. You are a problem solver and hiring you will lead to increased production, greater efficiency, better planning, less waste, higher profits, and more satisfied customers.

> I can save money for your firm by utilizing my experience in cost control. At Standard Products I reduced paper usage by 24% and photocopying costs by 30%.

> I can help increase the impact of your agency. While at Family Services I wrote a proposal that was funded for $22,000. This allowed us to significantly increase the quantity and quality of our services.

CREATE A TEMPLATE

Since most of the positions you will be applying for will be fairly closely related, you can prepare a basic template you can *massage* for each position. In most cases, up to 80% or even 90% of the content will be permanent. It is the remainder you personalize for each position.

In creating the template, first determine which of your key assets you wish to include. Select the ones that provide an accurate representation of your skill set as it applies to the types of jobs you are seeking.

Thus, if you are looking at retail management, which of your demonstrated skills and experiences will best showcase your value to the reader? Leadership, sales increases, margin increases, cost containment, company awards, and special assignments will count here.

If you are transitioning to a related field or seeking a promotion, select those pieces of your past that best support your argument. A project lead applying for management; a customer service specialist attempting to move into sales give you several options. Present the experiences and the achievements that most reflect those successes and, of course, inform the reader that this is just the tip of the iceberg, with more to follow in the resume.

Below is an example of a cover letter template. Can you build one like it for yourself?

Hiring Authority
Company
Address
Address

Date

Dear _____:

I would like to present my qualifications for the position of (<u>exact Job Title</u>) with (<u>Company</u>).

As you will learn from my resume, I have strong (<u>type of</u>) experience in (industries/-locations/etc.).

You will note that wherever I have worked I have established a reputation for (<u>quality/integrity/initiative/attention to detail/leadership/etc.</u>).

In my (<u>current/recent/etc.</u>) position, I _____
_____.

Previously, _____
_____.

I am excited about bringing my skill set to (<u>Company</u>). (<u>Why? What do you know about the company? Products? Services? Reputation? Track Record? Etc.?</u>)

I believe my blend of ability, experience, and achievement makes me an ideal fit for your (<u>type of</u>) team. I am confident you will agree.

I look forward to hearing from you.

Sincerely,

BE PROACTIVE

Most job seekers send off the resume and cover letter to the posted address to await the positive response that may or may not come. Unfortunately, no response is often the only response they get. Whether online or in the mail, it is becoming more common for companies to not even acknowledge receipt of your materials. Why? Lack of resources, for one. Corporations are operating "lean and mean!" So, even if a response requires little more than entering some personalized data into a response letter or email, chances are there is nobody around to do it. The best you might hope for is an autoresponse message acknowledging receipt. Not real warm and fuzzy.

If you did your homework, you sent your packet directly to the hiring authority. It may end up, unread, in HR, but at least there is a chance your intended target will read it.

With that in mind, take it to the next level. Instead of awaiting a reply, inform the hiring authority that you will be following up with a phone call to schedule a brief meeting to discuss the position and, perhaps, other opportunities within the organization. Do not use the word *interview*! An interview is a formal, by-the-numbers step in the hiring process. A meeting is a get-together of two individuals for the express purpose of sharing ideas. It is to learn more about the position, the type of work, and the company prior to making formal application.

Tailor your cover letters even if you develop a standard cover letter to be sent to a hundred or more companies. Write the cover letter so you can insert the name of the company somewhere in the body of the letter.

Review the sample cover letters, then simply start writing.

February 4, 2009

John Travis, Director
Home Energy Department
N. W. Center for Energy Efficiency
323 Sixth Avenue
Seattle, Washington 98021

Dear Mr. Travis:

Your recent efforts to promote energy conservation are of great interest to me. My experience as Energy Consultant for Seattle City Light would make me an excellent candidate for several positions in your organization.

While at City Light, I have inspected and provided energy savings estimates on over 500 homes. Eighty percent of the homeowners have acted on one or more of my suggestions and have averaged over 17% in energy savings.

I will call you next week to arrange a brief meeting.

Sincerely,

Brad Tolliver

January 11, 2009

Leslie Acosta
Regional Sales Manager
Peoples Pharmaceuticals
5825 146th Avenue S.E.
Bellevue, Washington 98006

Dear Ms. Acosta:

I was attracted to Peoples Pharmaceuticals when I read your annual report. My medical background and my customer service experience make me an excellent candidate for a sales/marketing position in your organization.

While at Danton Instruments, I was a key person involved in the writing and organization of new product manuals. My oral presentations to the sales force were always valuable and well received. District sales managers and the sales representatives themselves consistently expressed appreciation for the sales aids and information given to them. In addition, a large part of my time was spent working closely with our customers, successfully troubleshooting problems, answering questions, and informing them of new products or instrument applications that might better serve their needs.

I will look forward to hearing from you soon.

Sincerely,

Sandra Gulliver

Next is an example where the applicant has spoken to the employer by phone and is thanking the person for having given him some time. There was no opening, so the cover letter is also acting as a thank-you note. Notice that the first paragraph was written strictly for this one letter. The other paragraphs are part of the standard cover letter.

12/2/08

Paulette Meyers
National Sales Manager
San Sebastian Winery
San Sebastian, California 95476

Dear Ms. Meyers:

I very much enjoyed our conversation yesterday. As I indicated, I have always been impressed with San Sebastian Winery. At the Blue Panda in Portland, I was instrumental in taking San Sebastian wines from our sixth most popular wine to number two. I totally agree with you that a top sales rep must be highly knowledgeable about wines. I frequently invite wine reps to give wine tastings at the restaurant, both for my own benefit and for the staff. I think you would be impressed with both my knowledge and my palate.

At the Blue Panda Restaurants I have always been a producer. I run what has become one of the most profitable restaurants in the chain, and our wine sales are ranked number one. At each of the four restaurants I've managed, wine sales experienced dramatic increases. I am committed to remaining in the Northwest and am confident I can substantially increase your wine sales in this region.

I will call you in a few weeks to learn about any developments.

Sincerely,

Tom Reston

Dear Mr. Ronagen:

Your ad for a Western Region Dealer Representative was of great interest to me. I am very impressed with the Mitsubishi Company and the cars it produces. I would very much like to be a part of Mitsubishi, particularly in the area of dealer servicing. I can help Mitsubishi establish the reputation it wants for parts and service.

I know what is required to make service and parts departments run smoothly and profitably. I have always developed close working relations with dealership owners as well as parts and service managers.

In Oregon I worked closely with 16 VW dealerships. Most were poorly managed and barely making money. The service departments were all losing money. Within a year their appearances were tremendously improved, mechanics and service managers had received additional training, and quality control and inventory control systems had been established. Parts sales jumped 85%, and sales of new cars rose 45%.

I am committed to the automotive industry. My experience in Oregon is just one example of what I have been able to do with dealerships. Please feel free to contact me so I can tell you more about my background.

Dear Mr. Swenson:

As a Project Manager and Construction Manager for Danson Construction, I have overseen both large and small projects. As an architect I can design projects or work with an architect to come up with the best and most cost-effective design. I have hired contractors and have been very successful in making sure the projects were completed on time and were of high quality.

My degree in architecture, along with four years' experience in designing, cost estimating, and managing construction projects, plus nearly one year of drafting, make me an ideal candidate for your Facilities Engineer position. I am a person of high energy, which has enabled me to watch the many details of a construction project and make sure everything was completed correctly. That same energy and hard work will prove most helpful as I oversee projects at your many facilities along the East Coast.

Dear Ms. Glasser:

Since age eleven I have wanted to work as a flight attendant. I've been working in restaurants the last four years because I believed it would give me the best training possible for being a flight attendant.

I moved up into restaurant management so quickly because I proved I could handle the responsibility. I mix very well with customers and make each one feel important. This has increased the number of steady customers at each restaurant where I have worked.

I am also a problem solver. At Leo's I helped reduce operating costs significantly. At J. K. Jake's I reduced turnover by working more closely with the staff.

I am very much looking forward to interviewing for a flight attendant position.

Dear Ms. Preminger:

I have had a very exciting nine years in hotel sales, six of those years as Director of Sales. During that time I have developed highly effective techniques for attracting association and corporate business.

I would enjoy very much the opportunity to describe in more detail why those techniques have worked so well, and why I would function effectively as your next Sales Manager.

Make Your Resume and Cover Letter Work as a Team

On the next two pages you'll find Dante Jackson's resume and cover letter. Notice how he expands some of the points from the resume he included in the cover letter. Dante created a personalized letterhead for himself. The decision to do so is up to you. Dante used the Arial font for his cover letter and resume but selected Arial Rounded Bold for his letterhead.

How does it look to you? When in doubt, use the same header as on the resume. It provides a "branding" of your presentation.

Arial

Dante Jackson
2314 Cerrito Avenue
Oakland, CA 94611
(510) 745-0980
dante64@aol.com

11/5/08

Bob Hanson
Director of Operations
XYZ Corp.
2438 4th Avenue
Oakland, CA 94612

Dear Mr. Hanson,

I have a strong background in all aspects of shipping, receiving, and inventory control. I am very interested in your Shipping and Receiving Manager position.

I develop strong working relations with internal and external customers and I respond quickly to their needs. I have implemented systems which have significantly reduced costs and improved customer relations.

I'm recognized as an excellent supervisor. People like working for me and I have reduced absenteeism by over 45%. I cross-train my staff and they like the variety and knowing that their market value is increased. By developing a better scheduling system and through our cross-training, we have been able to reduce late shipments from nine per month to less than two per month. Largely because of the cross-training and the improved productivity due to lower turnover, our overtime in the shipping and receiving department has been cut by 25%.

XYZ Corp. is known for its customer service and its strong promotion from within policy. That is exactly the type of organization I want to be a part of. I look forward to meeting with you.

Sincerely,

Dante Jackson

Arial

Dante Jackson

2314 Cerrito Avenue
Oakland, CA 94611
(510) 745-0980
dante64@aol.com

OBJECTIVE: Shipping and Receiving/Inventory Control Supervision

QUALIFICATIONS

Broad knowledge of shipping and receiving and inventory control. Develop strong working relations with internal and external customers and respond quickly to their needs. Have implemented systems that have significantly reduced costs and improved customer relations. Excellent supervisor.

EMPLOYMENT

Simplotic Corp., Oakland, CA   6/01–Present

Shipping And Receiving Supervisor – 7/03–Present. File the daily shipping and receiving log and distribute all incoming materials. Work closely with department managers to resolve discrepancies on purchase orders. Keep production manager and other supervisors apprised of products with shipment priority, and ensure products ship on schedule. Negotiate with vendors and purchase all shipping materials.

- Developed a system that has reduced late shipments from nine per month to less than two per month.

- Developed an inventory control program that has reduced stocking levels of finished printed circuit boards from $1.6 million to less than $1.0 million.

- Reduced cost of shipping materials by ordering larger quantities and receiving staggered deliveries.

- Installed a system of packaging and boxing circuit boards that has resulted in a 99% shipment completion rate and 94% accuracy rate versus 66% and 78% in the past.

Shipping and Receiving Clerk – 6/01–7/03. Inspected incoming shipments and ensured all ordered parts and components had arrived. Made visual inspections to identify damaged items. Responsible for shipping finished circuit boards to customers.

EDUCATION

AA—Communications, Sequoia Community College   (2002)

Tailoring Your Cover Letters To Increase Your Interviews

While many employment ads provide only the barest information, some are quite explicit. Jobs posted on job bulletin boards or on the Internet are usually fairly detailed. To create a top quality cover letter in response to a detailed description, first analyze the ad by listing all of the key requirements, and then list your experience, knowledge, and the results that qualify you for each point.

If you have little knowledge or experience in any given area, do not let that stop you from applying. The ad has indicated the background of the ideal candidate and that person may simply not be available. The standard wisdom is that if you meet more than half the requirements, and know you could do an excellent job, take the time to create a cover letter that is tailored for that position.

THE MATCH GAME

All of the cover letters you have just read sell the candidates, but there is another type of cover letter format that can be very effective. It is a cover letter that lists the key requirements from the ad and then demonstrates how the applicant more than meets the requirements.

To use this approach you should meet or exceed each point *you select* to respond to. Respond to only those points you have strength in. Be careful not to skip over too many as it will appear obvious you are holding back for a reason—such as having nothing to say! If you cannot provide decent responses to the majority of requirements, reconsider applying. If, however, despite knowing your odds are poor, you really want the job and believe you could be successful at it, go for it. This strategy is designed mainly to get you past the initial screening, which is by and large weighted on minimum qualifications. The screener will almost assuredly not be an expert in your field and will be working off a checklist. If the items on the list are not obvious in the resume and cover letter, expect to be eliminated.

The following example demonstrates why you want to do everything possible to avoid being eliminated by a screener. Sandra, a mechanical engineer with two years' experience, applied for a position that she was excited about and felt she was perfectly suited for. Two weeks after sending her resume in response to an ad, she got a rejection letter. Rather than meekly accepting the rejection, she called the company and spoke to the hiring manager. She sold herself to him and intentionally made no mention of the rejection letter. Obviously impressed by what he was hearing, he asked her to stay on the line for a moment. While away from the phone he reviewed her resume and learned that a rejection letter had been sent out. He came back about three minutes later and told her to ignore the letter that might be arriving any day. He then set up an appointment with her. She interviewed for the position and got the job.

There are two major lessons to learn from this situation. It demonstrates how important it is for the resume and cover letter to fully sell you. In Sandra's case, her resume was good but not particularly tailored to the job, and her cover letter was only adequate. The screener simply did not see her qualifications.

It also demonstrates the importance of not giving up. Many people have ultimately been hired because they did things that their competitors did not. Sandra very much wanted the job and knew she would be great at it, so she overcame her natural timidity and made that call. Although her heart was pounding as she rang the manager's office, once she got him on the phone she comfortably described her experience and accomplishments. He immediately recognized her potential.

Obviously there was no guarantee that Sandra's actions were going to have such a desirable outcome. It didn't matter to her, however; she simply wanted a shot at it, and she gave it her best. While Sandra is to be admired for her gumption, a better-written presentation might have prevented its necessity.

ANALYZING AN AD

Accountant
For manufacturing and distribution business. Accounting degree, 4 yrs experience, strong PC and spreadsheet skills. Will have GL, AP, AR, and office management responsibilities. Knowledge of Real World accounting software and human resources practices desirable. Our accountant is responsible for all aspects of our accounting, works with our outside CPA firm and reports directly to the Pres. Send resume to A&B Concrete, 1348 NW Jubilee Road, Plano, TX 75075

Let's see how Jill responded to an ad for an accountant. Her first step was to determine the key points. Then she identified the parts of her background that met the requirements. At this point she was not concerned with quality writing, just the matches. By the time she finished her list, the cover letter practically wrote itself. Notice how she covered every point in her analysis and then produced a very strong cover letter.

Accountant / Manufacturing–Distribution

Requirements	*Qualified By*
Accounting degree	BA - accounting
4 years experience	3 years accounting plus one year office work
Strong PC skills	Excellent knowledge of Windows XP, Word, Publisher Trained in Vista
Strong spreadsheet skills	Heavy experience with Excel. Know how to create macros

Responsibilities

General ledger Accounts payable Accounts receivable	Three years working heavily with GL, AP, AR. One year with AccPac and two with Great Plains. Converted the GL, AP, and AR to AccPac and significantly improved those areas. Reduced receivables from 12% being 90 days or over, to 4% being 90 or over
Office management	Know how to run an office – handled most responsibilities of the office and reported to the office manager for one year
All aspects of accounting	Experienced in GL, AP, AR, internal auditing, financial statements, reducing receivables, payroll, cost accounting, taxes
Works with CPA firm	Have not worked directly with CPA firm, but my boss did and I know what is required

Desirable

Knowledge of Real World Accounting software	Experienced with AccPac and Great Plains Accounting software which have the same modules and similar techniques as RWA
Knowledge of human resources	Took a business course in human resource practices Knowledgeable of benefits, wage and salary administration, 401(k) plans, and retirement plans

Jill Josephson

13289 NE Piedmont Drive
Plano, Texas 75075
(806) 764-0098

2/5/09

Accounting Manager
A&B Concrete
1348 NW Jubilee Road
Plano, TX 75075

Dear Accounting Manager:

I graduated from the University of Texas three years ago with a BA in accounting. During the past three years with a medium-size manufacturer, I have had the opportunity to work in all aspects of accounting including GL, AP, AR, internal auditing, financial statements, payroll, cost accounting, and taxes. I have had one year of experience with AccPac and two years with Great Plains. I am especially strong in accounts receivable. In the past two years I have reduced our 90 day and over receivables from 12% to less than 4%.

Last year I had the opportunity to oversee a conversion from Great Plains to AccPac. The conversion went smoothly and we completed the process on schedule.

I have broad PC skills with excellent knowledge of Microsoft Office. I'm very strong with Windows XP and I recently attended a three-day course in Vista, which we will be converting to next month. I have heavy experience in Excel and have created numerous timesaving macros.

A business course in human resources gave me a good overview of the field. With my accounting experience I have gained knowledge of benefits, wage and salary administration, 401(k) plans, and retirement plans. I have also had exposure to health insurance and have worked closely with our HMO in several instances.

I also have solid office experience. During college I worked part-time in an office for three years and handled basically all of the office functions. During the office manager's vacations I functioned as the office manager and supervised a staff of four. I also trained several new employees.

I am looking for a new challenge and would welcome the opportunity to interview with you.

Sincerely,

Jill Josephson

Check out how Travis selected and responded to key points from a customer service job ad. Although this technique is not appropriate for everyone, it can be very effective when you respond to almost every point.

> **Customer Service**
> NetCare, Inc., a leader in the software industry, has immediate full-time openings for Customer Service Representatives to provide order processing and quality customer service through its national call center. Mon. - Fri., various shifts available. Qualifications include excellent customer service/sales skills, professional enthusiasm to support Internet products. Previous customer service, PC/Windows experience is required, software sales experience a plus. Please mail your resume to NetCare, 534 NE Fourth, Philadelphia, PA 19108. No phone calls please.

Customer Service / Software Distributor

Duties/Responsibilities

Order processing	Learn new systems quickly Excellent keyboarder
Quality customer service	Work hard to keep customers happy Four years of customer service experience

Qualifications

Excellent customer service skills	Get to know systems and procedures well so I can get a problem fixed. Know how to satisfy customers. Work hard to resolve problems. Excellent telephone voice. Always pleasant and helpful. Four years of experience
Excellent sales skills	Handled inside sales for two years for an electrical wholesaler. Know how to produce "add on" sales
Professional enthusiasm to support product line	Always enthusiastic and ready to help a customer
PC/Windows experience	Broad experience in Windows 2000, NT 4.0, XP, Vista

Desirable

Software sales	Sold electrical products to electrical contractors

3428 N Wankle Drive
Philadelphia, PA 19106
(215) 527-9191

NetCare
534 NE Fourth
Philadelphia, PA 19108

Dear NetCare:

I have an excellent background in customer service and am very interested in your Customer Service Representative position. I have over four years of customer service experience and have always been highly valued by both my employers and customers. My background fits your requirements very well.

Excellent Customer Service Skills
For both of my employers I quickly got to know their systems and procedures. This enables me to quickly assess a customer's problem and then resolve it. I work hard at satisfying customers and have frequently been told that I am friendly and helpful. I know the level of service that customers expect and I know how to deliver it. I'm told I have a very pleasant phone voice. I have four years of experience in customer service and have been given progressively more responsible assignments.

Excellent Sales Skills
For two years I handled inside sales for an electrical wholesaler. I was recognized as one of the best inside sales people on staff and was particularly effective at "add on sales."

Professional Enthusiasm to Support Product Line
I have always been viewed as a person with lots of enthusiasm. When I believe in the product and service of the company I work for, I am always enthusiastic and can sell our service or product. Because I believe in my company and the quality of my work, the customer always has confidence as well.

PC/Windows Experience
I have broad experience in Windows Vista, XP, and 2000, and I can install software. I have also trained many people on database and word processing software.

I look forward to a personal interview. The position appears to be very challenging and I would enjoy taking on such a challenge.

Sincerely,

Travis Johanson

This cover letter will sell Travis very effectively. He also has an excellent resume to accompany the cover letter. Obviously a cover letter like this will take a little longer to compose than merely using your standard cover letter. That extra effort, however, can make a big difference in the number of interviews you obtain.

USING YOUR OWN AD ANALYSIS TO BUILD YOUR COVER LETTER

After analyzing an ad, as demonstrated above, you can basically do two things with the information.

First, you can create a traditional cover letter as Jill did, touching on all or most of the ad's points, without referring to them directly (e.g. general ledger, office management, accounts receivable, etc.). Or, as Travis did, list each point and respond directly and in detail. Either way you will create an excellent cover letter.

Tip: Performing this analysis will also strengthen your interviewing responses.

Marketing Letters

How to Write Them—How to Use Them

Being different often brings positive results. Marketing letters are successful for that reason—they're different. The marketing letter presents your strongest accomplishments, often those with quantifiable results, to entice the reader. Dates and names of employers are seldom mentioned. The marketing letter acts as a substitute for a resume with a cover letter. In essence, the marketing letter is more like a lengthened cover letter than a resume. Compared to resumes, marketing letters are more personal in tone and more like business correspondence in appearance. Consequently, they tend not to be screened out by administrative assistants.

Marketing letters are perhaps the best-kept secret in job hunting. Less than 1% of all job seekers use marketing letters, yet few job-finding strategies can lead to more appointments and job interviews. By sending only the marketing letter, your resume is held in reserve for later use. The key to success is addressing it to a specific person and informing that person that a phone call will follow. Your goal is to meet as many hiring managers as possible, regardless of whether any openings exist at the moment. This is accomplished by requesting brief meetings (usually about 15–20 minutes).

The use of marketing letters has dramatically improved the way our clients find jobs. In the past we had clients cold-call potential employers to request appointments. They understood the importance of the calls, knew they would work, and had practiced what they would say. However, some failed to make their calls, and those who did call often procrastinated. Sending a marketing letter makes placing those calls easier. Knowing that a person is expecting your call, and is already convinced that you have something of quality to offer, makes a substantial difference psychologically. Using the marketing letter, combined with effective telephone skills, should get you in to see hiring managers 30 to 60% of the time. Contacting the most senior executives (e.g., CEO, president, CFO) reduces the probability to 10 to 20%. Still, not too shabby a return on a small investment of time and postage.

Notice the impact potential of the following marketing letter and you'll begin to see why this strategy gets results. It is especially strong because each accomplishment has been quantified, always a winner.

The marketing letter presents you in a way that is of value to the employer. It can highlight those skills and experiences you acquired at various times in your career without providing specific dates or even job titles. The essential information here is the quality of your experience and results that might be buried on the second page of a resume under unrelated job titles in an unconnected industry.

EMPLOYER MEETINGS

The philosophy of these sessions is that any good manager should be a good talent scout as well. Thus, a person with a valuable skill set and experience, making contact, even *unsolicited* contact, is someone who should be afforded consideration. Why? Because there might be a need for this person at any point in the future . . . from two minutes after the meeting to a few years.

Some job seekers feel comfortable just picking up the phone and contacting employers without having previously sent a marketing letter. They are the lucky ones; they are also the minority. Cold-calling is rarely anyone's favorite activity. It is more often their most dreaded one. The beauty of the marketing letter is that it "greases the skids." It prepares the person for your call. Then, when you are connected, you do not have to go through the painful cold introduction.

Put yourself in the role of an employer and check out the following marketing letter. Would you think it worthwhile to meet the author, even if you did not have a position available at the moment? If the person asked for just 15 minutes of your time, would you say yes? Remember, a responsibility of managers is to maintain a list of potential employees in the event a person quits, or changing market conditions require a special set of talents.

John Gaddly
1121 65th S.W.
Red Rock, California 92006
(916) 456-9874
jgaddly@infonet.net

January 20, 2009

John Campbell
Executive Vice President
Diversified Products Inc.
440 5th N.W.
Redding, California 96001

Dear Mr. Campbell:

When I joined my current employer two years ago as Production Superintendent, our quality control department was rejecting 6% of all printed circuit boards. Today that figure is less than 1% and continuing downward.

You may be interested in a person who has broad experience in solving production problems. Here are some other things I've done:

> Reduced absenteeism 42% and turnover 31%. With less turnover we were able to invest more in training, with a corresponding increase in quality and productivity. While rejections dropped from 6% to less than 1%, productivity increased 22% per employee.

> Introduced an idea program with incentives. The number of suggestions that were implemented grew from 11 in 2004 to 65 in 2008. In 2008 bonuses cost $25,000 while documented savings amounted to $197,000.

> Implemented an inventory control system. We increased production 34% with only a 6% increase in inventory. Production delays due to unavailable parts dropped from 72 to 11 during the first three years of the program.

> Instituted a company-wide safety program. Lost time due to accidents was reduced 21% during the first six months. Reductions in insurance premiums saved $85,000 in the second year of the program.

I graduated from the University of Wisconsin in 1985 with a degree in Business. Since then I have experienced rapid promotions during 24 years in manufacturing.

I'll call you next week to arrange a time when we might meet for fifteen or twenty minutes.

Sincerely,

John Gaddly

The next two examples demonstrate the flexibility of marketing letters. While they use a more narrative format and are less quantifiable, they also have a strong impact on the reader.

11918 Northeast 143rd Place
Kirkland, Washington 98034
(425) 821-3830

2/10/09

Peter Phillips
Sahalee Development Corp.
2119 Fourth Avenue
Seattle, Washington 98124

Dear Mr. Phillips:

In anticipation of the next development upsurge, you may be looking for a person with a broad background in land development and marketing. I have saved projects from failure, reduced development costs, and increased project marketability.

Recently, at the developer's request, I was retained to save a mobile home project that had been rejected during preliminary hearings. By creating a new marketing strategy, employing a more imaginative design, and representing the client throughout the remainder of the public hearings process, I was able to negotiate the project's approval.

As part of a team of consultants for a 1900-acre/$680 million new town development, I prevented costly delays by reducing agency review time and ensuring project approval with appropriate planning and design concepts. This saved the developer hundreds of thousands of dollars in additional consultant fees and penalty payments for an extension of the land-purchase option.

I have nine years' combined experience in civil engineering, land planning, and urban design. I graduated from the University of Washington with a B.A. in Urban Planning.

I will call you next week to arrange a time when we might meet briefly to discuss my background and your future needs.

Sincerely,

Roger Cricky

1298 N. Rosewood Avenue
Portland, Oregon 97211
(503) 682-9874

12/1/08

Don Harris
Vice President, Sales and Marketing
MicroCad
4309 Sepulveda Boulevard
Los Angeles, California 90030

Dear Mr. Harris,

I am currently looking at sales management positions with medium-sized high-tech manufacturers. During the last 15 years I have worked for Datacomp and Syngestics and am currently district sales manager for a major manufacturer of teleprocessing equipment.

I was given a mandate three years ago to strengthen the Pacific Northwest district. During that time we have increased sales an average of 35% annually, the highest rate in the region. I'm known as a motivator. I work closely with my staff to develop marketing strategies and I give them the independence they need to be effective.

I've been successful in both sales and sales management. As a senior account manager for six years with Datacomp, I took my territory from a ranking of 19th nationally to 5th and exceeded quota each year. I got my start in the industry with Syngestics. As a field marketing support rep for two years, my district exceeded its sales quota each year. Then as area supervisor for three years I supervised six field marketing-support engineers. The staff was rated number one in the region for providing technical support, two years in a row.

With a history of success behind me, I believe I can contribute to the further growth of MicroCad. I am strong in marketing, sales training, staff recruiting, and staff development. I will call you next week to learn about your future plans.

Sincerely,

Paul Sanderson

Writing an effective marketing letter requires that you first have a results-oriented and *empowered* resume. Once the resume is complete, the marketing letter almost writes itself. In fact, the results statements used in the marketing letter can come almost word for word from the resume.

The core of any marketing letter is the presentation of your results and experience. To write a strong marketing letter, review your resume and think through how you want to summarize your background. If you have some key projects or results that can be quantified, simply describe them, as was done in the first sample letter. If your career does not lend itself to that approach, the more narrative form might work best for you. Names of employers and key customers are seldom mentioned unless well-known or prestigious. Provide them only if you think they will sufficiently impress the reader and help your case.

Remember, the marketing letter is not a resume. The reader is not expecting to know everything about you. Your goal is to have quick impact. Your letter should cause the person to recognize your value and to remember you when you call.

Borrow freely from the resume. Take a look at your qualifications statement; in many cases parts of it can be imported almost verbatim. Even the results can be used with little or no change. Let it flow. Make sure sentences are complete, unlike the *telegraphic* style of the resume. Don't be concerned if your resume and marketing letter have similar phrasing; no one will notice. Lead-ins for your results could be worded:

You may be interested in my labor negotiating experience. Some of my additional accomplishments are:

My six years in customer relations could be valuable to you. This experience includes:

If your advertising department needs a person with strong experience, you may be interested in what I've done.

If you choose to describe jobs, as in the third sample marketing letter, phrases can again be lifted from the resume. Since this is a marketing letter, describe only the most important and relevant positions, even if they are not presented in any chronological order.

A good closing paragraph for your marketing letter might include a summary of your background, such as the number of years in your field, and information about your degree and alma mater. The final paragraph then prepares the reader for any follow-up contact you might make. In most cases this will be a follow-up phone call.

If the contact person is local, request a brief meeting and indicate this in the letter. Emphasize the term *brief*. Let these people know you understand the value of their time.

If the person is out of state but is likely to be in your area in the next two or three months, see if you can line up an appointment for that time. If the person has no plans to be in your area, polish up your phone skills because that is probably going to be the vehicle for the meeting. If you will be in the person's area in the near future, ask for a brief appointment when you're in town.

For more on how to follow up after sending a marketing letter, see Appendix B for examples of marketing letters and techniques for using them.

RESUME, COVER LETTER, AND MARKETING LETTER WORKING TOGETHER

The best way to understand how a resume, marketing letter, and cover letter work together is to see a sample of each for the same person. Here, the resume was written first, followed by the marketing letter. The cover letter borrowed some elements from the marketing letter, making it fairly quick and easy to write.

RANDAL JOHNSON
4045 NW Abilene
Denver, Colorado 80239
(303) 765-8967
rjzi@cortez.com

OBJECTIVE: Regional Manager

QUALIFICATIONS

Strong background in trucking with 17 years of management experience. Consistently increase market share and profitability. In a sales capacity, bring in large national accounts and significantly increase revenue from established accounts.

EDUCATION

A. A. - Business Management, Reginald Community College (2001)

EMPLOYMENT

Ryan Freight 12/00 to Present

Terminal Manager - Denver, CO, 7/03 to present. Responsible for the total operation and sales throughout Colorado. Planned and implemented a break bulk operation that reduced shipment time from 28 hours to 16 hours. Expanded the account base to include major national accounts such as Honeywell, Cisco, Goodyear, and Motorola, and ultimately attained "prime general commodity status" with each of them.

Through improved sales and customer service efforts, have increased revenue from $4 million to $19.5 million. Consistently ranked among the top five performers in customer service and on-time deliveries within the 42-terminal system. Won award for the "best average revenue per shipment" in three consecutive years.

Terminal Manager - Portland, OR, 12/00 to 7/03. Managed sales and operations for Oregon and increased revenue 74%. Significantly improved the transit service for Oregon accounts into the Rocky Mountain and Southwest regions. Took Ryan from 8th in market share to 4th in the Oregon region.

Longrider Lines 2/90 to 12/00

Terminal Manager - Scranton, PA, 2/97 to 12/00. Established primary general commodity carrier status with numerous accounts including GTE, Sears, Ralston Purina, and Mattel. Led terminal to achieve consecutive annual regional awards for exceeding revenue and on-time delivery goals (1998, 1999). Took the terminal from the 3rd lowest rated terminal in the 15 terminal region, to 4th highest.

Prior positions with Longrider: Operations Manager, Scranton, PA, 2/95 to 2/97; Supervisor, Terminal Operations, Scranton, PA, 1/93 to 2/95; Management Trainee, Pittsburgh, PA, 1/90 to 1/93.

(With the resume in place the marketing letter was easy to write.)

(Marketing Letter)

RANDAL JOHNSON
4045 NW Abilene
Denver, Colorado 80239
(303) 765-8967
rjzi@cortez.com

2/7/08

Ron Pitts
President
B&N Freightlines
1287 Wacker Drive
Chicago, Illinois 60626

Dear Mr. Pitts,

I have a strong background in the trucking industry with 17 years of management experience. With each company and at each of the four terminals managed, I significantly increased market share and quickly increased profitability. At each terminal I achieved one of the best on-time delivery records in the industry. I am now looking for a regional management position.

I have broad sales and marketing experience. At each terminal I devoted 40-50% of my time to marketing, sales, and sales management. Throughout my career I have brought in large national accounts and substantially increased the revenue from established accounts. I have achieved primary carrier status with such accounts as Honeywell, Cisco, Goodyear, Motorola, GTE, Sears, Mattel, and Ralston Purina.

With my current employer, our Denver terminal won the annual award for the "best average revenue per shipment" in 2006, 2007, and 2008, in competition with the 42 terminals in the system.

I have turned problem terminals completely around and I have strengthened those already doing well. One terminal moved from being the 3rd lowest rated terminal (out of 15) to 4th highest in a three-year period. I will call you next week to arrange a time when we might during my next visit to Chicago in late March.

Sincerely,

Randal Johnson

With the marketing letter in place, Randal's standard cover letter was a snap.

RANDAL JOHNSON
4045 NW Abilene
Denver, Colorado 80239
(303) 765-8967
rjzi@cortez.com

2/7/08

Jeff Olsen
President
RoadRider Freightlines
2312 Hennepin Avenue
Minneapolis, Minnesota 55403

Dear Mr. Olsen,

I have a strong background in all aspects of trucking line management. At each of the four terminals I've managed, I have significantly improved on-time records, revenue, market share, and profitability. I am now looking for a regional manager's position with responsibility for 4 to 8 terminals.

I have broad experience in both sales and operations. I have brought in large national accounts, and increased revenue with existing accounts. On the operations side I have taken over two terminals that were among the worst in the company. Within 10 months both were profitable for the first time in years. I came up through the ranks in the trucking business, so I have hands-on experience in all aspects of operations. I also have extensive experience with budgets and working with state and federal agencies.

I would very much like to meet with you to describe my background in more detail. I look forward to hearing from you.

Sincerely,

Randal Johnson

UTILIZING YOUR MARKETING LETTER TO MEET HIRING AUTHORITIES

Using a marketing letter effectively will get you in to see more hiring managers than any other strategy I know. These are not informational interviews where you are seeking information about a career field, an industry, or a specific organization. No, the people you are going to visit are managers who hire people with your background.

When you send out a marketing letter you will already know what fields you want to pursue and through Reference USA (see page 287) and other resources, you will have identified organizations that meet your requirements for size, location, and industry. These are organizations that you know, or suspect, hire people with your background.

You may previously have used informational interviews to nail down your career field and perhaps developed a list of industries. You move into the marketing letter mode when you have answered those questions.

Having identified prospective employers, you need to identify at least one person in each organization who has the power, the authority, to hire you. The person will probably not have an opening at the time you contact him or her. We say probably, because sometimes you'll meet a manager who just yesterday started seeking a person like you. Or, the person has become aware that it's time to add a person to the staff. If your marketing letter gets into her hands at this moment, you will likely be granted your request for a 15 minute appointment. Or, unbeknownst to the manager, a valued employee is going to quit in the next four weeks. If you can spend even two minutes with a hiring manager (15 minutes is what you'll initially ask for), you can cause the person to seriously consider you for future openings.

We each know a certain number of people from all phases of our lives—work, recreation, community, family, worship, etc. All of these contacts have similar circles they move in. So what we have is a nearly infinite network of potential contacts.

Getting to see someone on the inside brings you that much closer to the hiring authority. Here, at least you have someone with access to internal information, internal directories, email addresses, and more. If you make a good impression, there is the chance you will be referred to either the hiring authority or someone close. Repeat as necessary.

Contacts

Friends, relatives, acquaintances, business contacts can all provide useful leads if you approach them in the right way. Before they can help, people must know what you're looking for and what your qualifications are. About 26% of all job seekers find positions through such leads. This could be increased substantially if people made better use of this method. Include your banker, barber, broker, and butcher. Every person who has an interest in your success can be helpful.

Another 34% obtain their jobs through direct contact with employers. A significant part of the 34% is made up by folks who go straight to hiring managers seeking appointments with them, regardless of whether a current opening exists.

When directly contacting a manager, sometimes you'll contact that person at the pefect moment when they have an opening or are about to have an opening. At other times a manager will agree to a brief appointment, giving you an opportunity to kindle interest in you for when an opening does occur.

When you consider that approximately 70% of job seekers find their job through referrals and direct contact, you wonder why some job seekers devote 80% of more of their time browsing online job listings, when that source accounts for less than 10% of hiring.

Begin by handing or sending your resume and a list of your top 60-80 employment prospects to everyone you know. Enclose a note stating that you will call in a few days. Ask your contacts to review the list carefully and to indicate if they know *anyone* who works for any of the organizations. You truly want to talk to anyone, whether it is a janitor, secretary, or purchasing agent. By talking to that person you can learn if it is a good organization to work for, what its problems or strengths are, and even get inside information about the person who has power to hire you. Tell your contact what your strengths are and ask the person to call or email you if he or she hears of any openings. Tell the person that all you need is someone to contact and that you will take care of the rest. You are not asking for any great favors. You would certainly do the same for them.

Speaking to contacts is one of the most valuable things a person can do in a job search, yet few job hunters are willing to expend even the moderate amount of energy this strategy requires.

Create an Employer List

To conduct an effective job search you need a top-quality list of potential employers. The best resource to create that list is *Reference USA*, a database with 14 million U.S. businesses and 1.5 million Canadian businesses. *Reference USA* is available through most library systems. To use it you must have a library card for a library system that pays an annual subscription. *Reference USA* enables you to select organizations by industry, size, and location. The employer information includes all the industries the organization is involved in, its headquarters address along with branches, the names of key people, and sometimes bios of those managers. You can also save the information to your own database. The one limitation is that you can only access 25 organizations per day. If you access *Reference USA* from your home computer you can accumulate more than 100 per week. For more on how to use *Reference USA* see Appendix B.

Get Additional Help at Our Website

The full details of how to use a marketing letter, referrals, and direct contact, goes beyond the scope of this book. By going to Appendix B you'll be able to access the details for carrying out this highly effective type of job search on our website. Using a marketing letter is a critical element in the success of this strategy.

PART FOUR

Appendices

Appendix A

TIPS FOR IDENTIFYING RESULTS TO INCLUDE IN YOUR RESUME

Use these "Did you?" questions to get you thinking and to trigger memories, recalling experiences that you may have forgotten. You're looking for experiences where you played a major or significant role.

Ask yourself how people in your field are judged. How do supervisors and managers know that you are doing things that deserve kudos, salary raises, or promotions? How do you know you are successful and effective in your field? What have been your successes? Everyone in your field has similar duties. How do those most effective employees demonstrate their effectiveness and become recognized as bringing value to the organization?

As you read each of the following statements, say to yourself: Did you . . . ?

GENERAL TYPES OF RESULTS

Handle a growing workload with the same or fewer staff

Negotiate agreements, policies, contracts, etc., that benefited your organization

Control costs of purchasing supplies, raw goods, equipment, etc.

Reduce overdue accounts

Revise, design, or implement policies that improved operations

Help the organization through a growth period that strengthened its financial position

Update computerized systems relating to accounting, human resources, sales, etc.

Convert a system from manual to computer

Bring in new accounts as a rainmaker

Produce billable hours above the norm compared to those of others in the firm.

Through engineering, design, or marketing, create products or services that succeeded in the marketplace

Bring benefits to your clients or customers

Work on key projects

Improve file management, security, accuracy, ease of use

Open a new office/branch, help launch a start-up, start a new department

Accomplish more in less time and at higher quality

Become recognized for effectively completing key projects on schedule and within budget

Receive high ratings on reviews, for (teamwork, solving problems, etc.)

Create bids that obtained business and maintained sufficient profit margins

Produce successful funding requests for projects, research, services, etc. from your company, foundations, governments, or other funding sources

Improve the percentage of bids awarded on estimates and that were profitable

Keep disputes, claims, and litigation to a minimum

Improve customer relations

Demonstrate leadership skills

Bring consensus to groups/individuals on difficult/divisive issues

Gain community or business support for a controversial project or plan

Partner with community or volunteer organizations to meet a need

Recognize a problem or opportunity before others and take action to control/eliminate the problem and take full advantage of the opportunity

Improve relationships/increase cooperation with staff and other departments

Help departments work more effectively and more cooperatively to achieve crucial goals

Get a high percentage of your staff promoted to higher positions

Mentor/supervise employees to move them from marginal to highly useful

Get asked to train new employees or take it upon yourself to train them

Receive awards, recognition for your contributions

Effectively meet challenges/problems

Serve effectively on committees and task forces, enabling progress to be made

Act as a formal or informal mediator with friends, coworkers, department managers, etc.

Receive compliments from colleagues, community members, supervisors

Effectively define and clarify to staff the mission of your organization

Accept or take on a leadership roles

Complete projects that saved or made money for the organization

Work on a project that resulted in patents or proprietary ways to do things

Supervise outside consultants or contractors and obtain good results from them

Reduce dependence on outside consultants or save money by doing something in-house

Outsource work to organizations that could do it better or cheaper than in-house

Receive bonuses for completing projects ahead of schedule or for performing at a high level

Get selected to head up large or key projects

Produce excellent results while acting as a consultant or contractor

Manage or perform projects that received national recognition

Improve the financial strength of the organization

Establish new programs/profit centers

Receive high ratings from outside organizations that reviewed your organization, department

Obtain certification such as ISO 9000 from an outside certifying organization

Start new programs

Introduce new technology

Improve functionality by reorganizing your department or organization

Fix areas that were in noncompliance with your organization's policies or with certifying organizations such as ISO or hired firms such as a CPA firm, or a government agency

Work on noncompliance issues of any type

Turn around a money-losing organization or venture

Take on increased demands with no increase in staffing

Create loyal customers who tell others about the service and products

Make your organization more competitive

Make the best of a budget cut

Revise outdated policies

Help your organization adapt to major market changes

Turn around declining revenues/profits

Implement a cost-saving device or process

Implement better tracking, measurement, or metrics to know how the business is doing

Deal with integrity or accuracy issues of financial data

Get recruited to solve a major problem

Improve the quality of new hires

Build a personal reputation, or reputation of the organization that enables you to recruit the best and the brightest

Resolve labor or personnel issues

Direct facility expansions or construction projects

Open up new markets nationally or internationally

Handle damage control after a major problem or PR issue

Lobby a government entity to obtain desired changes or minimize the impact of undesired rules, regulations, laws

Get elected to some type of office or board of directors of a business, professional, or nonprofit organization

Bring new ideas or vision to the organization

Improve the recruitment of volunteers

Motivate volunteers

Improve community outreach

Create business partnerships/linkages within and outside the organization

Develop ideas that have been used as a model by other organizations

Play a role in strengthening the board of directors

Increase output

Improve efficiency

Decrease labor or material costs

Enable your organization to become a leader in technology

Adjust to radical changes in the market and prosper as a result

Develop excellent relationships with suppliers

Improve margins

Implement strategies that improved sales

Oversee successful projects

Instill in employees the desired attitude and behavior when dealing with customers

Carefully study sales trends and find ways to capitalize on that knowledge

Develop and introduce a market changing product or service

Fix specific procedural problems that led to errors or inefficiencies

Make effective use of your computer skills

Deal with heavy competition from a new player or long-term competitor

Bring inventory to appropriate levels and reduce out of stock situations

Introduce ideas or programs new to your industry

Start effective new programs

Implement innovative programs

Receive positive comments from colleagues

Create alliances with other agencies that benefited your organization

Become the office guru on any particular subject

College Results

Fund most of your college costs through your own employment

Complete your program in less time than normal

Have a high GPA

Complete dual degrees

Take difficult courses/electives

Hold leadership responsibilities on team projects or of volunteer projects/activities

Tutor students

Function as a teaching assistant

Study abroad (what did you gain from it)

Organize/plan events, activities, travel, or field trips

Hold student offices of any kind

Sales Results

Increase sales, market share, or profit margin

Add accounts and increase sales to those accounts

How many accounts did you add

Improve your personal ranking among the branch, district, region, or nation

Set any sales records

Restore inactive accounts

Introduce new products

Open a new territory

Win any awards

Increase the number of active customers

Increase sales with existing customers

Retain customers at a rate higher than the industry average

Build loyalty with customers

Increase market share

Appendix B

Go to www.careerempowering.com for additional information on topics in *Resume Empower*. Click on "Books by Tom Washington and Gary Kanter." Then click on "Additional Information on *Resume Empower*." Find your topic by the page number or topic name from *Resume Empower*, then click on the link. Not only will you find information on the topics below, but new resume and job finding information will be periodically added.

Appendix C

INTERNET RESOURCES

The Key Internet Trio

The following three websites are great because they provide outstanding advice on how to use the Internet for a job search and offer excellent links to other valuable sites. In essence these three websites individually and together open up the entire Internet. If there is a source of value relating to job finding, career exploration, or education, you will find those links on these three websites.

The Job Hunter's Bible (www.jobhuntersbible.com). This site is produced by Richard Bolles (author of *What Color Is Your Parachute?*) and Mark Bolles. We like this site because Bolles not only provides links to some of the best sites on the Web, but he provides a description of what you'll find and what makes each one useful. In his unique way, he also provides his view on how to best use the Internet. You can also access many of Bolles' articles on various aspects of job finding. Start with this site.

The Riley Guide (www.rileyguide.com/jobguide). This is Bolles' top pick for a must visit site. Margaret Riley Dikel has for years been showing job seekers how to use the Internet for job hunting. She also has great links to key sites with explanations of their value. There are also outstanding links to highly useful articles on job finding.

Career Resource Center (www.careers.org) Another key pick by Bolles. CRC has the most links to job, career, and educational sites of any resource on the Net. The site is continuously adding new technologies to make the job search easier. Their motto, "If it's about your career . . . it's here!"

Bibliography

THE CLASSICS IN JOB FINDING AND CAREER DEVELOPMENT

Interviewing

Interview Power: Selling Yourself Face To Face, Tom Washington, Mount Vernon Press, 2004

Sweaty Palms: The Neglected Art of Being Interviewed, Anthony Medley, Ten Speed Press, 2005

Memory Mining, Allan Hay, Book Publishers Network, 2007

Salary Negotiating

Negotiating Your Salary: How To Make $1000 a Minute, Jack Chapman, Ten Speed Press, 2008

Job Finding

What Color Is Your Parachute, Richard Bolles, Ten Speed Press, 2009

The Complete Job-Search Handbook, Howard Figler, Henry Holt & Co., 1999

The Wizard of Work, Richard Gaither, Ten Speed Press, 1995

No One is Unemployable, Debra Angel, Worknet Training Services, 1997

Internet Job Hunting

Job Hunting Online: A Guide to Using Job Listings, Message Boards, Research Sites, Counseling, and Networking, Mark Emery Bolles, Richard Nelson Bolles, Ten Speed Press, 2008

Guide to Internet Job Searching, Margaret Riley Dikel, McGraw-Hill, 2008

Career Planning

The Three Boxes of Life, Richard Bolles, Ten Speed Press, 1981

Finding A Job You Can Love, Ralph Mattson and Arthur F. Miller, P&R Publishing, 1999

Index

About The Authors

Tom Washington is the founder of Career Management Resources (1980), a career exploration and outplacement counseling firm in Bellevue, Washington. He has written and edited hundreds of resumes and has studied what enables clients to get more interviews.

Tom has shared his resume writing and job finding strategies on numerous radio and television talk shows. He is the author of *Resume Power: Selling Yourself On Paper* and *Interview Power: Selling Yourself Face To Face.*

Tom speaks to college audiences, career and job finding professionals, associations, and professional groups. He covers a wide range of topics and instills a motivation to conduct an effective job search. Tom holds a master's degree in counseling from Northeastern Illinois University.

Tom provides career counseling, job finding coaching, interview preparation, and outplacement assistance to people throughout the Puget Sound region.

Gary Kanter has taught seminars and community college classes throughout the Puget Sound region. His articles on resume writing and career search have been featured in regional and national publications. His development of the "clustered resume" has led to considerable success among his clients and students.

Gary   **Tom**

Prior to joining Tom Washington at CMR in 1988, Gary had developed a track record in providing employment services to special populations in the Canadian Maritimes, Middle Tennessee, and the Puget Sound Region.

In addition to his work at CMR, he served on the staff of Jewish Family Service of Washington as Vocational Guidance Consultant for 14 years.

Tom can be reached by email at tomw@careerempowering.com
Gary can be reached at gmkanter@yahoo.com

Career Management Resources • 1750 112th NE C-224 • Bellevue, WA 98004
(425) 454-6982   www.careerempowering.com

Resources
By Tom Washington

INTERVIEW POWER: SELLING YOURSELF FACE TO FACE

Interview Power is a complete and comprehensive interviewing guide. Filled with hundreds of practical ideas, strategies, and tips, *Interview Power* enables you to obtain more job offers and negotiate higher salaries. It provides you with the most up-to-date interviewing techniques—enabling you to have real impact on today's tough interviewers. (2004, 291 pages.)

Interview Power ...

Opens up the secret to effective interviewing—the art of selling your
   strengths by describing past accomplishments.
Provides the principles for answering 101 tough questions.
Shows you how to overcome objections and get the offer.
Prepares you for behavior-based interviewing—the fastest growing type of
   interview.
Reveals techniques that enable you to truly sell yourself.
Demonstrates how to deal with illegal questions.
Shows you how to quickly build rapport with your interviewer.
Gives you ways to prove you have the "right stuff."
Ensures that nothing will take you by surprise.

INTERVIEW POWER (THE DVD)

Written by Tom Washington (1995), this video takes key concepts from *Interview Power: Selling Yourself Face To Face* and uses video to *show* the viewer how to interview effectively. *Interview Power* demonstrates how to impact the interviewer with stories and anecdotes. You have the opportunity to see and hear how to best perform in an interview. This 70-minute video will enable you to get job offers that previously might have gone to your competitors. Purchase *Interview Power* and get a 30-day, money-back guarantee. This video continues to have the same impact as when first released.

What others are saying about *Interview Power:*

> This video will give viewers the skills, practice and confidence to interview well and get the job they want. Information is presented using dramatizations and graphics, interlaced with cogent on-screen comments by employment officers from Microsoft, Boeing, and US West. The pace moves along at a rapid rate with summary graphics at the end of each topic.
>
> —*Video Librarian*, November–December 1995 issue

> Anyone using these techniques will increase their self-confidence and effectiveness in selling themselves at an interview. The systematic approach given in this video provides the best method I've seen for fully preparing for successful interviewing.
>
> —John Knapp, Human Resources Consultant

> Every question you're likely to get about "Why should we hire you?" is covered with practical examples. It sets you up for no-surprise interviews.
>
> —Jack Chapman, author of *Negotiating Your Salary: How To Make $1000 a Minute*

What career and job finding professionals are saying:

Preparing a résumé that separates a person from everyone else is the first step in getting a great new job or launching your career. Standing out from the crowd, demonstrating your professionalism and presenting yourself as a high performer is an essential skill that's not easily learned. Luckily, Tom Washington and Gary Kanter have done the heavy lifting for you. In this remarkable guidebook, Tom and Gary will walk you step-by-step through what it really takes to put together a résumé that not only reflects who you are, but also what you're capable of doing. Whether you've just graduated and are looking for your first real gig, or a seasoned pro ready to jump start your career, start by following the invaluable guidance contained within *Résumé Empower!*.

—**Lou Adler,** author of *Hire With Your Head: A Rational Way To Make A Gut Decision*